Renew ~ at

A Century of
Air Power

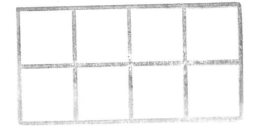

A Century of
Air Power

The Changing Face of Air Warfare
1912–2012

Dr Dave Sloggett

Pen & Sword
AVIATION

First published in Great Britain in 2013 by
Pen & Sword Aviation
an imprint of
Pen & Sword Books Ltd
47 Church Street
Barnsley
South Yorkshire
S70 2AS

ISBN 978 1 78159 192 5

Typeset in Ehrhardt by
Mac Style, Driffield, East Yorkshire
Printed and bound in the UK by CPI Group (UK) Ltd, Croydon,
CRO 4YY

Pen & Sword Books Ltd incorporates the imprints of Pen & Sword
Archaeology, Atlas, Aviation, Battleground, Discovery, Family
History, History, Maritime, Military, Naval, Politics, Railways,
Select, Social History, Transport, True Crime, and Claymore
Press, Frontline Books, Leo Cooper, Praetorian Press, Remember
When, Seaforth Publishing and Wharncliffe.

For a complete list of Pen & Sword titles please contact
PEN & SWORD BOOKS LIMITED
47 Church Street, Barnsley, South Yorkshire, S70 2AS, England
E-mail: enquiries@pen-and-sword.co.uk
Website: www.pen-and-sword.co.uk

Contents

Foreword

Arguably, in the first century of air power, the single most significant act was the bombing of London by the Gotha bombers of the Kaiser's fledging air force in 1917. This raid, coming on the back of the increasing use and determinant of air power over the battlefields of Northern Europe during the First World War, identified the key and enduring characteristics of air power: range, speed, agility and adaptability. If contemporary proof was required, it was these same aspects of the capability of air power that enabled the Royal Air Force and its sister air forces, from Europe, the United States and the Middle East, to rapidly launch the highly-effective operation into Libya in the spring of 2011. This multi-faceted action saw a major extraction of entitled personnel from under the nose of a potentially very hostile and militarily capable nation. The subsequent kinetic missions precisely and discriminately nullified the regime's military capability with the absolute minimum of deaths, injuries and damage to the regime's fighters, the civilian population and that country's infrastructure.

Air power has grown rapidly from an observer capability operating over the trenches of Northern France to a wide range of capabilities that give politicians enormous scope of action undreamt of at the start of the twentieth century. The projection, sustainment and application of military force would be almost unthinkable today without the fundamentals of control of the air, over the operational theatre, the ability to project and sustain deployed forces and the critical roles of providing intelligence, knowledge of what is happening in and around the operational area, and increasingly, through the Combat ISTAR (Intelligence, Surveillance, Target Acquisition and Reconnaissance) concept, ability to rapidly, precisely and effectively use that knowledge to bound and coerce the adversary and very much limit their options.

In this book, *A Century of Air Power*, Dr Sloggett provides a first-class analysis of the many varied, challenging and innovative uses to which air-minded commanders have put this third dimensional capability in the last 100 years. He ably and lucidly describes why and in what ways air power, commanded and controlled by experienced professionals, has fundamentally changed the nature of warfare and combat operations more broadly on the land, at sea and in the air. As we enter the second century of air power, that range of capability continues to increase. The use of space as the medium from which to observe; the adaptation of Remotely Piloted Air Systems and their potential for unparalleled persistence and reliability; and the precision, penetration and provability of air-delivered weapons continue to give political leaders and military commanders more options by which to achieve their aims. But, equally, the ability to project resources over long distances, rapidly and reliably, has given us the capability to react more effectively to natural disasters, be they caused by earthquakes, floods or any other means.

In this book Dr Sloggett has, yet again, demonstrated his mastery of analysis, synthesis and the ability to describe insightfully and effectively the use of air power. He does so clearly, dispassionately, but in a most readable style. He is to be congratulated on bringing the reader a comprehensive, thoughtful and incisive account of the first century of air power and I commend it to you.

The last 100 years have yielded many challenges in the air, innovations and lessons – mostly hard-won – and many brave and talented people have given their lives to the development of modern air power. Capturing all of this in such an effective work is no mean achievement. True to his character and his background, Sloggett presents the facts, the issues and some deductions but leaves the reader to draw the necessary conclusions. The challenge for those that follow, as the author knows well, is to translate these conclusions on the use of air power in its first century into its usage, capabilities and application for the next century!

Air Chief Marshal Sir Stephen Dalton
GCB ADC LLD(Hon) BSc FRAeS CCMI RAF

Preface

The Royal Air Force emerged from the end of the First World War as one of the pre-eminent organizations applying the new-found science of air power. During the Second World War that reputation became significantly enhanced as the Royal Air Force held off the might of the Luftwaffe during the dark days of the summer of 1940. Over Germany years later it was to provide the main instrument of the application of military power as the allied nations fought back against the Axis powers.

This was the point at which the baton for leading the western world left London and moved to Washington. The United States Air Force now comprises the greatest air force in the world. Russia and China are striving to catch up. China particularly is making huge strides with the rapid development of its fifth-generation fighter jets. As an economic powerhouse China is increasingly investing in its military forces. Within a decade it will have a formidable capability.

The Royal Air Force and the French Air Forces still retain a significant capability as they showed over Libya in 2011. Of the other countries in the world that recognize the application of air power, Israel is probably the leading advocate of its capabilities. Its experiences, forged in war, show the classic characteristics of air power when used in conjunction with forces manoeuvring on the ground. Through sheer experience in the kind of military operations it has had to conduct, the Israeli Air Force remains among the most pre-eminent in the world from a tactical perspective.

However, as defence budgets across the world come under pressure, the flexibility and agility of air power may help it to win increased spending at the cost of investment in land-based forces. The era of the air-land battle in Western Europe and in the Middle East may now shift to the development of the air-sea battle doctrine in light of the American 'pivot' towards the Pacific Rim. This shift perceptibly changes the geo-strategic context in which air power will be applied. Maritime air power will inevitably feature more strongly in the Pacific. Those familiar with the nature of the warfare conducted in the area of the Second World War will no doubt draw some interesting parallels.

The doctrine of the air–sea battle has to address the problems of a lack of strategic depth in the area. In Europe there was room to manoeuvre on the land to try to buy time for a political solution to be brokered. If conflict in the Pacific Rim develops over the abundant natural resources thought to lie beneath the South China Sea, the nature of the conflagration will be very different. The role of suppression of enemy air defences which was so prominent in the Cold War doctrinal thinking is bound to return to the forefront of military thinking. The decision by the Australian Air Force to convert a number of its F-18 aircraft into that role shows the concerns they have about what might develop in the Pacific Rim in the coming years.

In the aftermath of Afghanistan and Iraq it would seem few countries are about to contemplate stabilization operations of such a size again. This also reduces the importance of the air–land battle. Future upstream activities against terrorist training camps, insurgencies and trans-national criminal groups will involve a combination of law enforcement, intelligence services, Special Forces and air power, but the air power will come from a combination of unmanned drones and manned aircraft. Their task will be to watch sanctuaries and strike at times when terrorists are on the move, or when their locations have been revealed. They will also perform intelligence-collection tasks and help military forces to insert teams to conduct specific operations on the ground. As terrorists have moved out from Pakistan to the Yemen and Somalia and now across the Sahel into Mali the drones have not been far behind.

Long-term deployments of boots on the ground will move to a new paradigm in the absence of a major war. This will be one that focuses more on internal security sector reforms and training and building indigenous capabilities in vulnerable countries. Land-based deployments of troops will be small in number and will aim to remain in various theatres for short periods of time. The language defending these deployments will also change. In today's media-dominated world, political leaders struggle to find the right combinations of words to justify military action. That situation is not likely to change. After twenty years of war the public in the west will take a lot of convincing to join any new on-the-ground push against a perceived threat.

Over Libya in 2011 the time taken to mobilize an ad hoc coalition was relatively short and the lack of any political will to place boots on the ground very clear. The political consensus for action quickly converged. However, at the time of writing, despite very similar circumstances any concerted action in Syria seems a long way off. In the narrative developed by political leaders to justify military action the concept of warfare will be played down. The boundary between traditional defence applications and wider security tasking will become increasingly blurred.

Countries such as Mexico provide an insight into what is happening. Their air-power capabilities have been dramatically increased to deal with the activities of drug cartels that increasingly bring insecurity to large areas of the country. For Mexico the drive is to be able to rapidly manoeuvre troops into areas where the drug cartels are unable to be challenged by traditional policing methods. Mexico also has a major programme to develop its ability to project maritime air power. In a not-too-dissimilar way, Turkey has also sought to develop its air-power capabilities. The long-standing issues on its borders with Iraq require air power to enable them to intervene to tackle insurgents that use the northern border regions of Iraq as a sanctuary.

The role of air power in the rest of South America is less clear. The landscape there is quite patchy with some countries simply unable to afford large-scale programmes. Brazil's rapid economic development and hugely important indigenous aircraft development and production capability dwarfs the rest of the region. Its plans to buy new fighter jets and expand its military capability to guard its economically vital offshore oil industry are significant. Chile has an established air arm that also has an important maritime role designed to protect its significant coastline. It also maintains a wary eye on its long-standing adversary to the east. Oil deposits in the disputed waters to the south of Argentina and Chile could provide the catalyst for conflict. Argentina's air force still lacks investment. Venezuela, ever fearful of its neighbours, is building up its air force and buying Russian airplanes.

All of this bodes well for the future of air power as an instrument of military strength. Its time as the primary means by which military power is projected around the world by western military powers may have already started. In many countries around the Pacific Rim investments in new aircraft are drawing eye-watering sums from defence budgets.

Australia is among several countries in the region that are investing in new aircraft. South Korea, Japan, Vietnam, Singapore and Indonesia are also ramping up their air forces and capabilities. After clashes over the ownership of the Scarborough Shoal in the South China Sea the Philippines has also started negotiations with the United States about dramatically upgrading its air force. In the past it has focused on its own internal insurgency problems. Now it realizes it has to project military power on a regional basis.

It is in Africa where that global trend has not yet changed significantly. Armies remain a key element of any state's ability to project control over its citizens. If and when democracy spreads throughout Africa and all of the ethnic tensions that exist below the surface are addressed, air power might also see increased investment. At the moment only a few countries in Africa have a recognized capable air force, such as Egypt, Kenya, Ghana, Nigeria and South Africa.

In the Middle East Iraq is quickly rebuilding its air force and Iran has quickly developed its own indigenous development programme creating new aircraft to overcome the constraints imposed by international sanctions taken against Tehran's nuclear programme. To the east as NATO forces start to pull out of Afghanistan a debate on the nature of a future national air force has started. Like other countries concerned with suppressing insurgents, the air force will initially have a limited ground-attack and re-supply focus.

The Libyan campaign provides a cautionary note. It was to show up some deficiencies in the air power available to western powers when the United States chose to take a back seat. Without the fire-power that can be projected in the air domain by the United States, Europe lacks the kind of massed air power that can bring campaigns to a swift conclusion. The strategic stalemate that developed in Libya after the first two months of the campaign highlighted the difficulties of cuts imposed in the absence of a carefully worked out strategic context.

Doctrinal developments in the United States also point to a new paradigm emerging that focuses on the air-sea battle. In Europe in the Cold War it was the air-land battle that was the focal point of NATO's strategic thinking. The air-sea battle was of minor importance and involved maritime patrol aircraft and some land- and carrier-based maritime strike jets being deployed against sea-surface and underwater targets. While that was an important battle to ensure the free flow of supplies across the Atlantic Ocean to re-supply and reinforce NATO formations in Europe, the battle on the German plains was the crucial determinate of the outcome of any conflict. To conduct that battle NATO relied on the geography of Europe to give it strategic depth.

With the United States having pivoted its thinking from Europe to the Pacific Rim arena a change in doctrine is required. The geography of the area means that the United States has little strategic depth to reply upon. The development of the air-sea ideas is all about addressing how to deal with that lack of strategic depth.

With China emerging as a regional power, the ability to provide a counterbalance to their increasing military capability requires some careful consideration. The United States airbases in the region are very vulnerable to a pre-emptive strike. Chinese developments in the field of Anti-Access and Area Denial (A2D) weapon systems are creating a new threat environment. Against this backdrop the role of air power and the Order of Battle of forces need to be redefined.

For Counter-Insurgency (COIN) operations the A-10 proved to be a great asset. Its duration and ability to respond to calls to mass fire-power at a specific point proved its value. The A-10 is the latest in a long line of aircraft that have proven to be excellent assets in a COIN environment. Its demise in the United States defence reviews post-Afghanistan is understandable. To fight the air-sea battle the United States and its allies need a slightly new Order of Battle (ORBAT) in which to apply air power. It may be that surplus A-10 aircraft could be provided to the Afghans or to other countries trying to defeat a local insurgency.

The 'pivot' to the Pacific Rim will inevitably focus on a mix of air-to-air fighters and ground-attack aircraft that can be carrier-based as well as operated from dispersed airfields. If Chinese pre-emptive attacks against the main airbases, such as those at Anderson AFB, were to be successful, dispersal of the force throughout the region would be necessary. American efforts to consolidate its geo-strategic relationships with Australia and the Philippines show part of the thinking that is emerging.

China's countermove in trying to reach out to Indonesia provides a clue as to where they see the future lines of conflict being drawn. Indonesia, however, does have claims over the South China Sea that are in direct dispute with China. As the Indonesian economy develops and it becomes a new force in the region the dynamics may change. American rapprochement with Vietnam is also another indicator of the wide geo-strategic environment.

While speculating about the future is always difficult, these regional trends do provide some indication of the inevitable outcome of the strategic pivot the United States is taking towards the Pacific Rim. Economically it makes huge strategic sense. With Russia some time away from being able to emerge as a threat to Europe again, the strategic realignment makes sense. Russia's joint naval exercise in the early part of 2012 with the rapidly-emerging Chinese navy reveals a great deal.

China, it would seem, is ready to countenance renewing its geo-strategic relationship with Russia as a means of counterbalancing the United States' pivot. While the geo-strategic picture is emerging, the role air power will play in any future conflict in the area cannot be in doubt. That it will need to be based on a combination of air-sea thinking is also apparent. In moving from the air-land environment in Europe to the air-sea battle in the Pacific Rim the flexibility and agility characteristics of air power provide a reassuring point of continuity.

This book charts the development of air power since its inception over the carnage and destruction over the Western Front. The approach that has been adopted is not one based on a simple chronology of the evolution of air power. That has been done and will no doubt be done again as the centennial anniversary of the formation of the Royal Air Force approaches. Instead, the book attempts to look at air power through a slightly different lens, one that tries to draw out the various elements of air power and look at how their application has changed over time. Technological development has clearly been a major driver. Contemporary elements of air forces can now travel faster, are more inherently survivable, carry greater payloads and are flexible and agile in delivering a variety of military effects. These are generic characteristics of air power that apply to the fighter bomber and the transport aircraft and helicopters.

The book is structured in a way that allows the readers to see the individual elements of air power in their own right. Historical perspectives intermingle with contemporary examples. This is not an academic treatise. It looks at the issues of air power from a practical viewpoint. It does also draw on some excellent material sourced from a small number of key books which are referenced in the bibliography.

This is also not a chronological assessment, even if key events and examples are presented in time order. The aim is to take a holistic viewpoint. The accounts included in the book are used to build arguments about the utility of air power, not simply to provide yet another repeat of well-documented campaigns. The aim has been to provide the reader with some different viewpoints on air power, not to simply repeat tried and tested arguments. It is for the reader to judge whether the analysis and presentation add value to the debate on the future of air power.

Acknowledgements

It is always hard to write a series of notes that acknowledge the inputs I have received from so many people in writing this book. I am grateful to Air Chief Marshal Sir Stephen Dalton the Chief of the Air Staff for his guidance, encouragement and support. Air Marshal Stephen Hillier has also proved to be an expert mentor and tutor. Other members of the Royal Air Force have also been a source of constant encouragement and support. I specifically need to recognize the important feedback I received on the first draft of the book from Squadron Leader John McFall. His enthusiasm and positive reaction are sincerely appreciated.

Group Captain David Manning, the former Officer Commanding 99 Squadron RAF at Brize Norton, is always an inspiring figure to meet. A discussion in his office on the wider aspects of air power was always a pleasure. I am also grateful to the various Royal Air Force officers with whom I have had the benefit of working at the Defence Media Centre. Calling up and chatting to Group Captain Nicky Loveday was always a pleasure. During the week she rarely seemed to be away from the office. After Nicky had left her post, Wing Commander Mark Quinn provided an excellent and helpful interface with the Ministry of Defence Directorate of Media and Communications.

My interest in aviation started when I went to work at the Royal Aircraft Establishment at Farnborough. My first day of employment was 7 September 1970 after a chance remark was made by my careers' master at school. I have always believed that seven was my lucky number and on that day a career began to unfold that has been a brilliant experience. Few people can say they enjoy every day they go to work. For the vast majority of my working life that has been the case.

In the course of an eight-year career at Farnborough I was lucky to fly so many different types of aircraft. My flying logbook contains some interesting aircraft types, many of which are now centre-stage in aviation museums all over the country. The Comet, Beverly, Hastings and Andover aircraft at Farnborough all had important roles to play in supporting research into aviation. It was therefore obvious to me that I should get to a point in my career where I would wish to write a book that charted the history of aviation and the application of air power.

Of all the aircraft I was able to fly in those formative years the Dominie and the BAC 1-11 were the best. Flying a civilian airliner at 250 feet through the valleys of Wales, up through the Lake District and along the Caledonian Canal was special. Landing at RAF Leuchars for lunch and then setting off at low level down the east coast before landing back at Farnborough in the early evening was always a different way to spend a day. These were days when the Cold War meant that the scientific research had a real and important focus. Being able to reliably communicate and recall aircraft carrying nuclear weapons was important.

There were times as we flew through the Welsh valleys when we seemed to skim over the mountain-tops. If weather conditions deteriorated, my crew were ever watchful for the cloud that had a hard lining. For me these were hugely formative years. I had come to Farnborough having barely scraped together a basic set of academic qualifications. My academic development was to come later in life.

For allowing me that experience I would like to pay a specific tribute to my scientific colleagues and mentors Dr Paul Sudworth, Henry Spong, George May, Dr Boyd Burgess and other colleagues with whom I worked at Farnborough. I also want to thank the many officers from the Royal Air Force with whom I was privileged to fly. They were very special people to work with. That enthusiasm for aviation has never left me. Living in Farnborough I was always able to have a front seat at the Air Show.

To this day I marvel at the Red Arrows' formation flying. I will never forget watching them on my first day at Farnborough all those years ago. Of late I have been fortunate to return to flying with the Royal Air Force on trips to Iraq and Afghanistan. My last visit into Afghanistan was especially noteworthy as I was able to fly up front on the Tristar and Hercules. Whenever I return from such visits I never fail to be impressed by the professionalism of those I meet. They are an inspiration.

In researching this book I have read a great number of source publications. Many of them have provided important insights that have helped shape the arguments therein; none more so than the book *The Influence of Air Power upon History* by Walter Boyne. I am indebted to him for the detailed analysis he has undertaken of some air campaigns. The analysis of the strategic impact of bombing over Japan in 1944 draws on his unique and detailed examination of its outcome.

I am also privileged more recently to work with a number of editors of magazines that bring the realities of air power into the homes of many thousands of enthusiasts and practitioners on a monthly basis. Each title develops a specific set of themes to its readership. A glance at the shelves of any major retail distributor shows the plethora of titles that now provide coverage of all aspects of the aviation industry. It shows just how interested people still are in aviation. It has not lost its glitz and appeal. Titles such as *Combat Aircraft Monthly*, *Air International*, *Aeroplane Monthly* and *Classic Aircraft* are professionally-run titles in which I have had the pleasure to publish some material. They all exude a fine balance between the words and images on the page. Their readership does not need the academic tomes that appear in some publications. They need what are often complex subjects dissected to a level that can be easily understood, both by the enthusiast and professional readership.

Steve Bridgewater, the editor of *Jets Monthly*, and his team are a pleasure to work with and a source of constant motivation to look back at the history of jet-powered aviation. Gary Parsons, the editor of *Air Forces Monthly*, calmly and quietly produces the largest and most popular magazine to grace the High Street in the aviation sector. *Air Forces Monthly* is a great title that always provides up-to-date assessments of the many new and emerging facets of air power. I rarely fail to be impressed with the excellent balance of pictures and text that provides such a rich reading experience for the enthusiast and professional. Writing for both of these magazines provides a source of immense pleasure. Together they provide the means by which I can explore the full spectrum of air power and its application.

It would be wrong of me not to acknowledge the vital role played by my editor John Greham. His enthusiasm for history and for stories that interest the public knows no bounds. It is a real pleasure to work with a man who rarely fails to answer an email, no matter how trivial its query. His guidance in producing this book has been especially important. His professional approach also comes through in the production of the magazine *Britain at War* in which he is so closely involved.

At home, my wife has shown patience beyond the call of duty as I have retired on several occasions to write. Jo is a constant source of energy to me and I am indebted to her more than anyone for her kindness, support and love. In between the writings, the occasional text and emails from my three sons often provide a light moment. Richard, Chris and Anthony are sons that any father could be immensely proud of as their approach to their lives rarely diverts from the Latin maxim *carpe diem*. It is one that in the forty years of my working life I have tried to practise. I sincerely hope that the readers find this book enjoyable. It has been a huge pleasure to research and write.

Dr Dave Sloggett
Isle of Wight
October 2012

Chapter One

Introduction

Context

Today at the start of the twenty-first century people take aviation for granted. As we go about our daily lives the noise from an aircraft passes by without raising much interest, except of course when one flies low over a city. The collective psyche that developed after 11 September 2001 is not easily forgotten. On that day aircraft were turned into cruise missiles and the ideas of how air power could be projected entered a new phase. Leonardo da Vinci's vision of flight had been taken to a new and deadly extreme.

Ask any layperson what the first century of air power means for them and some might pause for a moment to think. A few, suspecting a question which is more involved than it initially appears, may wonder what the term actually means. They may be unfamiliar with its military overtones, preferring to ignore its role in delivering death and destruction upon an adversary. For many of them the discussion will evoke memories of a recent holiday, an unfulfilled desire to have flown on Concorde before it was taken out of service, or the trials and tribulations of getting through airports. The aviation industry is able quite literally to motivate a wide variety of responses from the general public.

Others, however, will quickly get the idea that the term 'air power' refers to its use as part of the military instrument of power in the land, sea, air and space domains. For many of them the term will quickly conjure up in their minds some stereotypical images. These may include dogfights over the trenches in the First World War, Spitfires and Hurricanes going toe to toe with Luftwaffe bombers in the Battle of Britain, the Blitz and D-Day. For the wider public the idea of air power will often be seen through the magnifying lens of history.

Deeper questioning about the way in which air power has evolved might also trigger a wider realization about some of the essential features of air power. One of those that many people will be capable of grasping is the notion of air superiority. First achieved over the battlefields of Verdun in the First World War, it is now the *sine qua non* for those planning military campaigns.

A widely-held view is that those who control the air are able to impose their tempo and will upon a military campaign. This is a somewhat simple perspective. The characteristics of air power, such as speed and flexibility of response, allow it to be delivered quickly over what can be large distances. While this notion grew out of the Second World War, through the Korean War, it was during the Vietnam War that some of this thinking started to change. Simply trying to bomb the North Vietnamese to the negotiating table did not work for a variety of reasons.

Those who are proponents of air power point out the political constraints on its application. Those who are the 'naysayers' offer equally robust reasons for its failure to break the will of a population. Over Iraq and Afghanistan nearly 100 years on from its inception some limitations of air power in a counter-insurgency environment became apparent. In the Libyan campaign in 2011 against a very different backdrop air power yet again found an opportunity to show how effective it could be when used in the right circumstances.

Of course, to achieve air superiority it is also important to project military power into a theatre of war. In Afghanistan routine movements of aircraft and crews ensure that the air superiority that has been achieved over that country can be maintained. As NATO moves towards its military draw-down in 2014 the issue of how the Afghan National Security Forces (ANSF) are provided with air support is critical. In Iraq the rebuilding of the Iraqi Air Force is only just taking place. This has left a gap in which the insurgents have been able to regain a footprint in the country. These are only examples of many that exist today where countries are investing increasing sums in air power.

Of all the examples it is perhaps China's rapid increase in its air force's capabilities that is most notable. The flight of the second variant of its new stealth fighter in November 2012 was the cause of much debate in aviation circles. It appears that China is taking the opportunity of its rapid economic rise to invest heavily in its air force and naval capabilities. These have traditionally lagged behind the army and its strategic nuclear force. As China turns outwards it has to provide itself with the capability to project air power over greater ranges.

In the Philippines recent concerns over China's intentions towards its claim over the South China Sea have forced the government to embark upon a re-equipment programme for the air force. Similar concerns have seen Vietnam, Singapore and Malaya updating their air forces. India, China's long-standing adversary in the region, is also rapidly expanding its capabilities.

In terms of speed and distance over which air power can be projected, no other means of deploying the military instrument of power has come so far in such a short duration of time. In the first half of that century of air power, it saw its initial application in the First World War.

While historical records can sometimes hide the specific date on which an event occurred, it seems likely that the first actual use of air power to bomb a target in wartime was on 25 October 1914. Two months later the United Kingdom received its first bombing attack when two bombs were dropped on Admiralty Pier at Dover. This was followed up four days later when a seaplane dropped bombs on a residence near Dover Castle.

In the intervening years new ideas emerged about how best it could be applied to support ground forces, obliterate an enemy's industrial capability or terrorize their population and political leadership into submission. In those early years the application of air power was primarily focused on its ability to deliver what today are referred to as kinetic effects: in short, the ability to destroy things during wartime.

Within years of the end of the Second World War the sound barrier was broken. In its second half-century the application of air power had to change. It could no longer be indiscriminate. Today precision is the watchword that governs the delivery of kinetic effect. This is coupled with the increasing emphasis on the projection of what now is called 'smart power'. This is the ability to apply the military instrument of power in ways that avoid human suffering. In the past wars have tended to result in large areas being laid to waste and in need of being rebuilt. Today wars seek to avoid destroying essential areas of infrastructure. Military strikes against utilities such as water and electricity are not placed on target lists unless it is imperative.

The lexicon associated with air power has also quickly grown. Terms like non-lethal effects have emerged as technology has delivered new ways of having an effect upon an enemy. In twenty-first-century warfare the avoidance of civilian casualties is also an imperative. This is a very different world from that of the twentieth century and the doctrine of air power has had to evolve. Today air power not only is applied in its traditional kinetic sense but also to help those affected by natural or man-made disasters.

Arguably, while navies and armies have also had to adapt to this changing military environment, it is air power that has undergone the most dramatic levels of development. While the rate of change of how air power is applied has gone through accelerated times, that does not suggest that in the intervening years it somehow stagnated. Far from it: as far as air power is concerned, change is constant. It is why its three underlying characteristics of flexibility, adaptability and agility are so readily applied.

Those minded to be pedantic about these points might highlight the rapid pace of development of missiles which are used across the land, maritime and air domains and they would be right to mention the issue. However, the simple fact remains that as far as the delivery platforms are concerned, land and maritime forces simply cannot project power over the distances and at the speed of response that is possible using air power. It offers unique abilities to political and military leaders at a time when the international security landscape has never been so uncertain. In such difficult times the versatility, agility and adaptability of air power are essential elements of any developed country's approach to defence and security.

One image that is easily recalled is of the flimsy bi-planes flying over the Western Front spotting enemy activity across the lines. Another is of the first attempts by the adversaries to contest the skies as they tried to shoot each other down. In just over a decade the aeroplane had moved from being a fantasy to reality. The dream of those who advocated how air power would play a critical role in military campaigns was quickly realized.

Early Beginnings

This was also the point at which air power was moving from the realm of the rich and famous and the dedicated enthusiast to its first hesitating steps as an operational capability. Those who flew in those early days were often driven by the sheer exhilaration of flying. They were the pioneers of military aviation.

Of all the achievements in that first decade the small but significant flight undertaken by Louis Blériot across the English Channel stands out. The flight itself was unremarkable. It lasted forty minutes and the average speed at which the aviator flew was 46 mph. The only interesting moment was when Blériot had overtaken the destroyer that was guiding him across to England and he nearly missed the English coastline. The shortest route was obviously the easiest but had he missed Dover and the weather deteriorated, his flight may have had an altogether different outcome. For some analysts, however, mindful of the implications of what they had just seen, it was a defining moment. It was now easy to see that the aircraft would not only be the plaything of the engineers, the rich and the famous. It would also become a weapon of war. The only question was when.

History shows that time would pass before it became accepted. Armies and navies were not about to stand aside and allow a new entrant into their domains without some resistance. Indeed, in a sign of the challenges to come, members of the cavalry complained bitterly that an aircraft, acting in a reconnaissance role on Salisbury Plain, was 'frightening the horses'. Be that as it may, the momentum to apply aviation in conflict was now unstoppable.

While the first serious applications of air power were to come in the form of the Zeppelins, the rapid developments in aircraft structures saw machines developed that would ultimately be far more versatile than the airships. The Zeppelin's impact on the military application of air power was very transitory. As airframes became increasingly robust, so important developments also occurred in engines. Aviators had quickly appreciated that the Holy Grail of flying was to find the right balance between weight and power. Robust structures often meant increased weight. That had an inevitable impact on the power requirements from the engines to get the aeroplanes into the air.

As with many early developments in aviation it was French ingenuity that pioneered early developments. Léon Levavasseur's Antoinette engines first flew on his Gastambide-Mengin I aircraft in December 1907. This was the forerunner to the successful Antoinette monoplane. An aircraft similar to this was to win the first prize at the inaugural *Daily Mail* Round Britain Air Race in 1911 flown by another Frenchman, Lieutenant Jean Conneau.

Early indications of the use of aviation in a military role appear in several accounts. Deciding which represents the definitive point at which aviation took on this role is difficult but some trends do emerge. Air shows became the place where the skills required to employ aircraft in a military capacity were first showcased. The first major air show in the United States took place at Dominguez Field outside Los Angeles in January 1910. At this meeting it was the French aviator Louis Paulhan who grabbed the most attention. Aside from setting several new records such as a new altitude ceiling of 4,164ft and taking a single passenger on a journey of almost 110 miles, he also flew a United States army Lieutenant called Paul Beck on one of the first recorded examples of a bombing sortie.

At a follow-up air show at Harvard Aviation Field in Atlantic Massachusetts a British pilot named Claude Graham-White stole the show with his mock attack on a model of a warship using a bomb made of plaster of Paris. It was from these highly speculative beginnings that the credentials of air power as an element of the military instrument of power were to emerge. It was a capability that was quick to catch on.

Within three years as the war clouds gathered over Europe the newly-formed Royal Flying Corps and the Royal Navy Air Service were able to call upon 113 aircraft and six airships. The French Air Force had 176 aircraft. The Germans and Russians, however, had invested more heavily and had assembled an inventory of 282 and 228 aircraft respectively. Austria-Hungary, the place where the fires of the First World War would be lit, only had forty aircraft. With aviation technology still in its earliest stages, how that air power would be applied in wartime became a central issue. Its debut was not glorious.

Television documentaries and re-enactments have shown the problems experienced by the various air forces in the early days of the war. In what were the first primitive attempts to contest the airspace, pilots carried pistols and observers' rifles. Their efforts to shoot at other planes could be thought of as almost comedic. The actual chances of hitting someone were slight. That was, however, not to remain a problem for very long.

The invention of metal deflectors that allowed bullets to pass through the propeller was to transform the ability of aircraft to contest the skies. The invention by the French aviation pioneer Roland Garros enabled him to shoot down five German planes in April 1915 in a period of sixteen days. For this achievement he became the first fighter ace of the war. The advantage that the Allies were to hold was, however, soon to be lost. When Garros was shot down over enemy lines a Dutchman called Anthony Fokker studied the design of the machine gun and the metal deflectors and quickly developed an equivalent system. When this was added to the advanced design and essential manoeuvrability of the aircraft he had devised, the Germans were quickly able to establish control of the skies over Europe. The 'Fokker scourge' had begun. Such was the dominance of the German Air Force at this moment that for many new recruits to the RFC their life expectancy was significantly reduced; a point parodied years later in the BBC television series *Black Adder*. While the origin of the term 'twenty-minuters' remains shrouded in mystery, the basic idea that new pilots had to learn fast to stay alive was true.

New Directions

Towards the end of the war as Germany unleashed its final desperate attempt to break the stalemate the aircraft moved from its reconnaissance and air-to-air duties into having a formal role as a bomber. The attacks on munitions dumps, enemy airfields and supply lines that were carried out by the RFC were crucial to defeating the German onslaught. The creation of the Royal Air Force in 1918 by David Lloyd George saw him send Handley Page 0/400 bombers into Germany. This was the time when the application of military aviation moved through its first tentative steps. It was to be the start of a long and sometimes challenging road. One year after the end of the First World War cutbacks in the capabilities of the RAF almost destroyed it.

Other images that would also surface would be those of the Battle of Britain. The connoisseurs might perhaps also recall the development of the Spitfire and its success in the Schneider Trophy races around the Solent off the Isle of Wight in 1931. The Schneider Trophy had originally been offered as a reward for the fastest seaplane by the French industrialist Jacques Schneider in 1912. The winners also received a cash prize of £1,000. This provides an important insight into the ways in which the initial pioneering efforts in aviation arose from non-governmental sources. The rather flimsy designs of the early aircraft did not generate a high degree of enthusiasm in military circles.

In 1913 a French airman called Maurice Prevost won the trophy flying at an average speed of 45.71 mph. A year later a Briton called Howard Pixton secured the trophy at nearly twice the speed (86.83 mph) of the year before. The First World War intervened and the races were resumed in 1919 when the honours were shared between Italian, British and American competitors with winning average speeds growing steadily year-on-year from 43.83 mph in 1920 to over 300 mph in 1931 when the race was held off Calshot Spit in the Solent. The race not only provided a catalyst for speed and engine design: it also fostered developments in flight control systems and aerodynamics that were to be pivotal to the forthcoming Battle of Britain.

The role of R.J. Mitchell as the designer of the S.6B prototype for the Spitfire is widely acknowledged. His design work was pivotal to the British successes in 1927, 1929 and 1931. However, at a time of economic depression his ability to attract funds to help him complete the development was not easy. The programme was saved by the vital financial contribution of £100,000 made by Lady Lucy Houston, the widow of a millionaire ship-owner, which rescued the development programme. It is sobering to think of what might have happened as the war clouds gathered over Europe had her philanthropy not seen the development of the S.6B variant. After overcoming some initial aerodynamic handling issues the aircraft went on to win the trophy on 12 September 1931. Flight Lieutenant J.N. Boothman achieved an average speed of 340.08 mph around the triangular 50km course.

This was a speed over the ground close to 6 miles a minute. Later that day one of the other pilots set a new speed record of 379.05 mph. A matter of two weeks later the same pilot, Flight Lieutenant G.H. Stainforth, went on to add nearly 30 mph to that figure when he flew at an average speed of 407.5 mph. The foundations for the crucial role that was to be played by the Spitfire in the Battle of Britain had been laid.

Applying Air Power

It was perhaps inevitable that with the advent of air power, key advocates of its capabilities would emerge. The names of Douhet, Trenchard and Mitchell are synonymous with developments in the application of air power. They were the air-power equivalents of Corbett and Mahan from the naval viewpoint. All three broadly subscribed to the view that as a result of the development of air power the way warfare was going to be conducted had been fundamentally changed. They were, however, quite different people. Trenchard was a patient man. Douhet was the complete opposite.

Arguably Douhet was the first of the air-power philosophers. Throughout his career he was a controversial figure, keen to buck trends in what he clearly regarded as staid thinking. He believed that by moving warfare into a third dimension those who exploited it correctly would 'wield offensive power so great that it defies human imagination'. Given the development of nuclear weapons within a short period of time of him publishing this assertion, it can be regarded as prescient. He also had a vision of a multi-purpose 'battle plane' that could both carry an effective bomb load and engage in air-to-air combat. Contemporary fighter jets like the Typhoon, Rafale and F-35 are the embodiment of what Douhet suggested all those years ago.

Douhet also suggested that if a state was to be defeated in the air it would lead to a situation where a country would be 'at the mercy of the enemy, with no chance at all of defending oneself, compelled to accept whatever terms he sees fit to dictate'.

Despite being written at a time when air power had yet to reach its full potential, his vision of the ultimate capability that it would afford military people was remarkable. In the skies over Normandy in 1944 that vision was to be applied. The air superiority enjoyed by the Allies gave them a huge advantage as they struggled to gain a foothold in occupied France. Once the Allies broke free of Normandy and General Patton raced for the German border, their application of tactical air power in support of ground forces was to be decisive.

Douhet's assertion that 'command of the air must be won' still applies today. His point that air battles must be avoided at all costs is reflective of the capabilities of aviation at the time. He saw the role of bombers to remove the threat at the outset of conflict. That desire to use the bomber as the principal instrument of air power was to have grave consequences for civilian populations.

The reminiscences of the history of air power might also bring back the dramatic pictures of the Blitz and the fire-storm over Dresden and Tokyo as bombers pounded cities in an attempt to shape the will of the people. Specialized raids that have been re-enacted through the medium of film might also come to mind, such as the raid conducted by 617 Squadron on three major dams in Germany.

Time, however, was to show that because of political constraints air power was often not applied in ways that its advocates suggested. Historians will always debate through many coloured lenses what might have happened in this or that instance if the political constraints on the use of air power had been untied. It is possible to argue that those who have written the doctrine have never been allowed to put its ideas into practice. The cost in human lives was simply politically untenable. That is, of course, until the events in Japan in 1945.

The pictures and films of the atomic weapons detonating over Hiroshima and Nagasaki and their aftermath might send a slight shiver down the spine. Once unleashed, the power of the atom clearly transformed the way in which war could be fought. Warfare had entered a new and very uncertain stage. Those such as General Curtis LeMay, who now moved into the forefront of its advocacy, were to find the lasting impact of those pictures would have a dramatic impact on their political masters.

In the Cuban Missile Crisis those military advocates of the use of such destructive power found their desire to go to war curtailed by political leaders who had dreamt of what life after a nuclear war might resemble. This was arguably the point at which strategic air power reached its apex. During the campaign in Vietnam in the late 1960s and early 1970s political restrictions placed on the application of strategic air power reduced its impact. Its huge destructive potential made political leaders wary of its application.

That was until President Nixon launched the Operation Linebacker raids over North Vietnam. For the first time he cut loose the advocates of strategic bombing and allowed targets in North Vietnam to be comprehensively attacked. For a brief moment it looked as if strategic bombing would have a major impact, but with media reports showing the scale of the impact in places like Hanoi the President was forced to call off the attacks once the North Vietnamese made overtures about reaching a political settlement.

They manoeuvred in the political space to negate the air force's manoeuvre in the physical dimension of war.

Since the Cuban Missile Crisis, aside from the United States bombing North Vietnam, the use of air power to try to coerce populations en masse on the ground has fallen away. As far as liberal-minded western political leaders are now concerned, trying to bomb a foreign country into submission by threatening its population at large is no longer acceptable. From this point onwards the definition of the strategic application of air power gradually changed.

Arguably over North Vietnam weaknesses in the application of tactical air power were also exposed. The missile era had started. It was to have an important effect on the combat tactics and equipment that needed to be developed. At the same time as one form of tactical air power was coming to terms with the next stage of its evolution a new form of air power emerged.

Air Power and Helicopters

The massed formations of helicopters flying into parts of South Vietnam were part of operations designed to flush the Viet Cong out of villages in and around the Mekong Delta. The scenes from the film *Apocalypse Now* with an airborne attack on a village being undertaken to loudspeakers blaring Wagner's *Ride of the Valkyries* provide a viewpoint of the way in which this relatively new formation of air power was applied.

This was a new form of manoeuvre using air mobility to place troops at short notice into combat with an insurgent that had the advantage of knowing the lie of the land. This form of air mobility depended upon operations in a relatively permissive environment. In operations in Afghanistan more so than Iraq the COIN operations saw a resurgence in the use of helicopters to deliver troops to a specific area where they wished to mass overwhelm an adversary.

Helicopters, of course, also have other roles. In Afghanistan today they play a huge part in saving the lives of servicemen injured or maimed in combat. One Chinook is maintained on stand-by all the time to conduct a medical evacuation (MEDEVAC). Similar roles had been conducted by Puma and Merlin helicopters in Iraq. The fearsome Apache helicopters can also deliver a range of fire-power as they fly close air-support missions. They have also on one notable occasion been used to recover the body of a serviceman who had been killed in action. On that day a serviceman tied himself to the side of the Apache and went to recover the body of his colleague under a hail of fire. For a two-seater helicopter carrying the additional load must have been challenging. It also provides a reminder of another of the elements of air power: the recovery of downed airmen or Combat Search and Rescue (CSAR) as it is known.

During the Vietnam War the issue of CSAR was enforced in the collective consciousness of the American people by media images of how airmen that had been shot down by the Viet Cong were treated. The stories and portrayal of the deprivations endured by captured airmen increased the resolve to try to rescue them if they had been shot down. Today CSAR is an integral part of any military campaign involving air power. In Libya in 2011 United States Super Stallion helicopters operating from the Royal Navy's HMS *Ocean* provided one element of that capability.

Widening the Applications Base of Air Power

The relative vulnerability of such formations to the kind of ground-to-air threat that could be deployed by the Soviets in the Cold War limited its application on the German Plain. There tactical air power would be crucial in trying to contain any onslaught through the Fulda Gap into what was then Western Germany. However, in the early part of the 1970s as the Cold War had yet to reach its peak NATO had to learn some salutary lessons about the limitations of tactical air power as the conflict between the Arabs and the Israelis erupted once more.

In the Yom Kippur War for a brief period of time tactical air power met its match as the Soviet-supplied Egyptian mobile air defence systems succeeded in destroying a high number of Israeli Air Force (IAF) aircraft. It is often thought that war can have a dramatic effect on the development of tactics and the application of new equipment. The Yom Kippur War was just such an event.

Twelve years later as it mounted Operation Wooden Leg the IAF was to project air power over 2,000km from its homeland to attack the headquarters of the Palestinian Liberation Organization (PLO) in Tunis. The raid by eight F-15 Eagles was supported by a Boeing 707 modified to act as an air-to-air refuelling tanker. To reach Tunis the aircraft flew a route that avoided Egyptian and Libyan radar systems and also contact with elements of the United States navy operating in the Mediterranean Sea.

The raid was carried out in retaliation for the killing of three Israelis on a yacht off the coast of Cyprus by the PLO elite group known as Force 17. This was the furthest distance the IAF had projected air power since the raid on Entebbe to release people hijacked by the PLO. The attack in Tunis had lasted six minutes.

Without the direct intervention of the United States in the Yom Kippur War in 1973 the Israeli position would have been precarious. The nature of the strategic airlift mounted by the United States Air Force to support the Israelis dwarfed anything it had tried to do previously. In Iraq and in Afghanistan the air-bridge from the United States and the United Kingdom into both countries became a crucial application of air power to help maintain their forces operating in theatre.

In one of the less easily remembered demonstrations of air power the United States demonstrated that a strategic cargo-carrying aircraft could not only carry military equipment to a friendly state but also act as a platform for the launch of a ballistic missile. In 1974 the United States Air Force flew a Minuteman ballistic missile to a height of 20,000ft in a C-5 Galaxy aircraft. Parachutes pulled the missile out of the back of the payload bay on a mounting rig. As that fell away the missile adopted an upright position before its engines fired. The tests that were conducted were completely successful. While the concept was never taken forward into an operational capacity, it provided another example of the flexibility and adaptability of air power. A new dimension had been added to the notion of strategic heavy lift.

For the Royal Air Force strategic heavy-lift operations have a long and important history that started after the end of the Second World War as British outposts in the Far East needed to be supported. The ten Shorts Belfast aircraft that provided the core of the heavy-lifting capability in the 1960s and 1970s in the lead-up to the British withdrawal from the east of Suez provided the capability that the eight Boeing C-17s perform today.

Their range and payload capabilities provide the Royal Air Force with an ability to project both hard and soft power across the globe in short order. From floods in Columbia, to deliver money into Benghazi at the end of the Libyan campaign, to the important task of evacuating the severely wounded from theatre, to the solemn duty of repatriating fallen colleagues back to the United Kingdom, the C-17s carry out a diverse range of missions on a day-to-day basis.

Of all the novel applications of air power, perhaps the mission to destroy low-orbit satellites is one of the most interesting and challenging. In the United States interest in what became known as Anti-Satellite (ASAT) missions started in the late 1950s. Russia had only launched Sputnik on 4 October 1957. It had lasted barely three months in orbit but its military significance was quickly appreciated.

Within two years the United States conducted its first ASAT test. The Bold Orion missile was launched from a B-47 Stratojet and passed within

4 miles of its target, the United States Explorer 6 satellite which had been launched two months earlier to conduct a range of experiments. The satellite also carried the first on-board camera and beamed cloud images to a ground station. It was to be the start of the use of satellites to monitor a vast array of things on the Earth.

While the mission was deemed a success, it would have taken a nuclear warhead on the ASAT to have destroyed the satellite. Between 1964 and 1967 the United States maintained a single Nike Zeus missile on stand-by in the ASAT role. It was nuclear-armed and had been originally designed as part of the first generation of Ballistic Missile Defence systems deployed by the United States to counter advances in Russian ballistic missile systems.

As the resolution of the instruments aboard the satellites grew, so too did their operational importance. At a time of war military powers may not wish to have an adversary looking into their backyard. Developing an operational ASAT capability was seen to be an imperative.

On 13 September 1985 at the height of the Cold War an F-15A aircraft that had been especially modified to carry an ASAT weapon called the ASM-135 destroyed an orbiting solar wind laboratory that had previously been launched by the United States. A previous test launch in November 1984 had failed to acquire the target. Two further successful tests were also accomplished in August and September 1986. In all fifteen ASM-135 missiles were built and five underwent flight-testing.

The new capability came at a time when concerns were being raised about a new 'space race'. Arguments were put forward that suggested it was perhaps a good idea not to target satellite systems after all. If the United States had the capability to destroy Soviet satellites in the run-up to war they would inevitably respond and develop a similar capability. Others argued that the whole thing was very destabilizing in an era of Mutual Assured Destruction (MAD). A pre-emptive move to destroy another state's satellites could be seen as the opening salvos in war.

These concerns had led the United States Congress to place limitations on the development of the ASM-135. In 1988 the plan to equip twenty modified F-15A fighters from two wings of the United States Air Force was abandoned. Its demise was principally down to cost overruns and delays due to the technical nature of the challenges involved. The military utility of an operational ASAT system was not sufficient for it to receive further funding.

Its potential role has been consigned to a starring role in a Tom Clancy novel called *Red Storm Rising* in which the ASM-135 engages and destroys two Soviet ocean-monitoring satellites called RORSATs. Had it ever crossed the bridge from fiction into reality the use of the ASM-135 would have had a strategic, operational and tactical impact on the battlefield had it been able to successfully destroy Soviet satellite systems.

ASAT development, however, has not been confined to the United States. During the Cold War reports emerged on more than one occasion of a site in Russia that was thought to have a capability to use a high-powered laser to damage the solar panels on low earth-orbit satellites or to 'dazzle' or blind their sensor systems. The actual role of the site remains the subject of speculation.

In 2007 China also showed its interest in ASAT technology. On 11 January a Chinese weather satellite named FY-1C that was based in polar orbit was destroyed by a head-on engagement by a multi-stage rocket deployed from mainland China. The debris from the test spread out in space over the coming weeks and caused a great deal of international reaction. It was the largest single event responsible for the creation of space debris that has occurred to date.

As a demonstration of the medium-term effects of such tests in 2011 and 2012 debris from the test threatened the International Space Station. Reports that quickly emerged from Washington suggested that this test had been the third in a series where the previous two had failed. Suggestions that the Chinese had also biased the test by making the interceptor 'home' onto a beacon on the satellite followed as well.

The development of such a capability fits well with emerging Chinese military doctrine. Its emphasis on what it calls the 'Assassin's Mace' is a reference to a historical weapon system known as the *Shashou Jian*. Armed with this weapon it is possible for an adversary to be quickly overwhelmed and defeated. In contemporary Chinese military doctrine the idea has been developed to embrace a number of new and emerging technologies that would help their military forces gain a swift advantage in the event of the outbreak of war.

Latterly tactical air power has shown yet further adaptations as it has had to deal with the issue of emergent targets. Instead of tactical combat sorties lasting around an hour, aircraft were deployed over Iraq, Afghanistan and Libya for up to eight hours at a time, being refuelled by air-to-air tankers like the VC-10 and the Tristar.

Over Libya this allowed air power to be available at a moment's notice, called in when ISTAR assets spotted a potential target, such as a Libyan army tank or other improvised military vehicles (the aptly-named 'technicals' based on the ubiquitous Toyota Land Cruiser) carrying GRAD rockets. Hardened fixed targets were engaged by strike missions that were flown from places like RAF Marham where Tornado aircraft carried the stand-off weapon known as Storm Shadow to help extend their range into the deepest parts of Libya.

Images of the Royal Navy ships destroyed by the Argentinian Air Force in the conflict over the Falkland Islands and the operations of the Royal Navy and Royal Air Force Harrier aircraft also reveal a time at which tactical air power was beginning to reassert itself. In the First Gulf War extensive bombing did occur in the build-up to the land war but that was directed at military formations. It is easy to recall the effect the bombing had on the Iraqi conscripts. The speed with which the ground war was executed to free Kuwait was clearly linked to the extensive effort to target the ground troops before the ground offensive began.

In 2001 and the early part of 2002 in Afghanistan extensive bombing of Taliban defensive positions also created the conditions for a successful and speedy ground attack by the Northern Alliance. Until that intervention, prompted by the terrorist attacks in the United States, the situation on the ground had come to a lengthy stalemate. The Taliban had been able to overrun most of Afghanistan but simply could not dislodge the Northern Alliance from its enclave in the north of the country.

As B-52 bombers struck the front lines of the Taliban tactical air power was being delivered by a platform that had been originally designed to perform a strategic mission in an example of the flexibility of the ways in which air power can be applied. Arguably, however, both of these examples represent operational uses of air power in contrast to their strategic application.

Perhaps of all the developments in air power at the start of the twenty-first century it is the use of unmanned aircraft to target the sanctuaries in Pakistan occupied by Al Qaeda and groups affiliated with the Taliban operating in Afghanistan that causes the most controversy.

The first use of armed drones to strike at key leaders of Al Qaeda occurred on 3 November 2002. A vehicle carrying the Al Qaeda leader Qaed Senyan Abu Ali al-Harithi was attacked by the Predator. Since then unmanned aircraft strikes by Predator and Reaper platforms have become routine. For those minded to criticize any use of military force the operations of the Predator and Reaper drones over the Federally Administered Tribal Areas (FATA) in north-western Pakistan are a specific rallying point.

The idea that a man operates the machine via satellite links several tens of thousands of miles away from the platform rankles them. Their argument appears to be based on the idea that if the pilot was in the cockpit and able to see imagery from the target area of the ground if he killed women and children he would be held accountable. Some parts of the media seem set on finding ways of undermining any moral case for the use of such weapons. Reports have even resorted to suggesting that as the pilots live at home and take breakfast with their children before going to work they become somehow immune to the realities of war.

The implication that those who are carefully trained to fight contemporary wars and are well aware of the legal minefields associated with the use of force somehow divorce themselves from the war zone because of the distances involved is frankly clutching at straws. While on a very small number of occasions procedures have not been followed to the letter, they are the exception rather than the norm. It is a fact that unmanned aircraft are now a feature of contemporary warfare and while that does seek to create an excuse for those occasions when mistakes are made, it does recognize that they do have a basic military utility that is hard to deny.

The Emergence of Soft Power Applications

Air power, of course, is not all about what is referred to these days as delivering kinetic effect. At a time when political leaders' sensibility to being accused of killing people has never been higher the doctrine writers have sought to develop a new lexicon that somehow waters down the actions that are being taken. Today terms like soft power and smart power have emerged to try to overcome the negative images of the use of air power for purely destructive purposes. When there are opportunities to use air power in this way it can bring real benefits to those in need.

When disaster struck in Haiti in 2010 it was air power that was in the forefront of the delivery of relief aid. It is an aspect of the way air power is applied that is sometimes easily overlooked. Air power can be applied in ways that help populations. Initial parachute drops were used to get aid to areas that were cut off by the severity of the earthquake.

After some operational issues in getting there, the main airport at Port-au-Prince was able to handle around forty aircraft unloading relief supplies. This was three times the usual number of aircraft that could be handled by the limited airport facilities, but it was still not enough and the lack of ground facilities proved to be a major bottleneck in getting relief supplies to those in need.

These are a small but important list of the ways in which air power has been applied in its first century of operations. They provide a broad cross-section of examples that show air power in a number of different lights and set the scene for what follows.

Characterizing Air Power

In trying to relate the story of the first century of air power it is worth trying to establish from the outset what the idea means. Definitions of air power abound in the doctrine manuals of air forces in all corners of the Earth. Each one, no doubt, represents some specific facet of air power that is of specific interest to that area and some general concepts about how air power should be applied.

It is an interesting point of debate as to how the doctrine of air power has evolved. Some might argue that the doctrine writers update their writings in the wake of military interventions and that helps develop the new generation of aircraft, their mission equipment and payloads. Others may take a different view that air power has always been enabled by technological developments and the doctrine writers simply have to catch up with the pace at which new capabilities are introduced. The truth no doubt lies somewhere in between these views.

Another issue over air power is that it is often applied to achieve different effects. Air power has in the past often been classified into its application at the tactical, operational or strategic level. Today there is even the notion of something that doctrine writers are tempted to call grand-strategic. When seeing such definitions it is important to remember that this is not a one-dimensional view of the application of air power.

Terms such as air policing, air superiority and air supremacy now frequently appear in doctrine. Air policing of course differs slightly from the other two terms. It is a mission. The others are a state which can be dynamic. One example illustrates the role of air policing as a mission.

Over the Baltic States NATO conducts operations to help protect the airspace of Latvia, Estonia and Lithuania. NATO aircraft, provided on force rotation from a number of states, ensure that the integrity of the airspace over the states is maintained. It provides reassurance to the populations of the Baltic States. With the Russian Air Force returning to conducting intelligence collection missions the NATO aircraft provide a visible reminder of states' membership of NATO.

Air superiority and air supremacy are potentially transitory states of air control. In a non-permissive environment an adversary may seek to contest the control of the skies. The parties that are involved in that contest for the skies will depend upon local circumstances. The means by which that airspace is contested does not always mean that fighter aircraft will become involved in air-to-air combat or dogfights.

During NATO's Operation Northern Watch mobile Iraqi air defence systems would frequently use their radars to illuminate the patrolling

NATO aircraft. These were often brief encounters. If the radar showed any hostile shift in its illumination patterns, suggesting that a missile launch might be imminent, then the rules of engagement allowed NATO aircraft to take offensive action. The Iraqi radar operators quickly learnt that to leave their radars on for any length of time was to invite retaliation.

During the coalition operations in Iraq a Royal Air Force C-130 Hercules aircraft was shot down as it left an airbase near Baghdad. It was brought down by gunfire from the ground. Those firing their weapons into the air were contesting the airspace. The impact of the crash and the death of all those on board the aircraft were to have an important effect upon the way future missions by C-130s were conducted. It also caused a major redesign on the wing tanks carried by the C-130 to supplement their fuel loads.

In the early days of the military campaign in Afghanistan the Taliban did possess some rather dated anti-aircraft guns. While relatively ineffective against fighter jets, they could pose a real threat to helicopters. The Taliban have often made repeated attempts to gain access to slightly modern versions of such weapons, and stories and rumours have often emerged of them adding to their depleted inventory.

Today when the Taliban try to contest the air they have had some success against NATO helicopters using Rocket Propelled Grenades (RPG) and some light-arms fire. During the war with the Soviets the Afghans did have help from the west with the provision of Stinger missiles which proved very effective in limiting the use of air power.

While rumours persist of some Stingers remaining in the Taliban inventory, problems with battery life and finding people who know how to use the weapon may restrict their operational use. As yet no open source-reporting suggests that the Taliban have been able to gain access to modern Man Portable Air Defence Systems (MANPADS). In Libya in 2011 NATO and coalition forces did report times when they were engaged by such systems. With today's active black market in such weapon systems, air power has to be exercised in any theatre of operations with due care. The air-bridge to Afghanistan does feature a final twenty-minute descent into theatre in total blackout on the aircraft to reduce the risk of being engaged by ground fire. Near to airfields some measure of protection is also afforded to air movements by patrols mounted by organizations such as the RAF Regiment.

Where a military actor is able to achieve a state of air superiority they are able to ensure that if an adversary resorts to the use of air power, any incursion into the controlled area will be met with force and that if required the encroaching aircraft will be shot down.

While few doctrine writers like to put a figure on the ratio of combat losses that represent a state of air superiority, recent operations suggest that it exists as a state when the outcome of any air-to-air engagement is a foregone conclusion. The state of air supremacy exists when an enemy's air force chooses not to contest the skies. In 2012 with Iraq's air force yet to become fully operational and equipped with its new F-16 aircraft, reports are appearing in the media to suggest that Turkey, Syria and Iran are routinely violating Iraqi airspace.

The term air policing arose from the NATO operations over north and south Iraq during the 1990s. This role was carried out to ensure that the Iraqi regime in Baghdad did not try to use air power to suppress the Kurdish people in the north or the Shia population in the south of the country. For many years NATO provided flights over the area. That their operations were contested cannot be in doubt. The game of 'cat and mouse' played out between Iraqi air-defence system operators and the patrolling NATO aircraft became an almost daily occurrence.

The Impact of the Media

In the twenty-first century air power can no longer be simply defined as being applied at the tactical, operational and strategic levels of command. It is more complex than that. A tactical application of air power, in a very specific situation, can have a major effect at the strategic level. What has changed is the ubiquity of the media.

At the start of the twenty-first century the international coverage of the media has changed how air power is seen and how people react to its application. Events that in the past would have gone unreported are now quickly beamed into the households of people throughout the world. The impact on the American population of the scenes broadcast from Vietnam into their living rooms has gone global. It is, however, a two-edged sword. It has both positive and negative connotations.

When humanitarian relief supplies arrive quickly by air in a region devastated by a natural or man-made disaster the long-term impact of such aid can be beneficial. The application of air power in such situations can literally change long-standing attitudes and beliefs. By contrast when air power results in what is known rather heartlessly as collateral damage, a phrase that almost seeks to deny the reality of what has happened, the backlash in the short and long term can be quite profound.

It is clear that now more than ever its use has to become highly selective. On complex and dynamic battlefields where the old division of enemy and friend is hard to establish, that nirvana of the selective application of air power has some way to go.

In contemporary military operations when civilians die in air strikes it can send shock waves through military and political coalitions. No one is immune from the backlash. Political leaders often find it hard to articulate the reasons behind the need to take such risks with the lives of non-combatants. Whereas one-off events may have a limited impact on public opinion a series of mishaps can quickly result in a tipping-point being reached. The problem for political leaders is that when such reactions occur it is very difficult to regain the initiative.

The solutions to these dilemmas are not easy. Where such actions are deemed necessary by political leaders they must also recognize the need to continue to invest in the development of the Intelligence, Surveillance, Target Acquisition and Recognition (ISTAR) systems that can help air power be applied selectively. If it is not, the international media will quickly sit in judgement, helping to shape public opinion.

Today against this backdrop of media scrutiny a tactical application of air power in a very specific situation can have huge strategic implications. Events in Syria in 2012 where the Assad regime applied air power against his own people were quickly revealed to the world by postings through the myriad of social networking sites on the internet. The international condemnation that follows rarely has an effect upon such regimes. They are used to acting with impunity. They create a narrative about dealing with terrorist groups, which is a line also adopted by the Gaddafi regime in 2011, and proceed to apply a range of military actions against their people. This provides them with what they believe to be legitimacy for their actions. They argue that by using their own military against the population they are seeking to stabilize a difficult situation.

That is not a viewpoint necessarily held by those who look at events through a different lens. They see a despotic regime desperately trying to maintain itself in power and willing to do anything to achieve that aim. In 2011 the regime in Tripoli was surprised when the international community drew a red line at the people in Benghazi being slaughtered. In Syria in 2012 that red line was erased. If the political will cannot be created the military instrument has no value.

A Military Instrument

To generalize a term such as air power is always risky. However, if air power is to mean anything as a part of a military instrument of power then it must be applied in ways that can affect a range of complex socio-political situations, from the national to the regional and global level. Ideally as a result of applying air power a situation on the ground must be improved, such as when the threat to the citizens of Benghazi was removed in 2011 by the NATO air strikes on the Gaddafi forces threatening the city. There are many examples that illustrate the current and past applications of air power.

Air power's first tentative steps in the skies over Europe in the First World War provided a reference point for all future developments in doctrine. Suddenly, rather than flying straight and level over the battlefield trying to spot the fall of shot of the artillery, aircraft had to be able to manoeuvre.

The dogfights involving aces like the Red Baron provided the first examples of the kind of air-to-air combat witnessed in Korea in the 1950s and in various brief exchanges between jet aircraft in the battles over the Bekkar Valley in the Lebanon or between American aircraft and the Libyan Air Force. Those actors involved in the conflict would, as technology permitted, contest the skies. In time it is highly likely that space will also be contested, although developments in anti-satellite missile technologies and hypersonic craft are still in their earliest stages.

It would be easy to suggest that the major developments in air power occurred during the two world wars that took place in the twentieth century. While some new ways of applying air power did arise and other established areas reached a new level of maturity, it would be wrong to suggest that the doctrine of air power was somehow driven only by the necessities of war. Being at war has a tempo all of its own. Developments in doctrine rarely emerge during wartime as those involved have precious little time to sit down and take stock of the situation.

The Germans, for example, used the 1920s and 1930s to do a lot of thinking and development of how they might fight the next war. The development of blitzkrieg and its subsequent application occurred in the laboratory of military schools.

Of all the missions that apply air power the defence of the airspace of the homeland is possibly the one that most resonates with the public. Given that the first duty of any political leader is the defence of his or her own country, the application of air power to ensure that any enemy is unable to breach their own airspace is paramount. The Battle of Britain is perhaps the foremost example of this kind of application of air power. As the power balance in the Second World War shifted it was Nazi Germany that had to erect its own fighter defence capabilities to deal with the incessant day and night raids on its industrial heartland.

Air power is not just about the application of what contemporary doctrine refers to as kinetic or hard power. It is also versatile and flexible enough to help apply what has been termed 'smart' power: making things happen without necessarily seeking to kill people or destroy property.

The delivery of humanitarian aid provides one example of a positive outcome. Of all of the examples of this the airlift maintained by NATO into Sarajevo during the Balkans conflicts ranks as one which provided a vital lifeline for the people of the embattled city. It had all the hallmarks of the Berlin Airlift. While not on a similar scale, forces deployed into theatres of operation also require re-supply. During the Second World War in the depths of the Burma jungle British troops operating behind enemy lines depended on the re-supply operations that were mounted by the Royal Air Force.

For troops on the ground hemmed in by insurgents a high-speed overpass by an armed fast jet can disperse the threat. If that does not have the desired impact then the insurgents can be attacked through coordination with a Forward Area Controller (FAC) operating on the ground. In the Second World War air power was applied in this tactical arena to help troops on the ground in the North African theatre of operations.

These are a few examples of the application of air power. They are not a comprehensive list. In the course of this analysis a number of pivotal moments in the evolution of air power will be highlighted. These are moments when the application of air power had a major impact. They would change the way the doctrine writers would think about the future evolution of air power.

The Gestation of Air Power

In the 100 years since man first took to the air to explore flying, the military applications of being able to master the art perfected by the birds since the dawn of time have widened and deepened. In some cases this development of the role of air power has occurred in very short periods of time.

Whereas warfare can be charted back to the dawn of civilization, air warfare has seen developments that have outpaced land and naval forms of warfare. In the century of air power the number of advances and innovations in the ways in which aircraft play a role in warfare has developed at a remarkable rate.

All of these developments are predicated on a simple view. Air power has a unique vantage point from which to observe the world and through which to provide effect. While that was an obvious military attraction, air power was nevertheless going to experience a difficult gestation.

Over time it has been able to apply that effect faster, with greater precision and over ranges that span the globe. That combination of speed, range and variety of effect is quite unique in terms of its application as an instrument of military power. Today the value of that contribution to military operations is clear as air forces around the world make their contributions to national, regional and global security.

Arguably in Libya in 2011 the tactical application of air power reached a new peak as it showed its other major characteristic of versatility. Over the century of air power this has not always been the case. From conception, through gestation to its birth, air power had to demonstrate that it could live up to expectations. In the early days there were many who remained unconvinced.

It is difficult to determine, as might be expected with the passage of time, when precisely air power passed its initial point of military acceptance. Navigating through what are often conflicting accounts of the period is hard when different historians cite stories that all appear to demonstrate the point at which air power moved beyond the amateur to the semi-professional and onwards into routine military application. The transition through each stage is not easy to identify.

In such a morass of evidence locating a single tipping-point is difficult. What is clear, however, is that once the genie of air power emerged from the pioneering research that solved the basic control function issues to maintain an aircraft in the air the speed with which it transitioned into military applications was rapid, spurred on by the imminent outbreak of war in Europe.

There is little doubt that in the immediate aftermath of the famous flight at Kitty Hawk there were a number of enthusiastic individuals who were keen to explore the potential of aviation. Many were wealthy people who were driven by the dream of being able to fly. It was easy in those days to label aviation as the sole purview of those with large amounts of money. There were notable exceptions. These were a small coterie of people with a genuine passion for developing aviation. They had faith that once the capability had been produced its application would be obvious. These were people motivated by a common vision but not necessarily by ideas of cooperation. Rivalry in the early days was intense.

As important developments around how to actually control an aircraft emerged others were quick to catch on. Legal action did occur on a small number of occasions as people sought to protect their intellectual property rights. While some might be easily labelled eccentrics, others carefully applied scientific principles to their quest. Governments, on the other hand, were initially slow to pick up on the potential with some dismissing aviation as the sole purview of the rich.

Many of those early pioneers did not take the risks they did because they had a dream of a supersonic aircraft flying from London to New York in just over three hours. They tried to fly because as wealthy people or enthusiasts it gave them a sense of doing something that was extraordinary at the time. They were conquering the final frontier, driven by all those who wondered if man could ever leave the ground and emulate the birds. One hundred years on their legacy is still recognized in the names of a number of highly successful aircraft companies that set out on that journey in the period beyond 1910.

These pioneers' mastery of flight came at the point when the foreboding clouds of war were gathering over Europe. As armies mobilized on what seemed an inevitable march to war the aircraft was just emerging in a simple enough form for governments to explore its potential role in a military situation. The first and most obvious role was to use the vantage point of the sky. Being able to fly over the enemy lines removed some of the fog of war. It was, however, an erratic source. On many occasions throughout the war the smoke created by bombardment allowed the fog of war to settle back over the battlefield. The bird's-eye view was not a complete panacea. It had its problems.

From the outset and even to today the issue of the timeliness of passing information derived from the aircraft to the ground has been important. When the fog of war cleared, albeit briefly on some occasions, what was seen from the air had to be quickly conveyed to the ground commanders to help their overall situational awareness. Ingenious methods were developed to solve this problem in the First World War.

Where cameras were mounted on aircraft their operation was often difficult. Whereas today airmen take for granted the benefits of automated navigation data being tagged to any imagery, in the First World War knowing where an image had been taken was not straightforward. After years of stalemate on the Western Front the terrain had become quite featureless. The vagaries of the weather also did not help.

The military value in the image depended upon its location being established accurately. This is referred to as geo-referencing the image. As the image was then analysed any changes in enemy dispositions could be accurately assessed. This was the start of the process of change detection which even to this day underpins the whole approach to photo-interpretation.

Given the circumstances on the ground that simple task of geo-registering the image was not easy to do unless the airmen involved had lots of experience over that area of the battlefield. These kinds of issues limited the tactical value of some of the imagery. Understandably senior army commanders involved in the war used these situations to bemoan the contribution made by the aircraft.

To many of them its potential had been overhyped. At best it could occasionally provide a detailed picture of a small area of the battlefield, but given the stalemate on the Western Front the intelligence value of images rarely interested ground commanders. They were operating on a much different scale of warfare. They were operating at the grand-strategic level of warfare. This was war on a continental scale. Images over a small part of the battlefield offered little of military value.

A series of images over an area of the Western Front of several hundred kilometres would have raised some interest, but assembling such imagery and creating a mosaic of the resulting pictures took time. Weather was an ever-present limitation to those conducting flying operations. With all these challenges to surmount it is perhaps understandable that the military value of air power took some time to catch on. Even on the few early occasions when aircraft were used in an offensive capacity their impact was minimal. The generals were unimpressed. Artillery barrages across vast swathes of the Western Front were still in their view the way to make progress. Air power's contribution was easy to label as puny and insignificant.

Already wary of its potential to erode the previously unassailable position of the army, senior commanders also used every opportunity to undermine the potential of air power. Among a cadre of senior commanders there was a very real antipathy towards air power. If it was to achieve its potential it needed to show that it could play a crucial role that could help ground manoeuvre at the grand-strategic scale.

On 22 August 1914 two aviators from 3 Squadron Royal Flying Corps (RFC) were operating in the Grammont area of East Flanders. They detected a large German formation on the ground that was passing through the area. What they had seen were elements of General Alexander von Kluck's plan to initiate the right wheel of the Von Schlieffen plan.

This was a strategic manoeuvre whose initial stages of development were detected by the RFC. This was a major breakthrough. The eye in the sky had detected the beginnings of a grand-strategic manoeuvre. It was to provide a base from which air power would finally be accepted as an important source of intelligence at the tactical, operational and strategic levels of warfare.

The plan envisaged defeating France inside six weeks before the might of the German military would be turned on Russia. The Von Schlieffen plan by-passed the defensive line of the fortified French towns and cities along the direct border between France and Germany. Instead of a direct onslaught the Germans would move to the north through Luxembourg, Belgium and The Netherlands outflanking the French positions. With speed and good fortune the Germans believed they could defeat France quickly.

Armed with the observations from the aviators over Grammont, Field Marshal Sir John French decided to commit as many forces as he could to make a stand at Mons. Ironically air power had helped prepare the British Expeditionary Force (BEF) for what was supposed to be an unexpected attack. By deploying forces at Mons the BEF thwarted the German offensive and created the conditions in which the Western Front would become stalemated. During what became an orderly retreat from Mons the RFC flew a series of reconnaissance missions that enabled the detailed movements of the German army to be monitored.

For the first time in history the vantage point of the air provided ground commanders with an important strategic, operational and tactical advantage. On 7 September 1914 Sir John French recorded his appreciation of the contribution made by the RFC when he wrote a dispatch recording that 'they have furnished me with the most complete and accurate information which has been of incalculable value.' If all the time up until this point had been the period when air power was gestating, arguably this was the point at which it was truly born into the world of military capability. Now it had to grow up and move through adolescence into being an adult.

This was the first of many incidents, often recounted in historical accounts of the time, that showed the speed with which air power played a key role in shaping events on the ground. Nearly 100 years later, had he been alive today, Sir John would have understood the value of ISTAR assets and the role they played in Libya in 2011 in helping focus air power on the battlefield. That, of course, would have been tempered with concerns over the emergence of air power as a decisive tool in a campaign.

Cold War Perspectives

For the years of the Cold War air power was focused on the air-land battle. In Europe air power was the key to the outcome of any conflict between the Warsaw Pact and NATO. It was where NATO had and maintained an advantage. While the Warsaw Pact on paper could mass superior numbers of land forces and use mobility to try to force NATO into retreat, it was in the air over the German Plain that the decisive element of the battle would be fought.

NATO warplanes would have to conduct three essential parallel missions. The first was to defend the airbases from which NATO was operating. The Harrier force deployed by the United Kingdom offered some mobility away from the fixed airbases, but it was the air power that could be deployed from the fixed airbases that was crucial.

A major investment in the deployment of Hardened Aircraft Shelters (HAS) and the development of complex taxiways and runways provided increased survivability from air attack. Interestingly in China today satellite observations of the main airbases show very similar patterns of development of the runways, taxiways and HAS. Chinese airbases are being built and modernized in ways that emphasize an ability to maintain a conflict should one break out.

At the height of the Cold War many of these airbases were also threatened by Russian Short Range Ballistic Missiles (SRBM). If they were deployed using conventional weapons it would have been hard to completely close down NATO airbases; some operational capability would have been retained. If the SRBM had been armed with even low-yield tactical nuclear weapons the ability of NATO to maintain any sort of operational tempo would have been seriously challenged.

NATO's second mission was to attack the leading edge of any Warsaw Pact encroachment into Western Europe. Blunting the tempo of that attack would have been essential. The whole NATO stance was based upon being able to then move relief supplies across the Atlantic Ocean. Securing those sea lanes of communications would be essential. That would involve a small-scale air-sea battle involving NATO maritime strike and long-range maritime patrol aircraft.

The last mission priority for NATO would have been to mount missions to conduct Follow On Forces Attack (FOFA). This was the need to get beyond the Forward Edge of the Battlefield Area (FEBA) and get into the second echelon troops that would be massing close to the border area ready to be launched into the battle. Their task was to maintain the momentum that the first echelon forces were expected to achieve given their numerical advantage. These three missions were the core of the air-land battle.

As the threat from the Warsaw Pact disintegrated and the Russian military became anaemic in its capabilities the overall security landscape in Western Europe dramatically changed. The threat was now seen to arise from long-range ballistic missiles being developed in Iran and North Korea. Theatre missile defence systems that had been a topic of interest for many years suddenly became a point of agreement in NATO.

Applying Air Power to Achieve Effect

Today the application of air power has moved well beyond its adolescence into adulthood. That transition has been accompanied by the writing of numerous works on the doctrine of how to apply air power to achieve effect. That has in turn been accompanied by a burgeoning lexicon of terms and language that describe its uses in a whole range of military campaigns.

It is characteristic of military doctrine and campaigns that with each new evolution of the technical capabilities to fight war new lexicons appear. Air power is no exception. ISTAR is one of numerous elements of the ever-changing military lexicon. The proliferation of three-letter acronyms grows exponentially. For those not directly au fait with the terminology a briefing room in a Royal Air Force base can be an intimidating location as terms are bandied about to describe the planning and conduct of a variety of different missions.

While technological advances have changed the ways in which aerial warfare is conducted, the essential element of air power, to deliver *effect* upon a target, remains the same. It is just the way the realization of that objective is achieved that varies.

Of all the recent changes to the lexicons of the military it is the term 'effect' that so dramatically illustrates the new world order in which some military planners, such as those working within NATO, find themselves. Gone are the days when air power was solely about killing enemies. The depiction of air power as a means by which one military can defeat another by shooting down aircraft in large numbers, destroying infantry, cavalry, tanks and battleships or carpet-bombing cities is far too narrow.

In the United States warfare has always been seen in quite mathematical terms. The objective is to reduce an enemy's capabilities by destroying a specific percentage of their forces. This can be thought of as quite a scientific approach to warfare, dominated by the Operational Analysts. The new era of effects-based warfare does not lend itself so easily to such an approach and in part explains why the United States military has struggled to adapt to the kind of COIN environments in which it has been operating in Iraq and Afghanistan. Had Sun Tzu been alive today he would have understood how effects-based warfare is less about science and mathematics and more about art. In the era of effects-based warfare the notion of the art of war has come full circle.

Air power today thrives on its selective application across a much wider range of missions. From humanitarian relief operations through to the destruction of a command bunker in Tripoli, air power is also showing how that rare combination of speed, range and type of effect can be innovatively applied.

One important thing that has also emerged through the first century of air power is that the distinction between its tactical, operational and strategic application has become blurred. One of the by-products of looking for effects is that the application of air power now can be seen through a two-dimensional lens in contrast to a single dimension.

In the past it has been customary to view air power as being applied at the tactical, operational or strategic level. The implication was that air power applied at the tactical level was only designed to have a tactical effect. The relationship between application and effect was assumed to be one-to-one, but with the advent of 'effects-based warfare' the single dimension now opens up into a two-dimensional world. Air power now may be applied at the tactical level to achieve a strategic effect. One of the enablers of that change is the ubiquitous presence of the media.

The strategic benefits of air power in the First World War arose from its tactical application. In the Second World War air-power enthusiasts defined a whole new vision. Air power was applied at the strategic level to achieve what they argued were strategic benefits. The Blitz and the subsequent application by the Allies of air power over Germany were examples of this new view of air power.

Today it is clear that tactical air power applied in a decisive way can have dramatic strategic consequences. The citizens of Aleppo know that when they are bombed by the Syrian Air Force, images will make it out onto the internet and provide a catalyst for calls for action. For western political leaders such coverage makes uncomfortable viewing.

Only a year earlier they had applied air power in what was a new and innovative way to remove a despotic regime. A matter of months later through the political intransigence of Russia and China the west seems paralysed and unable to act; seemingly incapable of even mustering the effort to create a no-fly zone such as was used over Iraq to protect the Kurds and Shia population in the south of the country.

Air power has other limitations. In today's world where the media pick up on any incident when civilians get caught in the crossfire there are ample examples of air power having been applied less than scientifically. Images from Kosovo, Iraq, Afghanistan and more recently Libya provide important reminders as to the continuing challenges faced by advocates of air power.

The move to using unmanned aircraft, or drones as they are often called, adds another dimension. Reports arising from drone attacks often play on the deaths of innocents. In practice the groups that are targeted know how to play to fears and debate in the west on the legality of using unmanned aircraft. Their utility in combating the increasingly geographically-dispersed franchises of Al Qaeda cannot be in doubt, but when things go wrong they do have a lasting impact from a military viewpoint. Tensions between Pakistan and the United States over drone attacks did not solely focus on their use. It also caused Pakistan to close down the logistical supply routes through Pakistan used by NATO to maintain their operations in Afghanistan.

The tactical application of air power against an enemy hiding in a sanctuary in Pakistan quickly translates into a geo-strategic issue for NATO, as it needs to open up new re-supply routes to ensure the operations in Afghanistan can be sustained. There are two keys to solving this difficult problem. One of those lies in better intelligence feeds to ensure that targets are very selectively engaged. The other lies in the development of even more precise weapons whose effect can be adjusted at the point of release. If NATO is to be engaged in any future 'upstream' conflict which may mature into a COIN operation these two areas are important points for development. However, that is not the whole story when it comes to the future of air power.

Wider Applications

Across the globe air power is being applied in an increasing number of ways to achieve effect. It is being used in various ways in both inter-state as well as intra-state conflicts to address local and regional security issues. Whereas in the past the focal point of air power was its projection against a backdrop of large-scale warfare between power blocks, its use in the twenty-first century is changing.

In Mexico air power is used by the government to move its forces into areas where drug cartels are rampant on the ground. This is an example of where the term 'enemy of the state' now gets applied to other Mexicans trying to run criminal business operations. In Columbia a similar application of air power against the drug cartels occurs.

In the Philippines the government has to use air power to try to disrupt the operations of insurgents who use the vast geography of the archipelago in which to manoeuvre. Before the break-up of Sudan the very small Sudanese Air Force was used against those in the southern territories that sought to break away from Khartoum. These are examples of where air power has to be used within the state to help maintain its own security. There are other contemporary examples.

In Syria in 2012 images emerged of raids by the Syrian Air Force against members of opposition armed groups trying to displace the Assad regime. This involved helicopters and aircraft in attacks against major population centres in Syria.

There are a number of other situations in which today air power is being employed across traditional state boundaries. On several occasions in 2012 Syrian jets have flown into Iraq to attack anti-Assad factions operating just across the border. With the Iraqi Air Force yet to be reconstructed into any sort of counter-air capability its borders are regularly transgressed by other nations with Iran using Iraqi airspace also to supply the Assad regime with weapons. Iraq's inability to be able to police its airspace effectively is leading to it being exploited by other nation states.

Turkey is one state that applies air power against insurgent bases located in a neighbouring state. In Iraq Kurdish rebels that seek to cede from Turkey have created bases from which they can project power across the border into eastern Turkey. While on a small number of occasions this has led the Turkish army to mount a cross-border invasion into Iraq, the trend is for the Turkish Air Force to bear the brunt of the attacks.

In contrast in Vietnam air power is applied from what might be regarded as quite a traditional viewpoint: that is to oppose the ability of another state to manoeuvre in the air, land and maritime domain. For Vietnam the argument with China over the ownership of the Paracel Islands in the South China Sea is a potential catalyst for war. This is one example of a number of potential flash-points in the South China Sea.

The ongoing dispute over the sovereignty of the Diaoyu Islands between China and Japan is another case study. South Korea is another state, with American help, that would use air power in a variety of roles if war with North Korea were to be resumed. Israel, like South Korea, finds itself in a similar position with air power being the principal means by which it could engage Iran if it decided to act against the Iranian nuclear programme.

In Georgia when Russian forces intervened over the status of South Ossetia air power was one of the elements used with airborne forces being dropped into the outskirts of Tskhinvali, the major population centre in South Ossetia. The Russian Air Force also conducted a series of well-orchestrated attacks around the Georgian capital Tbilisi.

Because navies operate air power they too can see its effect quickly transition from the tactical to the strategic. Without aircraft carriers navies would be limited to having an impact solely at the tactical and operational level. This is, of course, to leave out the strategic impact of nuclear-armed ballistic missile systems.

As the focus of this book is on air power the discourse will address nuclear-armed bombers performing a strategic role. The 'Doolittle Raid' by the United States on Tokyo launched from aircraft carriers off the coast in the wake of Pearl Harbor also provides an example of maritime air power having a strategic effect.

Today to have a military effect you need to have the capacity to do all of that and also apply air power selectively. In operations in Afghanistan the power of the low high-speed pass over the enemy to make them withdraw from close-quarter battle has been used on many occasions to tilt the balance of a battle in favour of the NATO forces.

As force sizes inevitably reduce as the bloody battles of Afghanistan fade from the collective memory, the need to be able to mass military fire-power at a critical point on the battlefield at short notice will remain. The British army is unlikely to emerge from Afghanistan in quite the same shape and capabilities as when it entered theatre in 2006.

Inevitably when small numbers of troops are deployed on the ground in efforts to bring governance and stability to a region, even if that is on a short-term basis, air power will be required in support. In Oman, Kenya and Malaya history shows that air power brings an additional dimension to the ability to prosecute a military campaign and achieve a desired outcome.

In Iraq and Afghanistan the application of air power has subtly developed. In Oman, for example, when air power was called in by ground troops it was often applied to have a kinetic effect. Destruction and disruption of the enemy's manoeuvres was the main aim. Today the military lexicon now includes the need to apply power in a number of other ways. Kinetic power must not be delivered in ways that place civilians in harm's way. If soft power can achieve a desired effect it should too become part of the arsenal of air power.

This ability to quickly mass is one of the things at which air power excels. Its ability to rapidly mobilize to a critical point on the ground gives it a unique ability to add military mass when and where it is needed. Once at the scene how that mass of military power that has been assembled is then employed is a tactical issue for commanders on the ground.

In some cases that may involve fast overflights of an area. In others a bomb may be released. Increasingly in places like Afghanistan crews return home from four-month rotations of duty reporting that they did not ever need to release a weapon in anger. Massing military power to a critical point on the battlefield is one thing. Applying that power once it has been assembled is another.

The massing capability also applies when air power is used to deliver relief supplies to communities devastated by natural or man-made disasters. Across the world the images of starving children or the aftermath of earthquakes, hurricanes or typhoons still resonate with western public opinion. Those that despite austerity measures still have a relatively secure lifestyle can quickly turn into benefactors when the immediacy of the need is made clear through the media.

This is where air power is able to quickly mobilize relief supplies. The Royal Air Force is one of a number of air forces that have the C-17 strategic and tactical heavy-lifting aircraft in their inventory. The order and delivery of the eighth aircraft in 2012 provides an indicator of the continuing need for operations to be mounted at short notice to provide assistance to those caught up in the aftermath of a disaster. This is an example of the flexibility and agility of air power. Its primary aim is to save lives.

NATO's other focus turned to Afghanistan in the aftermath of 11 September 2001. Some of the members of NATO were drawn into Iraq in 2003. While air power played an important role in the initial onslaught, when Baghdad was overrun the role for air power began to evolve. Core missions of casualty evacuation remained. Air power now became applied in several ways: one to move combat troops into areas to conduct sanitization missions aimed at removing insurgents from specific areas; the second to provide close air support to troops on the ground when they were engaged in a fire-fight.

The first of these two missions was always conducted professionally by air-crews but the mission effectives of such operations were quickly questioned. The enemy appeared able to melt into the background and re-emerge after the operation was ended. Sanitization operations rarely produced long-term solutions. Arguably they highlighted weaknesses in the apparent indiscriminate and non-proportional uses of force. They were certainly not able to help win the much sought-after 'hearts and minds' of the local population.

The second operation had echoes in other counter-insurgency campaigns. Close air support was always valuable to troops on the ground who in remote outposts may suddenly find themselves overwhelmed. In the campaign in Oman air power regularly came to the rescue when things looked bleak on the ground. The cavalry no longer arrived on horseback to save the day. In the case of Oman it was the Royal Air Force.

These variants of the air-land battle highlight the ability of air power to provide an important helping hand at a critical juncture in a fire-fight. On many occasions the Royal Air Force came to the rescue of ground troops, often flying in extremely dangerous situations. In Iraq United States close air-support aircraft such as the A-10 and the F-16 won recognition for their ability to mobilize and support ground troops often operating well out of range of artillery support from their home bases.

In Afghanistan this trend continued. Air power was applied increasingly selectively to assist troops on the ground. Operating in a multi-national force French Air Force jets might find themselves supporting American or British forces on the ground. In Afghanistan the air assets were available to meet the need, and while operations in support of their own troops were always afforded a priority where it was needed, the total air contingent was seen as a pooled resource.

In Mali in 2013, however, the French demonstrated that the strike element of air power does not always have to be applied in the context of a multi-national coalition. While the United States Air Force and the Royal Air Force supplied logistical support in the form of C-17 aircraft to help the French military deploy quickly into theatre, strike operations were conducted by French Mirage and Rafale jets flying from neighbouring countries. Quickly the United States also offered air-to-air refuelling tankers and the RAF provided a Sentinel R1 ISTAR platform to help locate targets on the ground in Mali.

The Sentinel R1 was specifically requested by the French due to the experiences they gained with its use over Libya in 2011. The speed with which the Islamic extremists were forced into a volte-face in Mali is yet another testament to the application of air power in surgical strikes supported by ISTAR assets.

The military effort in Libya may well turn out to be a one-off. It is unlikely to be repeated in Syria. China and Russia seem unwilling to sanction the use of air power in Syria and the result in Libya was not what they had hoped. When they agreed to the United Nations Resolution 1972 both Russia and China saw an outcome into which the regime in Tripoli would survive and NATO would withdraw having completed its mission to protect the citizens of Benghazi. The downfall of the regime was not an expected outcome. China and Russia became intent on not seeing that occur again in Syria.

NATO's use of air power in Libya will be seen by historians through a very constructive lens. The few occasions in which civilian casualties arose were nothing by contrast with those that had occurred in Iraq and Afghanistan. If anything the problem to emerge from Libya is that it sets new standards for low levels of casualties.

Arguably it may have set false expectations that will be increasingly difficult to live up to in the future. The precision with which NATO applied air power set new standards for future operations. The flexibility of its mix of weapons also contributed. This allowed each target to be attacked in ways that suited the prevailing situation on the ground.

If one new driver were to emerge from Libya, it is that it gives even more urgency to the need to link the outputs from ISTAR platforms to combat aircraft in real-time. Indigenous sensor systems on board fighter jets such as the Tornado and Typhoon based on the LITENING Pod have their limitations. Other sensor systems, operating in other parts of the electro-magnetic spectrum provide complementary sources of information that can help strike aircraft pilots build their situational awareness before launching a weapon.

NATO was formed to address the security of Europe. With threats emanating from Pakistan and Afghanistan arguments could be made about upstream interventions in those countries, either directly through boots on the ground or indirectly using unmanned aircraft such as the Predator or Reaper to prosecute targets in the remote and lawless areas of Pakistan. What is emerging is a new vision of the way in which air power is applied to achieve military effect. In the future it will arrive faster, on a global scale and with a much wider range of options about how it is actually applied.

Chapter Two

Airborne Intelligence Sources

Scene Setting

The task of collecting intelligence was the first to be undertaken by air forces in the First World War. The capabilities to drop weapons or to engage in air-to-air combat remained over the short-term horizon. When air power was first deployed on the battlefield its task was a simple one: find out what the enemy is up to and report back.

Doctrinally that task is divided into three subsets. The first is concerned with the collection and analysis of intelligence at the strategic level. This rarely requires real-time access to information. Its role is to collect information that helps analysts to build up long-term trends and detailed assessments of the current capabilities of a potential adversary. Photographing sites of interest in the optical, infra-red and radar parts of the electro-magnetic spectrum helps develop a comprehensive view of the current and future capabilities of an adversary.

The second and third levels of intelligence collection occur at the operational and tactical levels of command. This narrows down the geographic focus. In contemporary military engagements in places such as Afghanistan and previously in Iraq small unmanned drones play a major part in providing persistence over a target area. Of all the characteristics of air power it is persistence that is one of the major issues.

At the point the image is collected the data is accurate as far as it is able to penetrate any attempts to camouflage mobile activity on the ground. At that point the clock starts ticking. Data can become increasingly worthless depending upon the dynamic of the situation as time moves on. By being persistent any changes that are visible can be quickly detected and passed on to those who need to know. This explains why in the last two decades so much effort has gone into the development of long-duration drones, dirigibles and other airborne platforms. Increasing persistence over an area is one of the much sought-after characteristics for intelligence collection platforms.

In the Second World War the issue of capturing image intelligence was less dynamic. No ability to directly broadcast imagery to a remote ground station existed. That was to come with the technological revolution forty years later. The preoccupation was with trying to find ways of camouflaging fixed sites.

Aircraft involved in the conduct of long-range reconnaissance missions were often stripped to the bone of any form of self-defence capability. Every pound of fuel mattered to extend the range and to be able to look deep behind enemy lines.

Such was the concern about the increasing capability to collect long-range image intelligence that a great deal of effort was expended to try to hide airbases using camouflage techniques. This was just one example of a whole range of tactics used to try to disguise important armament factories and other parts of the critical war effort from prying eyes. However, as far as efforts to hide airfields were concerned, it had limited effect. To the trained observer, the distinct linear features of the runways and outer security perimeters were very hard to disguise.

The impact of intelligence collection platforms are of course very different in today's military operating environments. In COIN operations the need is often to focus on a location for a lengthy period of time to build up what is called 'pattern of life' indicators. These enable a base point of behaviour to be established from which any abnormal pattern would emerge bringing that activity to the attention of the intelligence analysts. This real-time dynamic environment contrasted markedly with the fixed-target analysis work in the Cold War. There warnings and indicators were derived when new security fencing was detected or new construction activity.

At the end of the Cold War the accent was on verification that sites to be dismantled as a result of the Conventional Forces Europe (CFE) Treaty were indeed being decommissioned. One of the complications that emerged in that period was the somewhat haphazard approach the Soviets had taken to military developments. When they handed over their statement of their inventory it was patently clear that they had no clue as to the role of some of the facilities that were known to western intelligence agencies. This was a difficult base from which to establish trust. Had the Soviets tried to hide the role of these facilities, or were genuine mistakes made in the development of the catalogue?

Air power was written into the heart of the verification process as countries were given the right to mount a number of no-notice inspections each year at specific sites with ground teams. They were cued to suspicious activity by surveys undertaken by aircraft filled with an array of sensing equipment. The swift collapse of the Soviet Union made the process of verification in balance a little easier as some facilities fell into disrepair and were abandoned. With the demise of the Cold War the world entered a new and arguably more complicated period. Countries that were not directly on the immediate intelligence collection horizon suddenly became important. For a juggernaut created to monitor the activities of the Soviets switching to other countries was not easy. The comparisons with the time it takes to turn a super-tanker from its course are obvious. In the Balkans in the 1990s and subsequently in Baghdad after 2003 the role of intelligence collection moved from an overriding emphasis on the strategic to the operational and tactical levels of command.

One indication of that shift started to occur over the Balkans. As NATO air power attacked Serbia during the air campaign strategic intelligence collection platforms, such as the Nimrod R1, adapted from its strategic role into one that also made an operational and tactical contribution. The main role of the Nimrod R1 was to hoover up radar signals and pass them back for intelligence analysis. On station over the Adriatic Sea, as the Serbians learnt from the destruction wrought on the Iraqi radar systems at the start of the First Gulf War, the Nimrod R1 found the levels of radar activity low.

The threats of the radar-seeking missiles used in the First Gulf War had made the Serbians nervous about leaving their radars on for any period of time. Unconfirmed rumours still circulate that the Iraqis helped the Serbians optimize their radar usage to minimize intelligence collection opportunities and the risks from radar-homing missiles. In this very quiet ELINT environment the Nimrod R1 operators tuned to providing a virtual real-time read-out of any radar activity they spotted over communications channels to inbound packets of aircraft seeking to strike targets in Serbia. A strategic intelligence collection asset that worked in non-real-time morphed into a real-time operational and tactical asset.

Over Baghdad at the height of the insurgency in 2005–07 numerous unmanned drones were flying over the city relaying their live data links to the ground to enable specific activities on the ground to be closely monitored. Where unusual or irregular activity was detected the drones could be assigned to pick up and track the evolution of that activity; for example, as a specific vehicle moved around the city. This tied up resources and intelligence cues were also additional important starting-points for image collection operations.

In Afghanistan unmanned platforms such as the Reaper systems operated by the Royal Air Force are also given real-time roles. One of their most important tasks has been to fly ahead of re-supply convoys heading out to Forward Operating Bases (FOB) to detect indications of insurgent activity along the route. People involved in the planting or detonating of Improvised Explosive Devices (IED) became of specific interest as the death toll from these rather crude but effective means of warfare grew.

Early Beginnings

The earliest form of airborne intelligence was based on aircraft operating above enemy positions. Cloud cover was often an issue, masking activities on the ground. On what were often featureless pieces of terrain navigation could also present problems. While getting back to an operating base was difficult, knowing precisely where specific military activities on the battlefield were located was often problematic.

It was therefore understandable that some generals openly stated that in their view air power was not ever likely to have a major impact on the war. Others, however, were more sanguine in their approach, taking the view that new technologies could and should be embraced. The naysayers were, however, to underestimate the speed of developments in aviation and the utility that would quickly emerge. Within what by other standards of warfare is a very short time air power's applications diversified.

It soon became apparent that air power could make a wider contribution beyond reconnaissance activities: it could deliver effect in its own right. It was all a question of how much could be lifted and how accurately it could be delivered. In the aftermath of the First World War as a traumatized European population came to terms with the mass slaughter that had occurred, anything that made warfare more precise had to be welcomed.

In between the two world wars, as is often the case, a number of military capabilities atrophied. Some of the lessons involved in collecting and processing imagery were lost. The profession of image interpretation became one that was regarded as a backwater for those incapable of being promoted to senior positions.

This thinking went along the lines that those who were good at image analysis were simply incapable of holding down a management position in the Royal Air Force. As the war clouds gathered in the middle of the 1930s some people realized that if war did indeed break out then the need for skilled photographic interpreters would again be paramount.

The story of how photographic interpretation developed from that point through the Second World War has been told elsewhere in great detail. Taylor Downing's book *Spies in the Skies* is a reference work centred on the specific tasks undertaken at Medmenham. His comparisons with the secret war being conducted at Bletchley Park make compelling reading.

The book is full of stories of the role of photographic intelligence and of the various skill-sets that people developed to understand everything from train timetables to the detection of German efforts to divert bombing raids, the reasons why runways were suddenly lengthened, to the stories behind the detection of major German naval units like the *Bismarck*, *Prince Eugen* and the *Tirpitz*.

One thing stands out in his accounts. His stories vividly illustrate the bravery of those who flew the missions to collect the imagery in the first place. For them every extra knot of speed or gallon of petrol conserved took them to their target and enabled them to bring back the pictures that helped provide the vital intelligence insights. Time was always an issue. Once the aircraft returned to its home base the imagery was given a first pass before being whisked off by car to have a more detailed examination.

Detecting Radiation

At the end of the Second World War the United States grew increasingly concerned about its inability to gain insights into what the Soviet Union was up to behind its closed borders. With the primary threat axis to the United States being the shortest route over the North Pole, initial intelligence collection efforts were made in what can only be described as extreme weather conditions. Aircraft were stripped bare of anything that they did not require. Defensive weapon systems were removed. This caused one B-29 crew to name their aircraft 'Sitting Duck'.

During the Berlin Airlift it undertook covert missions into Berlin, using these to collect intelligence on Soviet radar and communications emissions. Because of the nature of the equipment on board the aircraft it could not land and so had to abort the landing and return back to Germany. Soviet observers were no doubt amused by the apparent ruse.

These missions, which sometimes lasted over a day, were undertaken by a new unit especially set up to fly to the edge of the Soviet borders and over their northern areas. Early results showed the paucity of capability deployed by the Soviets. That was not a situation that was to last very long. As early as the middle of the 1930s the Soviets had been busy exploring what is today referred to as the High North. Quickly it became the location for a number of developments, one of these being the main Soviet atom-bomb tests.

On 29 August 1949 one of the missions to monitor this area was flying with some air filters designed to pick up specific nuclear particles that would remain in the atmosphere after an atomic test. When the aircraft returned to its base the analysis was conclusive. The Soviets had conducted their first atomic test. The technology of the atom bomb was no longer in the possession of a small and exclusive club of two.

This out-of-the-blue discovery shook the Americans and British. It was to profoundly affect the plans that were in their nascent stages for the next generation of intelligence-collection aircraft. After that surprise no one wanted the Soviets to break out in other areas such as ballistic missile technology or in strategic bombers. Put the nuclear capability with those delivery mechanisms and the world's security landscape just changed. Sixty years later those same arguments apply to the concerns over the Iranian and North Korean nuclear developments.

In the 1950s and 1960s such was the concern over the Soviets' increasing capabilities that some commentators have ventured to suggest that over 3,000 spy flights a year of one sort or another were being carried out either along the borders of the Soviet Union or over their airspace.

Non-Real-Time Image Acquisition

The delay from obtaining the image over the target to its initial processing on the ground and more detailed subsequent analysis has dogged the issue of ISTAR for many years. Even in the fast jet era of the Jaguar and Tornado aircraft being equipped with reconnaissance pods it was recognized that as soon as the aircraft had made its pass over the battlefield the data it had collected was starting to become stale. Getting real-time read-outs of the imagery would have to await the developments in digitization and miniaturization that came in the early part of the 1970s.

As digital technologies emerged it became apparent that ISTAR platforms could provide more of a contribution to the understanding of the dispositions of forces on the ground. Terms like searchlight and spotlight were used to try to picture how an ISTAR sensor system might focus on a specific area on the ground. The searchlight would illuminate an area that could then cue the spotlight to a specific target of interest.

Time was always the enemy. With ground-manoeuvre formations able to swiftly move on, even an overpass by a high-speed jet that sanitized an area (proved no targets were there at the point of the flypast) could quickly be out of date. If light levels could be used as a means of illustrating data currency the point immediately below the aircraft would be brightly lit. As the aircraft flew on, so the light levels over that point would reduce. Eventually it would be dark again. At that point another mission is needed as things could have changed dramatically at that location.

Even over Libya nearly seventy years later the time taken for imagery to be collected and processed in the air and being seen on the ground was an issue. In a fast-moving and uncertain ground conflict involving irregular forces from an opposition to the regime in Tripoli manoeuvring in highly uncontrolled ways on the ground, the need to avoid targeting those that NATO had sent to help was crucial.

For the Royal Air Force processing data derived from its new radar-based sensor systems aboard the Sentinel aircraft became crucial. During some lengthy sorties off the coast of Libya image interpreters were placed on board the aircraft to provide a real-time capability to analyse imagery. They then used the digital command links available to call in strike sorties where they were most urgently needed. In fast-moving situations where pop-up targets would appear on the screen and rapidly disappear this was an essential capability.

Many Royal Air Force and Allied missions were launched into the area not knowing the targets they were to engage. This tactic is called armed reconnaissance. To make it effective either the air-crews themselves detect the targets, which given their on-board sensor suites was difficult but not impossible, or they had to be cued. The source of that direction onto the target would sometimes come from an image interpreter based on an ISTAR platform. That reduced the time delays involved in processing the imagery. With no boots-on-the-ground in Libya, downlinking the live data for interpretation and analysis was simply not possible.

In Iraq as the COIN mission developed, the need for units on the ground to have a direct read-out from aircraft providing over-watch missions was the subject of an urgent development programme. In this the Long Range Maritime Patrol aircraft, the Nimrod, was converted to host a highly capable electro-optical sensor suite. Its ability to persist over a target area for long periods of time showed another facet of the versatility of air power.

The Nimrod was a highly versatile aircraft and the missions to support ground operations in Iraq in the latter part of the British military involvement in the southern part of the country at Basra simply added another string to the aircraft's impressive list of mission types it had supported. The real-time read-out capability allowed the Nimrod to broadcast the imagery its sensor system was seeing directly to a ground terminal. Image interpretation was then conducted by troops on the ground. The unique vantage point in the sky proved again to be a valuable asset to ground troops. In time as the Royal Air Force came to purchase and operate its own unmanned aircraft the need for the Nimrod over-watch mission passed.

The air domain also offered another important dimension to intelligence collection that was not simply focused on imagery or radar sensor systems. Collecting radioactive samples that resulted from atmospheric nuclear tests in the 1950s was hugely important. It enabled the progress of the Soviet nuclear programme to be monitored.

As the Soviet nuclear programme quickened in the aftermath of the Second World War it appeared that somehow they had been able to gain access to some of the design secrets that were supposed to be hidden away in Los Alamos. The 1950s was a period when several spies were involved in giving the Soviets access to nuclear secrets. Their arguments were often based on a need to have a balanced world where superpower blocks would face-off against each other. Those individuals could not have realized that their actions so nearly led to disaster in October 1962.

In the Second World War it was quickly recognized that air power comprised more than simply an ability to photograph their military preparedness, shoot down an adversary's aircraft or bomb them into submission. In the Second World War 100 Group RAF pioneered work to jam enemy radar systems. This can be argued as being the start-point of electronic warfare, when air power first moved beyond simply delivering kinetic effect to achieve a desired outcome.

To deliver that effect meant that aircraft also had to be modified to listen to an enemy's radar and communications systems traffic. Today we refer to this as Signals Intelligence (SIGINT). The first SIGINT war to occur in the air took place over Nazi Germany as Bomber Command and the United States bombers went onto the offensive conducting daylight and night-time bombing raids over Germany designed to wear down their industrial capacity and morale.

100 Group Royal Air Force

U-2 Incident 1960

Before the era of satellite-based reconnaissance and the development of the Keyhole series of military ISTAR platforms the United States relied upon getting pictures from the U-2 spy plane over countries such as Russia. Its design as a single-engine jet allowed it to operate at altitudes of 70,000ft. Its sensor suite provided an all-weather mapping capability. It allowed the United States to peek over the horizon at what was actually happening inside the Soviet Union.

In the course of its operational service from 1957 to the current day eighty-six U-2 spy planes have been built. It could fly for up to twelve hours at a time and cover a range of over 5,500 nautical miles. However, it relied on altitude to evade air defence systems. Its maximum speed of 434 knots and cruise speed of 373 knots made it an easy prey had it not been operated at high altitude. When it was developed in the early part of the 1950s the surface-to-air missile threat was still in a nascent stage.

When the U-2 entered service the capabilities of the Soviet air defence system were improving dramatically. It was as a result of these improvements that on 1 May 1960 a U-2 was shot down near Degtyarsk in the Soviet Union. The pilot, whose name was Francis Gary Powers, managed to survive the shooting down and was initially imprisoned in the Soviet Union. He was exchanged months later in a scene reminiscent of one from the famous spy thriller series *Tinker, Tailor, Soldier, Spy* written by John le Carré.

That one incident was to have far-reaching consequences for the application of air power. Altitude was no longer a safe haven. One limit to the application of air power had just been found. At the start of the twenty-first century as designers contemplate the development of ramjet technologies that would allow aircraft to fly halfway around the world in a matter of hours, some additional manoeuvre room may be about to reappear.

The mission that was to end in calamity both militarily and politically had been the subject of an initial delay. The U-2 was flown from a number of then highly secret locations around the world to give it a start when it came to over-flying the Soviet Union. Gary Powers, as he preferred to be known, had taken off from a secret airbase at Peshawar in Pakistan.

Fifty years later the United States used the same airbase to launch drone attacks into the areas of Pakistan where Al Qaeda and its acolytes had taken refuge. Due to another calamitous event the United States was thrown out of Peshawar after pressure was brought on the Pakistan government following some of its soldiers being accidentally killed in a drone strike.

On this day the U-2 lumbered into the air and Gary Powers set a north-westerly course initially towards the Aral Sea. At this point he turned right and headed virtually due north towards Yekaterinburg. The mission, code-named GRAND SLAM, was to then to continue to Plesetsk, Arkhangelsk and Murmansk before landing in Bodø in Norway.

Before the U-2 had taken off the Soviet air defences had been on full alert. Earlier on in the year another U-2 mission had successfully penetrated Soviet airspace. On 9 April a U-2 piloted by Bob Ericson had photographed secret bases at the Semipalatinsk missile test site before heading on to the Dolon Air Base where many of the Soviet Union's TU-95 strategic bombers were located. Once that area had been photographed the U-2 had gone on to image the Soviet SAM missile test site at Saryshagan before completing its intelligence collection activities over the Tyuratam missile test range at the Baikonur space centre. The flight had been monitored by the Soviet air defence systems but the height of the aircraft placed it out of reach. For the Soviets this was an incredibly frustrating experience. The U-2 landed at another secret airbase in Iran.

On the day Gary Powers took off from Pakistan the Soviet air defence system was waiting for him. Being unable to bring down the previous U-2 mission was tantamount to a national disgrace. Humiliated, the Soviets had decided to take drastic measures. One possible tactic was to try to get a fighter jet close enough to the U-2 to ram it. In the Second World War the Germans in their desperate state adopted similar tactics against the massed bomber formations of the United States Air Force.

Mystery does still surround the actual means by which the U-2 was finally brought down. The fact that Gary Powers survived suggests that the aircraft was not hit by a missile as is generally assumed. This has led to a number of competing claims circulating about the actual events that saw the demise of the U-2. One account suggests the Soviets fired the first of three SA-2 (NATO Code Name: Guideline) missiles. An earlier version offered a slightly different view based on a salvo of fourteen SA-2 missiles being fired.

Another variant was published in 1996 when a Soviet pilot named Igor Mentyukov claimed that he had been ordered to ram the U-2. He claimed that he had managed to catch the U-2 in the slipstream of his Su-9 fighter and flipped it over. He confirmed that one of the pursuing missiles did hit an aircraft but that it was not the U-2. In fact the Soviets actually shot down one of their own MiG-19 fighters. At the time this was covered up, but years later this part of the story appears to be confirmed when a Soviet pilot named Sergei Safronov received the Order of the Red Banner.

In an account published in 2000 that appears to draw some of the threads together into a plausible story, the son of the former President of the Soviet Union Sergei Khrushchev noted how Mentyukov did indeed attempt to intercept the U-2. His MiG had been stripped of all unnecessary equipment in order to give it a chance of getting close to the U-2. He failed to get visual contact with the U-2 and withdrew. Three SA-2s were then fired, of which two failed to launch. The only missile to fly exploded close to the U-2 and did sufficient damage to bring the aircraft down. While the wings of the U-2 buckled under the explosion, the cockpit in which Gary Powers sat remained intact and broke away from the main body of the aircraft.

As the aircraft broke up Gary Powers remained initially in the cockpit of the U-2 which was falling quickly. He remained on oxygen and waited to leave the cockpit and deploy his parachute until he was below 10,000ft. As a result of the break-up Sergei Khrushchev's account then states that thirteen other missiles were salvo-fired and it was one of these that shot down the MiG-19 piloted by Sergei Safronov.

Of all the various claims, the account by Sergei Khrushchev appears to make most sense. It draws together threads that appear to fit into a plausible account. His access to the story through his father also adds credulity, as does the passage of time.

Whatever the real truth that lies behind the story, and the Soviets have a track record of manipulating history to suit their own propaganda aims, the simple fact is that Gary Powers was quickly captured and placed on a show trial in Moscow. The Soviets milked the occasion for all it was worth. They had been humiliated by the ability of the United States to fly over their territory; now it was time for payback.

For the United States the need to still maintain a careful watch on Soviet military developments did not go away once the U-2 was compromised. Their options were limited. One programme called Project Rainbow had tried to reduce the radar signature of the U-2. That had failed to achieve the levels required to allow the aircraft to fly undetected over the Soviet Union. Other solutions had to be explored. Those involved going faster. While that may sound simple on paper, it was to demand a great deal of the design engineers, both of the platform and the optical intelligence collection systems. To fly faster required the designers to build a titanium airframe. Getting titanium was not easy as most of the world's supply was in the Soviet Union. Clandestine programmes were established to obtain the material. The development of the optical systems took image reconnaissance to a new level that also pioneered techniques that were to appear in the satellite intelligence collection programme.

Their development of the first generation of satellite-based sensor systems called CORONA, and its replacements called GAMBIT and HEXAGON, was accelerated. The United States also invested heavily in new technological innovations that sought to take the air platform to new levels of speed to outpace the Soviet air defence systems capabilities.

The development of the Lockheed A-12 OXCART supersonic spy plane was one solution that was explored. The programme behind this had initially been called Archangel. This followed on from the original nickname for the U-2 which was known as 'angel'. As the concepts for the aircraft evolved each design was assigned a different number. The first serious design to emerge was called A-11. The next iteration saw additional measures taken to reduce the radar cross-section.

On 26 January 1960 the operators, the Central Intelligence Agency (CIA), ordered twelve A-12 aircraft. It first flew in 1962 and completed 2,850 sorties in the course of its career. On operations the A-12 flew missions over Vietnam and North Korea. Its speed (Mach 3) enabled it to cross the continent of the United States in seventy minutes. Its on-board camera system was able to detect objects 12in in size. This was an improvement over the 30-in resolution of the U-2 camera. The A-12 was retired from service in 1968. It was to be replaced by the iconic SR-71 Blackbird aircraft. In the early 1960s Lockheed also started to develop the D-21 unmanned drone, pioneering the technologies that are now in routine use today targeting terrorist sanctuaries in remote corners of the world.

The story of the A-12 is also one that is fascinating. Declassified material released nearly fifty years on from the initial development programme shows that the A-12 was operated from the Area-51 facility that Hollywood depicted in the film *Independence Day*. Maintaining the secrecy behind the developments that were being tested at Area-51 required the people involved to go to quite extraordinary lengths to cover up stories that could emerge or to prevent Soviet intelligence satellites from watching the facility.

Fortunately the orbits of spy satellites are very predictable. At the time the Soviets were flying between four and six satellites that were capable of imaging Area-51. Many of these only remained in orbit for relatively short periods of time. These were, after all, the earliest generations of satellite-based sensor systems.

When an overpass occurred the aircraft could be moved back into the hangars, but on occasions that was quite disruptive to the development activities. The security arrangements surrounding the programme were intense. Everyone on the team held a special access clearance. However, if the aircraft had been outside for a long period its infrared shadow would remain on the ground for some time. That thermal signature was durable. Today on open-source imagery such thermal signatures are readily detected at airfields all over the world. History shows that despite the lengths the United States went to in order to protect the secrets of the A-12, the Soviets had a good idea of what the shape of the aircraft looked like.

This created an internal market within Area-51 for creative deception ideas and a number of weird objects were placed out in full view of the Soviet satellites to give them something to think about. Another programme to emerge from the A-12 saw the development of the SR-71 Blackbird. Its design was driven by a need to reduce its radar cross-section which ended up as 10 sq m. That is not a specifically stealthy figure by modern-day comparators such as the F-117 Nighthawk which had a radar cross-section often compared to the size of a ball-bearing.

A key design feature of the SR-71 was the adoption of chines. These were sharp edges that started at the nose of the fuselage and carried around to the rear. While these helped reduce the radar cross-section of the aircraft, it posed a series of problems for the aerodynamicists involved in the programme. Not all of these, however, proved to be bad. The designers found that the chines actually increased the vortices that were present close to the surface of the aircraft generating additional lift. These also helped the aircraft as it landed, making it harder to stall.

One other advantage was that the angle of incidence of the main wings could be reduced which had an impact on drag and helped improve stability. This had another positive effect on fuel that could be carried to increase the operating range. These aerodynamic developments were to have an impact on other aircraft designs, such as the F-5, F-16 and F/A-18. Soviet design teams also incorporated chines into the MiG-29 and Su-27. They remain an important design feature of many contemporary aircraft such as the X-45, X-47 and the Dark Star. The chines provide solutions that improve stealth without compromising stability.

The SR-71's first flight was in December 1964. The final aircraft of the thirty-two that were built went into retirement in 1998. Not all those built had the same configuration, with twenty-nine built to SR-71A, two SR-71B and one SR-71C. Of those built, twelve were lost in accidents. There was no repeat of the Gary Powers incident. In 1976 it gained the world record for the fastest air-breathing aircraft. If a SAM was launched against the SR-71 it simply accelerated and outran the missile. A similar approach was adopted when a Soviet MiG-25 tried to intercept an SR-71.

Throughout its service life the SR-71 flew over 3,500 sorties on operations. Through its development activities the total number of missions flown exceeds 17,000 resulting in over 50,000 flying hours. On operational tasking the aircraft flew just over 11,000 hours of which around a third were undertaken at Mach 3.

The increase in the tempo of SR-71 sorties is highlighted by the growth in its mission generation rate. In 1968 as the aircraft entered service over North Vietnam and Laos the SR-71s were flying a single-mission sortie on average once a week. This operational tempo was maintained until 1970. By the end of 1970 the SR-71s had increased their tempo to two sorties a week. By 1972 this had further grown to around one sortie a day.

The drive to obtain better imagery over the Soviet Union came at a time when the Cold War was in one of its routine periods where the level of trust between the United States and the Soviet Union was low. The launch of Sputnik and the speed of development of Soviet nuclear technologies surprised the United States. Used to being in a dominant position from a technical viewpoint, suddenly the Soviets seemed to be catching up quickly. In the Presidential election campaign in 1964 the Republican nominee criticized President Johnson for a lack of investment in new defence systems. This was a time when American paranoia over Soviet capabilities reached new heights. To try to counter the attacks President Johnson decided to make the development of a variant of the secret A-12 programme public.

Incorrect CIA estimates also accredited the Soviets with an accelerated build-up of their ballistic missile and strategic bomber fleet. This led to the so-called 'missile gap' and the 'bomber gap'. American concerns about Soviet developments were also driven on by events elsewhere in the world where the Soviets started to use other countries as proxies for creating tensions with the west.

That need to really understand what the Soviets were up to was a major factor in driving the CIA efforts to explore the utility of air power as a means to collect intelligence information. The development of those systems and the advanced image-collection systems employed was to lead to the discovery of a major clandestine operation on the island of Cuba. It was to lead the world to the edge of a nuclear abyss.

Nuclear Air Power and the Cuban Missile Crisis

Background to the Crisis
The routine sortie over Cuba on 15 October 1962 was to have profound political consequences. It was to lead within a matter of days to the world standing on the edge of a nuclear Armageddon. Within hours of the data collected by the U-2 spy plane being processed an urgent meeting was called in the White House with President Kennedy.

For some time the President and his staff had been suspicious of what appeared to be increased military movements into and out of Cuba. The fiasco at the Bay of Pigs when a United States-sponsored effort to displace the Castro regime in Cuba failed left a legacy. The Russians clearly wanted to retain a foothold in the Caribbean. It was a useful point for intelligence collection. The threat of some follow-up invasion of Cuba and its loss from the Russian sphere of influence caused the Kremlin to contemplate how they could best offer military aid to Havana.

The Russian President also saw an opportunity to redress an imbalance that existed militarily. The United States, through its NATO alliance, had based Thor and Jupiter missile systems in the United Kingdom, Italy and Turkey. These missile systems lowered the nuclear threshold as they were only a matter of minutes' flying time away from striking targets in Eastern Europe. Why not counter-balance that deployment with one of our own, went the reasoning in a small coterie of staff inside the Kremlin.

The plan to install nuclear-armed ballistic missiles was hatched. The build-up of the capability was carried out slowly; there was to be no obvious intelligence spike that would alert the Americans to what was going on. With any luck, the people involved reasoned, the missiles would be installed and operating before the United States realized what was going on. Once they were operational the Americans could do little to see their removal.

The chance encounter of the U-2 over Cuba with ballistic missiles in the final stages of being deployed therefore came as a shock to the Kennedy Administration. They had not anticipated such a reaction to the attempt to overthrow Castro. The deployment of a few Surface-to-Air Missile (SAM) sites to increase Cuba's military defences was thought to be the extent of the Russian ambition. However, Moscow was not being quite so constrained in its thinking.

Preparations were also made to deploy four nuclear-armed submarines into the Caribbean. Once the land-based missiles were operational Russian submarines would also operate from Cuban ports. This gave them greater operational flexibility as previously they had to sail from Murmansk past the SOSUS sensor arrays on the floor of the North Atlantic to get to their patrol stations off the Eastern Seaboard of the United States. The land-based missiles were therefore part of a comprehensive strategy for putting pressure on the United States. Cuba would be a virtual aircraft carrier-cum-Soviet missile base right in the back yard of the United States.

The missiles deployed by the Russians consisted of a mix of Medium and Intermediate Range Ballistic Missiles. Had they reached an operational status they would have been capable of targeting all of the main population centres in the United States. Once President Kennedy realized the scale of the problem he faced he quickly realized it would be something the American people would not tolerate. Something had to be done to remove the missiles. The question was how to achieve that when they were clearly in the final stages of being deployed.

The reaction of some hard-line elements of the military was perhaps understandable. United States Air Force General Curtis LeMay was scathing in his assessment. He had always regarded the Kennedys (as he liked to brand them) as appeasers. In doing this he was recalling the belligerent stance taken by President Kennedy's father against becoming involved in the Second World War. LeMay's view was that this had rubbed off on the sons. They could not be trusted with the defence of America. As the crisis quickly unfolded LeMay took every opportunity to lay out his views that this was the confirmation he had been warning about for some time. The Russians, he would regularly assert, could not be trusted. For LeMay here was the evidence that his views on the Russians had been right all along.

LeMay's view of the crisis was that this meant the Americans now had the perfect excuse for attacking Russia. He could see a long hard Cold War ahead (a point that turned out to be right) and wanted to 'cut to the chase'. He felt now was the time to 'remove the threat of the Russians once and for all'. In one of the initial meetings called by the President, LeMay took the opportunity to rub it in, opining that 'you are in a hole, Mr President'.

Kennedy, showing irritation in his voice, informed LeMay that he should not forget that 'he was in it with him'. The taped records of the conversation show that those in the room laughed nervously at this point. This was not a joke. What LeMay was advocating was that America should use the Cuban Missile Crisis as a pretext for launching the Third World War.

This conversation was to be satirized two years later in the film *Dr Strangelove* which envisaged a situation not unlike the Cuban Missile Crisis in which America and Russia went to war. It was to be the first in a genre of films that explored the issues about how to control an escalating situation when a nuclear holocaust lurks in the background, ready to engulf the world in a conflagration.

Over the next three days President Kennedy asked his brother and close confidant to take a small team of people away into a secret location and come up with some options. Meanwhile the President would continue with his public engagements, creating the impression that nothing was awry.

Robert Kennedy's small team laboured over the following three days to give the President a plan. Arguments ranged across a number of options from a pre-emptive military strike against the missile sites in Cuba to a full-scale invasion. When these were discussed with the President he asked a simple question of LeMay. Could he guarantee that all the missile sites would be eradicated in a first strike?

Despite LeMay's pugnacious character and desire to fix what he saw as the communist menace in a single all-out nuclear strike he replied that he could not give the President that assurance. For President Kennedy, even if one Russian missile could be launched at an American city, that was too high a price to pay.

In those days intelligence-collection systems, such as the Keyhole satellite systems in use today, had barely left the drawing-board. Air-based intelligence collection platforms made high-speed passes over an area at low level. They did not have the persistence characteristics of contemporary air intelligence-collection platforms.

Robert Kennedy's team completed their deliberations on 19 October. After searching for solutions and being sent back to explore other options they had narrowed their selection to the idea of enforcing a blockade around Cuba. This would prevent any further equipment reaching the island and buy some space in which a political and diplomatic solution could be found.

Within days on 22 October President Kennedy went on television and radio in the United States to broadcast his assessment of the situation and what he proposed to do about it to see the Russian missiles removed from Cuba. As he spoke the alert levels of all United States military forces across the world were raised from the normal peacetime state of DEFCON-5 to DEFCON-3, two levels below the state of all-out war.

It is fair to say that General LeMay's view of this was less than enthusiastic. It seemed to him to be a low-key response, which is exactly what the President wanted. On 24 October, as the crisis worsened, United States Air Force General Thomas Power (a person close to LeMay) took the decision, without consultation with the President, to raise this alert level one stage higher to DEFCON-2. The instructions to do this were sent out in an uncoded form that he knew the Russians would be able to read. As a direct result of this signal one-eighth of the Strategic Air Command bomber fleet was mobilized into the air. They were now beyond the immediate threat of a pre-emptive attack by the Russians.

What was not clear at the time, however, and did not emerge until several years later was as the crisis broke the Russians had already pre-positioned 158 strategic and tactical nuclear weapons on Cuba. Of that total, forty-two were capable of being launched against anywhere in America. Had the Americans chosen to launch an attack on the island to occupy it some commentators have ventured to suggest that the invasion beaches may well have been targeted by low-yield Russian nuclear missiles.

The United Kingdom's Response

In the United Kingdom the evidence from declassified Cabinet meetings shows just how much of a shock the Cuban Missile Crisis was for the government. On 16 October, as the U-2 was flying over Cuba collecting the evidence of the Russian actions, the Cabinet had held one of its routine meetings. Cuba was on the agenda, but declassified records show that the conversations were focused on the indications of a Russian build-up of military support to the regime in Havana. None of the records that are available indicate any hint that the Russians may be trying to base nuclear-tipped ballistic missiles on the island.

The first time the United Kingdom's Prime Minister Harold Macmillan became aware of the dangers that lay ahead was when he opened a private letter from President Kennedy on 20 October. He had been forewarned by the American ambassador to expect such a private communication only hours earlier. As Macmillan read the letter his blood must have run cold. He had lived through two world wars. He knew what that had collectively cost mankind. This was on an altogether different level. As Hiroshima and Nagasaki showed, the threat of nuclear war was in a very different league. At the very least it would be an order of magnitude worse. This was hundreds of million dead, not tens of millions.

Macmillan's first reaction was to council caution. This was understandable. He had concerns over the idea of a blockade which President Kennedy outlined to him in a second follow-up letter. He noted those doubts in his private diary at the time and asked the Lord Chancellor to establish a United Kingdom government view of the legitimacy of the American proposals. Macmillan felt it was also important to do everything possible to gain international support for the American situation. Acting precipitously on the blockade may see international support and even NATO allies ebb away in the coming days.

In the course of the crisis Macmillan made two hugely important interventions to dampen down the headlong dash that appeared to be happening towards nuclear war. The first of these was to suggest to the President that he make the U-2 pictures public. It was in his view the strongest diplomatic weapon that could be employed to reveal Russian complicity. In the White House there were strong reservations about doing this. It would remove the veil of uncertainty that hung over the United States intelligence-collection systems. Intelligence organizations like to live under such a shroud as it requires potential adversaries to second-guess their capabilities.

If a future enemy did that they may have to take a position that somewhat overestimates the capabilities. Once the U-2 images were in the public domain that veil would be gone. While no direct connection has ever been made to the subsequent high levels of investment in satellite intelligence-collection platforms, President Kennedy's decision to release the pictures necessitated that next-generation systems had to be developed that were even better. That would bring down the veil again and restore the status quo. Macmillan had got his way. In a rather theatrical occasion Adel Stephenson, the United States Ambassador to the United Nations, revealed the imagery in the course of a sharp exchange at a Security Council meeting as the crisis unfolded.

Macmillan's second point was equally important. The initial American proposal had been to establish a blockade at a radius of 800 miles around Cuba. If any vessels approaching Cuba tried to cross this imaginary line they would have been stopped and boarded. The boarding teams would then conduct a comprehensive search of the vessels. If military equipment been found the vessel would have been impounded and escorted to a United States port. For some commentators this was tantamount to piracy on the high seas. The blue-water ocean was supposed to be a place where merchant vessels could make innocent passage without facing any form of confrontation.

Macmillan successfully argued that the blockade should be enforced at a range of 500 miles from Cuba. This bought time as vessels steaming at 15 knots would take longer to reach the blockade line. At that point no vessels detected by the United States navy were close to the blockade line so it gave the President a little more time to think about how to actually deal with a confrontation on the high seas.

Macmillan's other intervention was focused on the domestic preparedness for war in the United Kingdom. He did not wish to create any indications that the United Kingdom's military deterrent, some of which was committed to NATO, was being mobilized. At the time of the crisis the responsibility for the deterrent was held by the Royal Air Force. Its Vulcan bombers were equipped to carry the Blue Danube nuclear weapon with a yield close to that used over Japan at the end of the Second World War. It had entered service in 1953 and was available to the Valiant bombers that were the predecessors to the Vulcans.

On the NATO front Macmillan made it clear that he would not agree to a NATO-wide mobilization. This, he felt, would also have the potential to ratchet up the tensions. He also made it clear to the senior commanders in the Royal Air Force that there should be no overt manoeuvres associated with the Vulcan bomber force that might suggest the United Kingdom was moving onto a war footing.

It happened that at the time of the crisis the Royal Air Force was already engaged in one of its periodic tests of the ability to mobilize the nuclear deterrent. These exercises were often called at short notice. Their aim was to test the ability of the Royal Air Force to generate aircraft that were ready to execute predetermined missions over Russia and Eastern Europe.

These exercises often involved the Vulcans being flown away from their nominal operating bases to dispersed airfields, awaiting a signal to launch an attack on Russia. The Royal Air Force had twenty-six pre-prepared airbases across the United Kingdom to which the Vulcans could be mobilized if a pre-emptive attack against their airbases was thought likely. These dispersed airfields were part of a programme designed to improve the survivability of the Vulcan bomber force. In those days it would have taken the Russians a long time to find the dispersed aircraft and target them. That complicated their targeting efforts.

Fortunately as far as Macmillan's instructions were concerned the exercise that the Vulcan bomber force was then engaged upon did not involve the dispersal of aircraft. Macmillan knew that a mass scramble of the Vulcans was a noisy affair and that the Russians had ears on the ground that would alert them to any large-scale movement of the force.

However, under the cover of the exercise Royal Air Force commanders did take a number of measures to ensure that the Vulcan Force was as ready as it could be within the political constraints set by the Prime Minister. Despite rumours to the contrary and accounts of situations where aircraft were dispersed no full-scale 'flushing' of the airfields occurred. Accounts from the time also vary in detail on the degree to which the Vulcan force had been armed and was ready to be launched.

That the crews were on Quick Reaction Alert (QRA) is beyond doubt. If dispersal was not possible then the aircraft simply had to be available to fly in a four-minute window. The time taken to scramble was one that was fiercely contested among air-crews with squadrons vying for position as to which had achieved the fastest time into the air.

At the 'Blue' alert state Vulcans were held at thirty minutes' readiness. At the 'Amber' state of alert crews would be seated in the cockpits ready to start up the aircraft. Timings were based on an assessment of the notice period that would be derived from the Fylingdales Ballistic Missile Early Warning System (BMEWS). For medium-range ballistic missiles being fired from Russia against the United Kingdom it was held at the time that fifteen minutes' warning of a nuclear attack might be forthcoming.

However, it would be wrong to think that this was a launch-on-warning-based approach. That would have reduced the nuclear tripwire below a threshold that was comfortable.

In practice that alert time had a political reaction time built in to ensure that the telephone line from Fylingdales to Number 10 Downing Street could be used for a quick consultation with the Prime Minister before the Vulcan bombers were scrambled. False alarms also plagued the early introduction of the BMEWS capability. Meteorites were sometimes thought to be re-entering warheads that had been pre-positioned in space to reduce the alert time. Over time ways of eliminating the false alarms improved and the systems became very reliable. Other measures were also put in place to alert the two sides of the Cold War about up-and-coming launches. This had a marked effect on reducing tensions.

During peacetime the rivalry between crews and some innovative approaches to start-up procedures saw the time to get airborne from the initial scramble signal reduced to a low point of just over one minute. This was achieved after the Cuban Missile Crisis by four Victor aircraft departing RAF Cottesmore. Whenever exercises were called crews felt obliged to beat the four-minute nominal window to scramble. The worst recorded figure has been noted at two minutes and forty-seven seconds, still well within the time window available.

Slight changes to the schedule of the exercises were made to maintain the fleet at its highest level of preparedness. Additional Vulcans were generated above those that had planned to be involved in the exercise. At RAF Marham in the east of England Vulcans assigned to NATO were also discretely if somewhat chaotically prepared. These measures, personally put in place by Commander-in-Chief Bomber Command, were sensible and adhered to the political guidance given by the Prime Minister.

The airbases on which the Vulcans were based moved quietly onto a war footing. Civilians and non-essential staff were sent home. No one was allowed onto the sites. Guards were deployed to prevent any coordinated efforts at sabotage by fifth columnists. For the next few days, until the Royal Air Force Vulcan bombers were stood down at the start of November, the air-crews did not leave the side of their aircraft.

Of all the rumours and conjecture that surround the actual level of readiness of the Royal Air Force throughout the Cuban Missile Crisis, the issue of whether the Vulcan bombers were actually armed at any point remains shrouded in some mystery. Some reports from the time suggest that the Vulcans were all armed with Blue Danube nuclear bombs, while others have suggested that only part of the fleet had been armed.

Given the fact that the airbases were in lock-down and that the United Kingdom did not have an extensive stockpile of Blue Danube bombs at the time it seems unlikely that every Vulcan that could have participated in an attack would have been fully armed. One report has suggested that only one aircraft each on ten airfields actually was loaded with its nuclear bomb. This is probably at the lower end of what actually occurred. Some of the British stockpile of nuclear weapons was dispersed anyway to locations that could support the dispersed airfields, so it is unlikely that the entire inventory of weapons was instantly available.

Once the crisis was over Macmillan commissioned a small group of people from across government to undertake an analysis of the preparedness and to draw lessons from the Cuban Missile Crisis. This was to be a review of the government's War Book planning to make sure the system was as responsive as it now appeared it needed to be as the world had moved on from the Second World War.

It is highly likely that the team found lots to debate as they deliberated on the way the crisis unfolded. In their terms of reference, laid down by the Prime Minister, they were asked to specifically address issues around situations where there were only two to three days' warning of war and where other countries were engaged in tense stand-offs with each other. Macmillan had clearly noted for himself some issues in those dangerous days and wanted another viewpoint to consolidate into his own recollections. If there was to be another occasion, next time the United Kingdom government would be better prepared.

That next time occurred during the Yom Kippur War in 1973 between Israel and an Egyptian-Syrian axis. As the Israelis fought back and regained lost ground they made a daring crossing of the Suez Canal. Once on the Egyptian side they turned north and drove towards Cairo. At one point it seemed to some observers that the Israelis were intent on dealing a final blow against the Egyptian political leadership.

The Americans who had militarily bailed out the Israelis called for a halt at the same time that the Russians started loading parachutists onto transport aircraft in Bulgaria. That move was detected by the United States intelligence agencies and an increased alert level across NATO was declared. The United Kingdom Vulcan bombers which still held an important role as part of the nuclear deterrent again went into their QRA procedures. For a very brief period of time the United Kingdom again was on the nuclear precipice.

The Crisis Unfolds

As the Cuban Missile Crisis wore on the Americans mounted additional over-flights of Cuba to update their intelligence assessment. Each flight over the country was extremely risky. On one occasion two United States A6 Corsair aircraft flew at low level over the country photographing the missile sites. This was not an incursion by a high-flying U-2 spy plane operating at altitudes over 60,000ft: this was up close and personal.

General LeMay was looking all the time for a pretext for moving the confrontation on to the next stage. In the Hollywood depiction of the events in the film *Thirteen Days* one of the Corsair pilots is asked to accompany the photographic film back to Washington to be interrogated by the military chiefs about the mission. In the film LeMay asks the young pilot 'Did they fire a shot at you?' The pilot, who had been appraised of the situation, was economical with the truth in his reply.

His aircraft had indeed been peppered with bullets but he chose not to mention that to the military chiefs. While the depiction of that scene may emerge from the creative thought processes of the film's writers and bear little resemblance to reality, it drives home the point that the American political and military leaders were on somewhat divergent paths during the crisis. Had the chain of events that occurred in the coming days varied slightly there could have been a devastating outcome.

The 27th of October has become known in historical accounts as 'Black Saturday'. This was the low point in the crisis. Events seemed to have a momentum all of their own. At around 10 o'clock in the morning a U-2 spy plane flown by Major Rudolf Anderson, the pilot who had conducted the original mission over Cuba twelve days previously, was killed when his aircraft was shot down by a Russian SAM. The order to engage the spy plane had been given by the commander of the Russian air defences in Cuba. Apparently he had not felt the need to consult with Moscow.

Within hours over Siberia another U-2 on a spying mission had made a navigational error and drifted into Russian airspace. As Russian MiG aircraft were scrambled to engage the threat United States interceptors based in Alaska responded. It seemed as if a 'chain of events' had been put in train and, in a similar way to the build-up to the First World War, the outcome was now a foregone conclusion. The stage was set for the Third World War. Political leaders, for whatever reason, had lost control and seemed unable to pull back from the brink.

These two events on Black Saturday were not alone in defining the sombre mood that descended over the White House that evening. Russian merchant vessels were rapidly approaching the 500-mile blockade line and the messages emerging from Moscow seemed confused. At one point it even appeared that the Russian President had been deposed in a military coup.

That the Cuban Missile Crisis did not lead to a devastating world war is a matter of history. At the crucial moment the Russian President blinked. Within days an orderly stand-down of nuclear forces commenced. The world had stood at the edge of an abyss and had taken a step back. In the aftermath the awesome nature of what the world had faced became clear. Measures to improve communications between Moscow and Washington were overhauled. There would be no next time.

Throughout the crisis intelligence collected by aircraft that placed themselves in harm's way was a crucial element of the overall assessment of the situation. The need to see what the other side was doing became clear in fast-moving situations. The lessons from the false intelligence assessments that led to the bomber-gap and the missile-gap now also sharpened the response. From that point onwards investments in technologies to place sensor systems in space and to maintain the airborne capability would be a priority for spending. Today the unmanned platforms that carry the latest versions of those technologies still provide the data sources for assessments of the capabilities and readiness of potential enemies.

Sigint and the Hainan Incident

On 1 April 2001 a United States Lockheed EP-3E ARIES II Signals Intelligence (SIGINT) aircraft collided with a Chinese J-8II fighter jet close to the disputed Paracel Islands in the South China Sea. The EP-3 was assigned to Fleet Air Reconnaissance Squadron One (VQ-1, 'World Watchers'). It had left base at Kadena in Okinawa in the depths of the night.

Six hours later it was confronted by the Chinese jets operating from Lingshui airbase on the Chinese island of Hainan. One J-8II made two close approaches to the EP-3 in an obvious attempt to move it away from what the Chinese regard as a highly sensitive military area. On the third pass the jet collided with the EP-3. Accounts vary as to the cause of the collision. Whatever the truth of the matter the EP-3 was severely damaged and its pilot had to use all his flying skills to recover the aircraft.

Once he had regained (partial) control of the aeroplane the pilot had little time to consider his options. Reluctantly he concluded that to save the crew he had to fly to the nearest airbase. That was in China, on Hainan

Island. Despite numerous emergency calls and dialling the necessary code into the Secondary Surveillance Radar (SSR) transponder on the EP-3 his arrival at Hainan was a surprise.

When the aircraft landed it was quickly seized by the Chinese. In the coming weeks it would be dissected looking for anything of value. In the few minutes the crew had between the collision and their unexpected arrival in Hainan they had done all they could to destroy and render useless the sensitive intelligence-collection equipment they had on the aircraft.

The EP-3 had been on what was as far as the Americans were concerned a routine intelligence-collection flight. This was not the first time such aircraft would fly in what the Americans regarded as an area covered by international conventions as one protected for free navigation for all countries' aircraft and ships.

During the Cold War SIGINT flights became a vital part of the armoury of the west in positioning its military to fight a war with the Russians. The Royal Air Force also used its equivalent systems, such as the Nimrod R1 variant, to conduct eavesdropping missions. Its task was to collect information on radar systems and their associated communications infrastructure. Unlike the incident near to Hainan Island a great deal of this work could be relatively dull, flying patterns up and down what was then the East German border. The data recorders on board these aircraft would faithfully record every pulse and glitch. The tapes were transferred to ground-based intelligence-collection systems for processing.

The information derived from these missions was used for a number of different forms of assessment. Some were strategic in nature, as in assessing advances in Russian technologies. Others were more operationally focused, allowing radar warning receivers to be programmed with a library of pulse types that could be used to characterize possible threat radars should they be detected.

As surveillance radar systems built tracks to hand off possible targets to tracking and engagement radars that controlled SAMs their signature would vary. Pulse rates might increase or the rate at which the radar illuminated the target would change. All of these were warnings that a launch of a SAM might be imminent. Collecting the operational parameters of the Warsaw Pact radar systems used along the border gave those flying aircraft a better chance of survival.

They also provided the information needed to develop electronic warfare jamming systems that might escort ground-attack aircraft as they sought to penetrate mobile SAM shields protecting advancing Warsaw Pact columns. The Order of Battle of the Warsaw Pact and specific Russian divisions was well known to NATO. If the Cold War ever turned hot the ground-attack aircraft trying to attack the massed formations of tanks crossing the Fulda Gap would have had to penetrate the SAM shield to attack the tanks and reduce the tempo of the movement. To achieve that on occasions they would have been escorted by aircraft such as the variant of the F-111 fighter-bomber (the 'Wild Weasels') that had seen its bomb bays filled with electronics instead of bombs.

Chapter Three

Air-to-Air Case Studies

Of all the applications of air power the air-to-air environment is arguably the most glamorous. The images of Baron Manfred von Richthofen's red Fokker tri-plane engaging and bringing down Allied airmen have received widespread coverage, even being satirized in a BBC television comedy series. The reality as ever was somewhat different. The idea that air-to-air combat was somehow a refuge for gentlemen who knew how to conduct warfare was far from the truth.

The notion that warfare could be conducted in a spirit of noblesse oblige among men who had a certain standing in society brought to the emerging world of air warfare the paradigm of air combat being conducted by officers and gentlemen who played by a set of rules. Warfare is rarely something that is fought in such an arranged environment. It is a chaotic and often bloody affair.

The losses in air combat in the First World War showed that to be the case. Efforts to romanticize air warfare possibly as a counter to the bloodshed that was occurring in the trenches may have initially worked on a public horrified by the carnage on the Western Front. In time, however, that myth has been dispelled.

In the Battle of Britain, over the skies of Burma, the war in Korea, the Yom Kippur War and the air battles over Iraq in 1991 the realities of life and death have been shown to be very different. Shooting pilots as they glide towards the earth on their parachutes is hardly the act of a gentleman. Air-to-air warfare is combat at the leading edge of human endurance. Pulling 12 Gs to try to avoid being killed by a missile system is something the human body cannot do that often. The enduring relevance of manned missions in the air defence environment is also subject to debate.

Some commentators have even questioned if pilots need actually be involved in air combat any more. Why not let missiles fired from unmanned drones take on the task of air defence? They can withstand much higher levels of stress and in a situation where the technological advantages traditionally enjoyed by the west are being eroded the next leap in air-to-air combat must surely be to dispense with pilots.

With the end of the Cold War the potential for air-to-air combat to occur over the North Sea in scenes reminiscent of the Battle of Britain receded. Air-to-air combat occurred infrequently. Over Libya in 2011 there was not a single incident when Allied fighters were confronted by the Libyan Air Force. Arguably this meant that some of the missions flown by the international community over Libya were rendered worthless. Political restrictions placed on the contribution that some air forces deployed into the coalition neutered their effectiveness. Their presence in the coalition was purely a political signal. Militarily their value was close to worthless.

In recent history when air-to-air combat did happen it was very one-sided. A combination of on-board sensor systems on the interceptors and complex C3I networks gave a huge advantage to one side over the other. This was to lead to a period in the 1980s and early 1990s when some quite extraordinary claims were made about the impact on C3I systems on the battlefield. This was, according to some writers, nothing less than a revolution in military affairs. The creation of the United Kingdom Air Defence Ground Environment (UKADGE) provided an example of the ideas in practice.

In fact its similarity in operation to the systems put in place for the Battle of Britain and for the Battle of Malta showed that the basic ideas behind the creation of an air defence system remained intact. Soviet developments of long-range stand-off missiles throughout the Cold War did, however, change the dynamics. No matter what systems are in place time was still of the essence. In the early part of the Cold War over the North Sea the English Electric Lightning provided a way of getting airborne quickly but its armament of two missiles provided a limited capability against what were likely to be large-scale attacks against United Kingdom airfields in the early stages of a new world war.

Only for the Cold War warriors such as the RAF FGR4 Phantom the issue was that it had to be deployed as far forward as was practical on Combat Air Patrol. Supported by tankers and Airborne Early Warning Systems (AEWS) the aircraft could get at the Soviet bombers before they could launch their missiles. Airborne radar in the AEWS and the interceptors became crucial to the ways in which engagements were planned and executed.

Arguably UKADGE was the pinnacle of air defence systems: a step-up in terms of flexibility and responsiveness that genuinely took the basic ideas forged in the heat of the Battle of Britain and made them effective in the modern era. As the Cold War faded the role of air defence also seemed to have had its day. As ever in the military field, those anxious to reap a peace dividend need to be careful.

As we come towards the end of the first century of air power the Russian Air Force is resuming flights into the United Kingdom's airspace at an apparently increasing rate. Rather than the occasional singleton that was often seen en route to Cuba that typified day-to-day life in the Cold War, the Russian Air Force is now sending several bombers at a time to test what remains of the UK air defence capability. Add to that the fear of a possible hijack scenario and a repeat of the dreadful attacks in September 2001 in America, and the need to maintain a flexible and responsive air defence capability over the United Kingdom remains.

These concerns over the ways in which some countries are rebuilding their offensive air capability are mirrored elsewhere. In America concerns over a resurgent Russian Air Force and rapid developments in Chinese fighter technologies are also leading some to suggest that the reduced purchase of the F-22 Raptor aircraft may need to be revisited. Across the South China Sea many nation-states are also turning to new fighter-jet technologies to provide a counter-weight against Chinese military investments.

Systems-of-Systems

The claims made a great deal of the ability of C3I systems to create situations where commanders would enjoy a position of being 'dominant' in their ability to appreciate the dynamics of the battlefield. The veracity of these claims was quickly to be disproved in combat. To achieve that level of comprehensive situational awareness defence doctrine writers now speak of 'systems-of-systems'. This implies that every individual system (radar, electro-optical sensor, missile, airplane and ground elements) now needs to be joined together to help create the recognized air picture. While it is easy to write such concepts, it is not quite so straightforward to bring them into service.

That said, through many international collaborative efforts a great number of improvements have occurred in creating systems-of-systems, often driven by operational necessities in places like Iraq and Afghanistan. Multi-national collaboration in such systems-of-systems thinking has also dramatically advanced in recent years to support more integrated ground and air operations.

An enemy does have a vote and when faced by numerically superior forces will adopt the simplest of measures to achieve their aims. The idea that C3I systems could give one side a technological edge may have been justified in some analysts' minds in a Cold War situation where one side had greater numbers of aircraft and the other side relied on technology to cancel out that advantage.

In the future it may be in cyberspace where such asymmetric conflicts are fought with outcomes being decided before a shot is fired. The more dependent nations and alliances become on the notion of systems-of-systems, the more they need to heavily invest in cyber-defence. It is the Achilles' heel of the whole concept.

As the sun set on the Cold War the dynamics of conflict were to change dramatically. A new term entered the lexicon of the military doctrine writers. The talk now was of asymmetric conflicts. While asymmetry had existed in the past in purely numerical terms and C3I provided a counterweight to that problem, the move towards the new tactics of asymmetric warfare was to cast a long shadow over the claims that C3I systems could create dominant decision environments. To achieve this required the C3I systems now to be persistent. That was to drive a whole new series of platform developments and the evolution of the unmanned drone.

Today the much-heralded gap in technological capabilities is being closed. China is one country that has spent a huge amount of time in its military academies studying the outcomes of past wars and confrontations. Its huge investment in C3I systems shows that it appreciates the value of networking aircraft and their indigenous sensor systems with ground, air, sea and space-based sensor systems to help develop the RAP (Recognized Air Picture) and distribute it to all those participating in the conflict.

In May 2012 the Pentagon initiated studies with industry to look at the design alternatives for the sixth generation of fighter jet. For those starting to sketch out their ideas on the computer graphics screens a number of very interesting trade-offs need to be considered. The F-22 Raptor clearly emerged at a time when the west enjoyed an advantage of stealth technologies over its potential rivals. That gap is closing rapidly.

The Chinese J-20 and the Russian T-50 demonstrator aircraft all provide illustrations of how ideas now proliferate through the internet. Design concepts can be stolen by states seeking to readdress apparent technological asymmetries or knowledge can become what academics like to refer to as democratized, or shared. Design features on the J-20 are similar to those emerging in America and Russia.

With the advantage of supercomputing now being lost to the west the physics of the highly granular models of aerodynamic behaviour are now well understood in aircraft design teams from Tehran to Beijing and Moscow. This inevitably allows some countries such as Iran to skip development cycles that have been tackled in places like American and

European aircraft design teams. That same trend is being seen in the civil airliner marketplace.

The west puts in a great deal of investment to develop the new technologies, only for their design ideas to permeate into the rest of the world where low-cost production capabilities enable larger quantities of aircraft to be manufactured. The high cost, for example, of stealth developments may soon reach a point of diminishing return. The design concepts that emerge from the studies into the sixth-generation fighter may provide an indication that continued benefits from stealth technologies are reaching a point where it is hard to argue the cost-benefit calculus.

In this situation the balance of investment in giving the fighters more agility versus making them stealthy and equipping them with indigenous ISTAR and C3I capabilities becomes very interesting. The decisions made in the studies will provide a legacy of military capability that will have to extend beyond the middle of the twenty-first century.

As technology proliferation continues apace the outcomes of those trade-offs will determine the relative military advantages that will exist in a world where resource depletion and climate change is almost bound to be the source of new conflicts. From 2030 onwards, as the sixth-generation fighter emerges from the drawing board into production its operational life may well have to contend with a situation where the Chinese and Russians have achieved parity on the technology front. With the west's traditional advantages eroded, the decisions made by the designers are going to be really interesting.

Despite the evolutions in the tactics of air-to-air combat and their associated technological developments one essential truth remains. To paraphrase the head of Fighter Command in the Battle of Britain one side has to shoot down more of the adversary's aircraft than the other. Sir Hugh Dowding's actual words were that it was the 'essential truth of the matter'. That simple fact holds true today. The ratio of combat kills is important and will be a central aspect to this analysis. How you achieve the objective of shooting down the enemy has changed from the early days of air-to-air combat but that you need to do that remains critical.

Shooting Down the Enemy

Over the history of air warfare the nature of air-to-air combat has changed. The early attempts to fire guns at an opposing pilot from what was already an unstable platform were very much a hit-or-miss affair. After the development of the machine gun that could fire through the propeller air warfare took a new turn. The manoeuvrability of the machine and the skill of the pilot using the flight envelope became the means by which air-to-air warfare could be waged. Get on the tail of the enemy and do not let him shake you off whatever outrageous manoeuvres they pull and then fire some form of weapon to shoot them down. The solutions to that problem saw several innovations in the last 100 years, some of which proved remarkably enduring in their in-life service.

For the Germans their initial superiority in aircraft design and development gave them an advantage. For the pilots of the Royal Flying Corps air-to-air combat was a risky business. The number of times armaments, such as the Lewis gun or the French-designed 20mm Hispano-Suiza type 404 cannon jammed added an unpredictable element to many air-to-air engagements. The Lewis gun was prone to freezing and the HS.404 cannon often saw explosive shells jammed in its firing mechanism.

It also became increasingly difficult to achieve that aim as advances in metallurgy made the airframes more robust. In simple terms the bombers increasingly became harder to shoot down. With these developments it became clear that the machine guns that had been used had to be replaced. The first upgrade that occurred saw the two guns installed in the Spitfire Mark 1B replaced with four 0.303-in Browning machine guns in each wing with the simple aim of bringing more fire-power to bear on the target. Although these were more reliable in combat Royal Air Force pilots consistently complained about running out of ammunition before being able to bring down an enemy aircraft. Evidence in support of their claims can be found in the number of partial kills awarded even to distinguished fighter aces. On many occasions the statistics show it took bursts from three separate aircraft to achieve a combat victory.

Despite its initial problems and the advent of the missile age the option to keep a gun or cannon for the very close-up forms of air-to-air combat has remained. The six-day war between Israel and the Arab States, the Yom Kippur War and the battles over Vietnam all proved the enduring utility of the cannon. One example of this was the ADEN cannon. It could fire rounds at 1,200–1,700 a minute. Although the muzzle speed of the fourth iteration of the design was only 741m per second (2,341ft per second), which was lower than the Hispano-Suiza figure of 850m per second (2,789ft per second), the ADEN cannon was more lethal.

Even accounting for the reduction in kinetic energy which scaled as the square of the velocity, the heavier and larger round in the ADEN was better able to shoot down enemy aircraft. It was not the velocity of the projectile that saw a German bomber brought down; it was the damage radius of the round. Over time the ADEN was to become a standard fit for many air-to-air fighter aircraft including the A-4S Skyhawk, the Hawker Hunter, and Saab Draken, SEPECAT Jaguar, the Sea Harrier and more recently the Hawk trainer. The Sea Harrier retained the ADEN cannon until they were prematurely retired from service in 2006. The ADEN had been in service for just over half a century.

From its design inception in 1946 it went on to serve with over thirty air forces around the world. A series of new designs saw the basic capabilities continually improved until the attempts to build the ADEN 25 failed. Design problems had plagued the programme and it was cancelled in 1999.

The use of the cannon was all about dogfights that are up close and personal. Today the developments of stand-off cruise and long-range air-to-air missiles mean that early detection of the threat is critical. If the bomber carrying the cruise missile can be detected and engaged before it reaches its launch-point then the likely targets, such as the airbases from which the defenders have flown, can be protected. For the RAF over the North Sea in the Cold War this race to engage and destroy inbound Soviet bombers from the north or the east was crucial.

Today the doctrine of air defence speaks of 'first look, first shot, and first kill'. In an era when stealth technologies are making life harder for defence systems to gain that first look at the target the nature of the air-to-air battle is changing. The first look in the past was carried out by eye. Today the first look depends upon on-board sensor systems on the fighters.

The fifth-generation fighter jets need to be able to carry advanced sensor systems with them as they try to establish air superiority. In the air-land battle of the Cold War the close proximity of airbases in Eastern Europe meant that ground and airborne radar systems would quickly spot any incoming raid from Warsaw Pact countries. As the environment in which future warfare changes and the air-sea battle becomes a crucial focus it is important to re-examine past assumptions and determine whether they remain valid. The air-sea battle also has an element in it of the air-sea-air battle: where the control of the air-sea battle is now moved away from the land environment into warships. During the Libyan operations control of the airspace in and around Libya routinely passed from HMS *Liverpool* to an AWACS aircraft and back again, showing flexibility in the delivery of the point where control of the air was conducted. With the United States now pivoting its forces towards the Pacific Rim and away from Europe one thing is clear. The dynamics of the air-to-air battles envisaged over Europe have changed.

The traditional role of ground-based radar systems will be somewhat diminished. This will shift the priority of taking the first look to the fighters themselves. If they are not to give away their position to a potential enemy they must remain covert. Any indigenous radar systems will need to be used sparingly. This shifts the emphasis in on-board sensor systems towards the Infra-Red Search and Track (IRST) systems, such as the equipment due to be flown on the F-35 Lightning in an operational context.

In the context of the Pacific Rim this will also mean that the decision not to equip the F-22 Raptor with an IRST capability will need to be reviewed. For the F-22 to make a contribution to any future conflict in the region the task of early detection of the threat will fall to the IRST. Tracks developed from fusing the information derived from different aircraft will then enable the RAP to be built and for that to form the basis of the following battle to achieve air superiority.

To achieve this air superiority needs to be established over an increasingly large area. As the air-land battle gives way to the air-sea battle the interaction between aircraft deployed from aircraft carriers and those that are launched from fixed airfields will be important.

Should any future conflict break out in the South China Sea, for example, the United States and its allies in the region would have to create a series of layers through which Chinese and/or Russian aircraft would have to penetrate before reaching vulnerable American and allied airbases in the area. The first layer of that defence will be the land-based air defence fighters in Korea and Japan. The second layer will be the F-18 aircraft and the carrier-based AWACS. The final layer will be the F-22, AWACS and air tankers that would be operated from airbases such as Guam from which the strategic bombers would need to operate.

In September 1940 in the skies over the United Kingdom the Royal Air Force fought the first air-to-air battle where a command and control system enabled the commanders to allocate fighter aircraft to the battle. In the future the C3I systems will still play a hugely important role providing the glue that hooks together the individual components into a coordinated and layered defence system. The timelines of the activities, however, are going to be very compressed. In the Battle of Britain, while the tempo of the operations over the United Kingdom was high there was at least some downtime for the defenders. In the future the timelines and pace at which battles will be conducted will be frenetic. The outcome of any future conflict will be decided in hours, not the weeks and days of the summer of 1940.

Airframe Developments

The turning-point for the fortunes of the Royal Flying Corps in the First World War came when they introduced a new aircraft. The introduction of new aircraft types saw the German advantage in machine manoeuvrability eliminated. Air-to-air warfare over the trenches would now become a battle of skills. Those that were the best flyers survived, adding to their heroic caricature. These were people who lived on the edge, seconds away from being killed.

The images and anecdotal tales told by those who fought in the Battle of Britain often understate the nature of air-to-air combat in the Second World War. The modesty of some of those involved can create a perception that shooting down German bombers was a relatively easy affair. That overlooks the degree of armament carried on a Junkers 88. This was an aircraft that could shoot back laying down several arcs of fire through which the Spitfire and Hurricane pilots had to dive in order to bring their guns to bear on the target. When flown in formation those arcs of fire could create a deadly barrier to the pilots who had to get up close to the German bombers to try to shoot them down.

The trajectory chosen to attack the Junkers was always important, as was the speed of the engagement. Royal Air Force pilots knew that if they lost speed in the air it could have fatal consequences. They could not close on the bombers and bleed off speed to be sure of the kill. The tactics adopted by the Royal Air Force pilots evolved quickly to reduce the risks from the gunners in the German bombers. The early formation tactics adopted by the Royal Air Force also had their weaknesses which the Bf 109 exploited in the early days of the Battle of Britain.

Insight into the nature of the problems faced by the Royal Air Force was to come from an unlikely direction. In the early part of the Battle of France a Bf 109 pilot became disorientated in fog and landed at a French airfield. The Bf 109 was quickly flown in a series of trials by the French Air Force before being handed over to the scientists and combat trials teams at the Royal Aircraft Establishment at Farnborough. Over a really short period of time a detailed comparison was made between the performance of the Spitfire and Hurricane in a range of combat situations with the Bf 109.

The common perception that either the Messerschmitt Bf 109 or the Spitfire was a superior aircraft was clarified. In some situations the Bf 109 did indeed have a superior performance. In others the Spitfire outclassed its opponent. The real issue was to learn the lessons from these trials in sufficient time for them to have an impact upon the outcome of the Battle of Britain. History shows that some minor adjustments to the configuration of the Merlin engines helped improve the Spitfire's abilities in a dogfight.

The main drag on the ability of the Royal Air Force to respond to the insights gained from the captured Messerschmitt was the large investment in training that had already gone into preparing pilots for combat. The initial tactics deployed by the Royal Air Force did not help. Marauding Bf 109s used their performance to exploit the inherent weaknesses in the Royal Air Force V-shaped formations that had been documented in the Fighting Area Attacks paradigms published in the 1938 Manual of Air Tactics. As ever with improvements in doctrine unauthorized and locally-developed tactical developments were introduced at the squadron level.

The Germans also benefited from capturing three combat-ready Spitfires after the invasion of France. They too were evaluated in detail by the Luftwaffe's Rechlin Test Centre where the ease with which the aircraft could fly was noted by the German pilots. However, their evaluation also exposed key weaknesses in the performance of the aircraft. In truth the Spitfire and Messerschmitt were well matched and it came down to the skill of the pilots in flying the aircrafts' envelope in combat as to who gained combat victories.

Often they came as one pilot made a crucial mistake in manoeuvring that opened a brief window which, if exploited by an attacker, would lead to the demise of that aircraft. Those lessons still apply today. Air-to-air warfare is a deadly affair if your skills do not match those of your enemy. It can be very one-sided and the pilots only have one life to play with.

Flying air-to-air engagements in the Second World War was something that required men who were able to live at the very edge of their flying skills and levels of situational awareness. When the engagement did occur the firing rate of the guns could often see all the ammunition expended in a matter of seconds. The average time of engagements in the Second World War was fifteen seconds.

To bring their rather crude gun-sight to bear on an enemy for any length of time and to then fire the guns required immense concentration and a single-minded purpose. Royal Air Force pilots quickly became aware that the effective range of engagement of an enemy was about half of the distance they had been trained to fly at around 200–250m. They simply had to get close to the enemy to ensure they could shoot them down.

Even then the guns could jam, preventing the kill shot being taken. Some of these modest men have been known to describe engagements in a language of getting into the right position and then 'hammering away on the guns in the hope of hitting something'. If they did succeed they also had to have the ability to avoid some of the debris that would inevitably fly off their opponent ahead of the aircraft disintegrating or entering the death spiral.

The pilots of the Second World War did not enjoy the technological advantages afforded to those that have followed them. Despite the technological advantages enjoyed by their heirs the essential element of air-to-air combat has not changed. Throughout the century of air-to-air combat pilots have had to be quick-thinking, able to seize an initiative when an opponent loses their situational awareness, and be able to move in for the kill.

Contemporary Perspectives

Today pilots have some new terms in their lexicon that their predecessors might initially find confusing. The language of defensive counter-air and offensive-air missions may seem a little remote from the terms that they used to describe aerial warfare. In part the terms have been introduced to reflect the many ways in which air power can be applied. Developments in electronic warfare are partly to blame for this changed lexicon.

Suppressing an adversary's air defence system using jamming techniques does give a pilot an advantage. It is one that does not solely apply to the air-to-ground environment. The same arguments apply to trying to reduce the effectiveness of an adversary's on-board sensor systems, such as radar and electro-optical detectors.

It was during the Korean War when technology allowed pilots to start to engage each other with missiles. Air-to-air warfare was able to be conducted as a remote affair. The pilot's task was to manoeuvre his aircraft into a suitable firing position and allow the missile to home onto its target. When missiles could not be used the pilot still had a gun.

From the mid-1950s air-to-air missile system developments could be broadly characterized into two main groups. These were those that were designed to operate in visual range in the classic dogfighting roles and those that were to be used beyond visual range. Those that are to operate within visual range utilize infrared heat-seeking missiles to latch onto the signature that inevitably arises from fighter aircraft as they engage in high-speed manoeuvres.

With today's developments in stealth technologies the head-on heat signatures that are available to an attacking aircraft make long-range detection in the infrared part of the electro-magnetic spectrum exceedingly difficult. New technology infrared systems are required to operate at the levels of sensitivity required to detect the much fainter signatures of an aircraft's skin that has been warmed by flying at supersonic speeds. Attacking from the rear still provides the highest heat signature.

For beyond visual range engagements, where infrared systems could become confused by false alarms such as sun glint from clouds, radar-based seeker-heads are the preferred solution. Missile guidance uses information from the host platform to lock the missile onto the target. Guidance to the target can be achieved in one of a number of ways.

One approach employs a variety of ways of utilizing radar technology. Active radar homing provides another approach where once fired the missile locates the target. This has the advantage of providing what is called a 'fire and forget' mode of operation, reducing the workload on the pilot and allowing them to position the aircraft for the next engagement. Semi-active homing relies on back-scattered signals from the target aircraft as a result of its being illuminated by the attacking platform.

For the aircraft under attack a variety of counter-measures exist. If the attacking missile is thought to be guided by an infrared seeker, the pilot can deploy flares. Their temperature profile is designed to seduce the incoming missile away from the aircraft. The duration of the flares and their own infrared signatures make them vulnerable to being rejected by a smart seeker-head. If the seeker-head is thought to be based upon radar technologies then chaff can be used to create a false target. Again this has a limited time span in which it is able to act as a decoy.

In air-to-air combat today's pilots have a much wider range of issues to deal with as they try to shoot down an adversary's fighters. The speeds, rates of turns, manoeuvrability and diversity of missile systems provide the pilot of the F-15E and its equivalent fourth-generation fighters with a much higher workload than those that fought in the Battle of Britain.

The advent of the missile has created a challenge for the designers of future weapons systems and platforms. Where in the design trade-offs do you find the right balance between the manoeuvrability of the aircraft and that of the missiles? While airframes have become more able to withstand very high-G turns, the physical limits placed on the pilots do constrain one aspect of the engagement.

The missiles, however, have no such issues. They can happily pull high levels of G-forces. It is not difficult to see why a new debate is emerging about the balance of investment in the host platform and the money to be spent on missiles and specifically their ability to home onto a target and destroy it no matter what manoeuvres the target aircraft undertakes. If survival of the host platform is important, i.e. if it is manned, then those arguments can cancel out. The host platform has to remain manoeuvrable to the same level as the missiles or have a suite of defensive aids that are able to defeat the seeker sensor of any incoming missile.

The next evolution of air-to-air warfare could well involve deploying a combination of manned and unmanned fighters into the battle. A new paradigm would emerge. Manned aircraft could carry swarms of small unmanned aircraft into an air-to-air battle. The unmanned aircraft would be stealthy to avoid detection. Their weapons fit could well see smaller missiles carried in the unmanned aircraft. The host platform would run the air battle, assigning targets to the unmanned aircraft. Protection of the host platform would fall to the unmanned aircraft, some of which would be dedicated to that task. An alternative solution could see a mix of manned fighter aircraft being tasked to protect the host platform.

Of course this vision of the future of air-to-air combat has to be seen against a backdrop of the austere environment which is likely to hamper large-scale military projects in the future. With fighters now costing over $100 million for a single platform, something does have to be done. In the limit, instead of developing potentially costly unmanned aircraft that could be deployed in larger numbers, the traditionalists might suggest that each unmanned aircraft is in fact just another missile. While the technologists might salivate at the prospect of yet new technologies being developed to change the dynamics of air-to-air combat, pragmatism may set in and determine that the fifth-generation fighters are not the last manned aircraft that history will see in that role.

As ever in these situations at a specific point where combat occurs the relative advantages of one side over another would be difficult to appreciate until the first combat sorties were analysed. Rapid technological advancements can give one side a small but significant advantage. This is the battle of technologies. As one side introduces a measure that is effective it takes time for the adversary to counter that with their own advancement. As events during the Yom Kippur War showed, overcoming that temporary asymmetry can be critical.

Of all the contemporary images of air-to-air combat the legacy of the film *Top Gun* is one that has become ingrained in the mindset of the public at large. This is one of a genre of films that depict warfare and it remains in a class of its own. The way the scenes are filmed brings the audience into the reality of the cockpit. The speed of thought, reactions and sheer hard work of pulling high levels of G-forces during an encounter that could last for several minutes provides an updated view of the airmen involved in air-to-air combat.

Of all the images from the film the teamwork of the pilot and the weapons officer is enduring. Their ability to work together was an important element of air-to-air combat as the twentieth century came to an end. The advent of the F-15 fighter saw that teamwork broken up as the single-seat cockpit evolved. At the start of the twenty-first century, as China races to develop its military capabilities, the single-seat fighter is now the accepted design. The F-22 Raptor, the F-35, the Russian T50-PAKFA and the Chinese J-20 are all single-seat configurations.

Should these planes ever be engaged in air-to-air combat in the future one of the serious issues that the pilots will face is detecting the enemy. These fifth-generation fighter jets are all designed to compress the battle-space to their advantage. The longer the enemy spends trying to detect them the better their chances are of achieving the kill shot. Initial assessments of the Chinese J-20 fighter have drawn distinct comparisons between its design and that of the F-22 Raptor. From an airframe viewpoint it is hard not to conclude that the Chinese have used the F-22 Raptor as a model from which to develop their fifth-generation fighter jet. The airframe design appears to include all of the classic design elements required to reduce the radar and infrared signatures of the J-20. The head-on radar cross-section of the J-20 and its significantly reduced heat signature will make it difficult to detect beyond visual range. This compresses the battle-space. The enemy may literally be capable of sneaking up on aircraft flying on an offensive air or a defensive counter-air mission.

This is a new paradigm for the air-to-air domain. Tactics will have to evolve. While stealth characteristics can reduce signatures in one aspect, they cannot in others. Aircraft flying defensive counter-air missions will have to split up to try to 'paint' the incoming enemy aircraft from a number of directions. The classic head-to-head manoeuvre to visually identify a target may no longer be possible. It would simply involve too many risks. The historical naval dictum of 'he who fires first' wins the battle may yet become one that applies in the air-to-air domain.

It is no wonder then that films such as *Top Gun* come under the category of classical realism. The pilots in the film are the ones who operate at the edge of the flight envelope, just like their forefathers in their flimsy flying machines over the Western Front. While the timing and range over which air-to-air combat is conducted has changed, it still comes down to reflexes and situational awareness. It was in the area of situational awareness that one of the most important and enduring lessons from the air-to-air environment has emerged.

Situational Awareness in Combat

In Korea one of the most important insights to arise from analysing the air-to-air environment investigated why American F–86 Sabre aircraft were so successful at shooting down their MiG-15 counterparts. Initial claims made by the United States Air Force suggested that the ratio of combat kills was 15:1 in favour of the F–86 with over 700 MiG aircraft having been shot down. After an enquiry, where footage of the gun cameras involved was re-analysed, this ratio was reduced to 7:1.

The United States tactics over Korea were helped greatly by the defection of a North Korean pilot with a MiG-15. The aircraft was flown to the United States and over a four-day period was extensively tested. Its superior rate of climb, higher operational ceiling and its faster initial acceleration were all characteristics of the MiG that helped it compete with the F–86, but at over Mach 0.94 the MiG-15 became unstable. With this knowledge the training on the F–86 was revised to maximize its advantages over the MiG-15.

Despite all of the obvious aerodynamic advantages enjoyed by the MiG it was an advantage in other areas that helped the United States gain an advantage in air-to-air combat. That focused on the situational awareness of the pilot. The insight, from the work led by Colonel Boyd of the United States Air Force, led to the development of a term that remains in widespread use sixty years later. The Observe, Orient, Decide and Act (OODA) loop has now firmly become part of the military lexicon. It is widely used to describe the way in which a military commander establishes that vital commodity: tempo on the ground. The argument goes that if you can operate inside the OODA loop of your adversary you will prevail.

In looking at the combat engagements Colonel Boyd realized two crucial things. The all-round view afforded to the pilot of the F–86 Sabre aircraft was superior to that available to the MiG. The pilots of the MiG had limitations on their peripheral vision. To add to this the F–86 had one other advantage. While overall it was poor aerodynamically in comparison with the MiG, it could move between flight states faster. The combination of these two relatively small-scale advantages, placed in the hands of a well-trained pilot, enabled them to think ahead of the enemy in air-to-air combat. In effect they could get inside the adversary's OODA loop and make the kill shot.

The OODA loop became a way of illustrating a command decision cycle. The pilot would observe the enemy, orient his aircraft to maximum advantage in combat, decide what to do next and then act to carry out the manoeuvre, whereupon the cycle would restart as the pilot would keep assessing and updating his position relative to his adversary. This idea of a continuous loop of decision cycles provided a template for anyone seeking to describe how military commanders react to changing situations.

It is a paradigm that has stood the test of time. It is also recognized that in a military campaign several OODA cycles are in train at the same moment. At the strategic level there is one that is relatively slow and ponderous and driven by political decision-making and its limitations on military commanders. At the operational level in a theatre of war several OODA loops will be in train at the same time. At the tactical level every engagement or contact with an enemy has its own OODA loop.

Colonel Boyd's work is now accepted as an almost universal paradigm for warfare and merits discussions at military academies that have elevated his analysis to the status of the work of that well-known bastion of the blindingly obvious in military insight, Sun Tzu.

While the pilot's appreciation of the situation in an engagement was critical, it also became important over time to be able to place a fighter in a good initial position from which to initiate combat. The development of the airborne early-warning aircraft, such as the E-2 Sentry and its maritime equivalent the E-2C Hawkeye, provided a solution to this problem. Surface-based radar systems are subject to horizon limitations on detecting incoming raids. Deploying a specifically configured high-powered radar system on an airborne platform extended the detection horizon. In an age where fast jets could move very quickly and fly low close to the sea to try to sneak under the radar horizon this solution was critical if defending aircraft were to be mobilized in sufficient time.

Through combining data from the AWACS and the ground radars a picture not unlike that developed in the Second World War by the Battle of Britain systems could be created. This was known as the RAP. Its aim was to provide the definitive view of the allegiance and status of aircraft in the area. The RAP allowed the defender to decide which incoming targets should be engaged. It is a paradigm that, having been created just ahead of the Battle of Britain, still provides the basic building-block on which air-to-air combat engagements are conducted, albeit with some slight regional variations across the world.

A Basic Air Defence Paradigm

When it comes to analysing the Battle of Britain the bookshelves of major retailers illustrate the degree to which the various insights that can be drawn from the battle have been gone over with a fine toothcomb. It was a hugely significant campaign within the war. Had it been lost, the invasion of the United Kingdom would have followed. Whether or not the Royal Navy could have prevented the crossing of the English Channel is a subject that historians will no doubt debate for many years to come. The only comment to make is that had the German Air Force been able to establish air superiority over the designated landing beaches for Operation Sealion, the Royal Navy would have had to sail south into a decidedly non-permissive environment.

In defeating the German Air Force the Royal Air Force scored a hugely important strategic victory. That was, however, to lead to the Blitz. The people of London bore the brunt of the outcome of the Battle of Britain. It had been a desperately close-run thing. The arguments over the effectiveness of the so-called Big Wing concept advocated by 12 Group over the different tactics adopted by 11 Group who were charged with the front-line protection of the country against the full might of the German Air Force rage on. Air Vice-Marshal Park was clear in his own mind that getting airborne as quickly as possible once a raid had been detected was crucial.

Park took those same ideas into another theatre whose role in the war has been less analysed and documented. These were the air battles that took place over the small island of Malta in the Mediterranean Sea. While the island is geographically small, its location was of huge strategic significance and enabled it to play a crucial part in disrupting the logistical supply routes upon which Rommel's army in the North African desert depended.

The small bomber force based in Malta was able to use its airfields to launch attacks against the re-supply convoys travelling across the Mediterranean Sea. Using intelligence derived from Enigma the bombers could readily locate the convoys, although before bombers were dispatched each convoy had to be sighted by reconnaissance aircraft to ensure the penetration of Enigma was protected. For Rommel the small garrison in Malta was more than an irritant. His problems with his supply route were well-known to Montgomery who used this to plan the battle at El Alamein to achieve the maximum effect upon Rommel's already stretched forces.

To sustain the ability to disrupt the convoys Malta had to survive an onslaught brought about by the German Air Force operating from airbases in Sicily. The Battle of Malta has so many parallels with the Battle of Britain. The importance of radar, the distance the German Air Force and their Italian partners had to fly to get to the island, the warning times and need to get the Hawker Hurricanes and Spitfires airborne quickly to harry the bombers before they could try to bomb the three airfields were an eerie replay of the Battle of Britain.

In attacking Malta the German Air Force showed that it had learnt from its mistakes in the Battle of Britain. Attacks did not commit the full bomber force. The ratio of bombers to fighter escorts was sometimes as high as one bomber to ten fighter escorts. Raids would arrive over Malta at dawn, noon and at dusk. In the afternoon as the pilots of the Royal Air Force were trying to snatch some sleep Messerschmitt fighters would mount sweeps over the island at low level just to prevent the pilots from having any rest.

The bombing of Malta conducted by the German and Italian Air Force saw the capital Valletta designated as the most bombed place on the Earth. Fortunately its strong fortifications built in the sixteenth century helped the people of Malta to withstand their very own form of Blitz.

The experiences from Malta showed that fighter tactics could evolve and that the ratio of fighters to bombers could also change. In time as aero-dynamic solutions created more versatile platforms the differences between the fighter and the bomber became less distinct. As the move towards precision delivery of weapons to help avoid civilian casualties also quickened in the light of experiences in the First Gulf War in 1991, newer types of aircraft appeared that were classified as fighter-bombers. The Typhoon operated by the Royal Air Force started its design life as an air-to-air machine capable of defeating a Cold War adversary. Over Libya it gained its first battle honours as an air-to-ground fighter.

The Cold War Routine

For many pilots flying over the North Sea in the course of the Cold War the battlefields of the First and Second World Wars must have seemed a long way away. The threat of nuclear war hung over all of the activities of the various air forces based in Europe.

For the Royal Air Force the next instantiation of the Battle of Britain was to come from a clash with Warsaw Pact aircraft, principally Russian bombers and their fighter escorts, flying over the North Sea to target airfields in the United Kingdom. This was an era of stand-off weapons where Russian bombers did not have to overfly the United Kingdom's territory to inflict damage on its defence capabilities. As with the Battle of Britain, time was of the essence. Fighter aircraft were held on Quick Reaction Alert (QRA) to intercept Russian bombers that often flew provocative trajectories towards the United Kingdom before turning away, either to head off to Cuba or to return home.

For the Royal Air Force the intrusions by the Russian bombers, such as the TU-95 Bear, were an exam question. Every time they flew to intercept them they knew the Russians would be setting a stopwatch on their response time. Each reconnaissance trip was just another test in the Cold War to help build up insights in case war ever came.

As in the Battle of Britain NATO benefited from a range of radar stations that enabled early warning of Russian flights leaving bases such as those in Murmansk to be alerted to the UKADGE system. The model for the operation of the United Kingdom's air defences had not significantly changed since the Battle of Britain.

What had changed were the dynamics of the intercept. Initially the Lightning aircraft provided a fast-response interceptor to attack Russian bombers that would have to close on the United Kingdom's airspace. However, as stand-off weapons were introduced by the Russians, so the Royal Air Force had to counter with its own developments. The iconic FGR4 Phantom, the Air Defence Variant of the Tornado and now the Typhoon interceptor were designed to fly fast to a point of intercept. To prevent the Russian bombers launching stand-off missiles the Royal Air Force interceptors had to be capable of remaining airborne for potentially long periods of time. That required in-flight refuelling.

With time being such a precious commodity in warfare the deployment of Airborne Early Warning (AEW) aircraft became essential. For the United Kingdom the venerable Shackleton provided the initial, albeit limited, capability. The ill-fated attempt to produce a Nimrod variant then saw the purchase of the Boeing E-3 aircraft which remains in service today. The need for an airborne command and control facility was dictated by the timelines of the air battle. If the United Kingdom airbases and other strategic assets were to be protected the Royal Air Force needed to move forward. Simply being on QRA was not enough if war had broken out.

In that situation the priority for the air defence interceptors of the Royal Air Force would have been to try to shoot down the Russian bombers while also trying to defend the AEW assets from being shot down by Russian escort fighters. The refuelling tankers upon which the interceptors would depend would also need to be safeguarded. Like most air-to-air combat situations it would have been a chaotic environment not unlike the Battle of Britain. Its outcome would have been highly uncertain. For the Russians, desperate to disable the United Kingdom's airbases and prevent their use for flying in supplies across the air-bridge from the United States, the attack on the United Kingdom would have had a high priority.

An example of an Airco DH.2. Designed by Geoffrey de Havilland, the DH.2 was the first effectively armed British single-seat fighter, though because of its sensitive controls, and at a time when service training for pilots in the RFC was very poor, it initially had a high accident rate, gaining it the nickname the 'Spinning Incinerator'. Fourteen aces scored five or more aerial victories using the type. (*Historic Military Press*)

Pilots and personnel of 22 Squadron, which operated Bristol F.2B single-engine two-seat biplanes, pictured at Vert Galant on 1 April 1918 – the first day of the RAF. From left to right: Lieutenant W.S. Tout-Hill; Lieutenant G.H. Traunweiser; Lieutenant J.H. Wallage; Lieutenant B.C. Budd; Lieutenant G.S. Hayward; Lieutenant J.J. Hunter; Lieutenant R. Critchley; Lieutenant W.F.J. Harvey; Lieutenant J.L. Morgan; Lieutenant H.F. Moore; Lieutenant H.F. Davison; Lieutenant J.E. Gurdon; Major J.A. McElvie; Lieutenant N.T. Barrington; Captain R.S.P. Boby; Lieutenant H.F. Harrison; and Captain D.M. McGoun. (*Historic Military Press*)

The use of aircraft in a military capacity soon led to the development of numerous roles – one of the earliest of which was the gathering of aerial photographs – as evidenced by this image, taken at a low altitude, of French soldiers during an attack on the Somme Front. On 1 April 1918 (the first day of the RAF), for example, no less than 1,047 pictures were taken, the plates brought back, images produced and then sent by dispatch riders to the command HQs. (*Historic Military Press*)

The wreckage of a German Albatros D.III fighter pictured in Belgium in 1917. The legend O.A.W. D.3 on the tailplane suggests that this aircraft was produced at the Ostdeutsche Albatros Werke at Schneidemühl. (*Historic Military Press*)

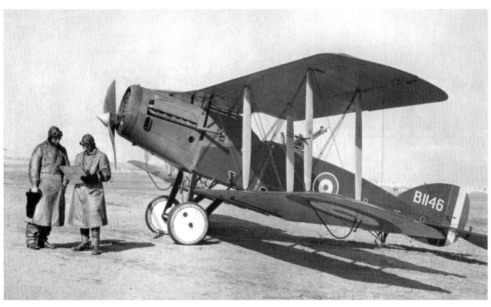

Lieutenant Ross Smith and his observer by their Bristol F.2B of 1 Squadron AFC in Palestine during 1918. In 1919 Ross Smith was part of the crew that set the record for flying from the UK to Australia. (*Courtesy of the Australian War Memorial*)

Though difficult to handle, to an experienced pilot the Sopwith Camel provided unmatched manoeuvrability. A superlative fighter, the Camel was credited with shooting down 1,294 enemy aircraft during the First World War, more than any other Allied fighter. It also served as a ground-attack aircraft, especially near the end of the conflict when it was outclassed in the air-to-air role by newer fighters. (*Historic Military Press*)

An Airco DH.4 pictured over a desert camp during the inter-war period. The type remained in service with several nations until well after the end of the First World War. (*Historic Military Press*)

A Hurricane Mk.I pictured during a mock combat just before the outbreak of war in 1939. (*Historic Military Press*)

Lockheed Ventura Mark I, AE742 'YH-M' of No. 21 Squadron RAF flown by Warrant Officer L.L.G. Jones and crew over the docks at Ijmuiden, Holland during the second of two daylight attacks on the coke ovens of the Royal Dutch Steel Works, made by the squadron on 13 February 1943. Both raids, each consisting of twelve aircraft escorted by fighters, were led by the Commanding Officer, Wing Commander R.H.S. King. (*Historic Military Press*)

Sergeant Victor A. LaBruno, a cameraman on board a B-17 of the 388th Bomb Group that had attacked the oil plant at Brüx (the German name for the city of Most in the Czech Republic), pictured this Me 410A-1/U4 as it pulled 'away to start a dive less than twenty-five feet off the bomber's wing'. (*Historic Military Press*)

The devastating effects of Allied air power by the end of the Second World War: a view of the bombed-out historic city of Nuremberg, Germany, taken in June 1945. (*Historic Military Press*)

A line-up of Vulcan B2s at RAF Wittering in July 1963. (*Historic Military Press*)

Ready for action: an RAF Tornado. (*Crown copyright*)

An RAF Hercules conducting a parachute drop. (*Crown copyright*)

Maritime air power: the USS *John C. Stennis* at sea. (*Crown copyright*)

Awaiting the call: RAF Tornados at sunset. (*Crown copyright*)

Essential element: Airborne Early Warning. (*Crown copyright*)

Tanking force: an RAF VC-10 keeping two RAF Typhoons and a Tornado topped up with fuel. (*Crown copyright*)

Armed and dangerous: a British army Apache on HMS *Illustrious*. (*Crown copyright*)

A Merlin helicopter being unloaded from an RAF C-17. (*Crown copyright*)

An RAF Chinook kicks up a dust storm in Afghanistan. (*Crown copyright*)

Future tactical life: the A-400M. (*Crown copyright*)

Tactical airlift in action: an RAF Hercules over Afghanistan. (*Crown copyright*)

Night-time helicopter operations from the deck of HMS *Illustrious*: a Chinook and Apache in action. (*Crown copyright*)

Sensing danger: the huge radome of the RAF Sentinel R1 which contains its main sensor system. (*Crown copyright*)

British army Apaches in the United States on exercise. (*Crown copyright*)

In a hurry: an RAF Typhoon lifts off at an air display in southern England. (*Crown copyright*)

Remote control: flying the RAF Reaper. (*Crown copyright*)

Armed RAF Reaper unmanned aircraft over Afghanistan. (*Crown copyright*)

Future warfare: an RAF Reaper unmanned aircraft. (*Crown copyright*)

Darwinian Aces

Inevitably for someone with such a reputation the exploits of Baron von Richthofen have given him a cult status. In the First World War no other pilot achieved his level of air combat victories: he is credited with eighty. That achievement alone gives him a premier status among the century of aces that have followed in his footsteps. However, as with others who are revered, the circumstances surrounding his death are also subject to detailed comment. Having placed someone on a pedestal it is hard for some to accept they could ever be defeated. His downfall must have arisen, they reason, from subterfuge to trickery. The real reasons are often more prosaic.

In the case of the Red Baron and his downfall on 21 April 1918 at the age of 25 an array of theories have been offered to explain how this combat veteran could have ever come to meet his end. One explanation suggested that Baron von Richthofen had simply succumbed to combat stress, failing to observe the routines that had served him well in the war. Others have taken a more mathematical approach to suggest that a combination of wind direction and speed drove him over the British and French lines at the Morlancourt Ridge near the Somme River. Whatever did happen on that day, a legend passed into history, the like of which may never be seen again.

That is not to suggest, however, that the total number of victories achieved by the Red Baron would not be surpassed. In the table of aces that reports combat victories in the Second World War the German Erich Hartman stands out as the top ace of all time with 352 combat victories. Behind him a list of other aces appear that are predominantly German. Indeed, all of the top fifteen in the list with over 200 combat victories are German airmen from the Second World War.

Their aggression and tactical evolution just gave them a numerical edge over the Royal Air Force. Over the four months of the Battle of Britain 361 Spitfires were lost in combat and an additional 352 were damaged. Over this period the Royal Air Force received 747 new Spitfires as the improved production processes that came into force ahead of the outbreak of war were able to provide more machines than were being lost. German fighter losses in total were 610 Bf 109Es. In total Fighter Command lost 1,023 Spitfires and Hurricanes, giving the German fighter pilots a kill ratio of 1.2:1.

For the Royal Air Force, however, it was not the issue of having sufficient aircraft to fly: it was having the men trained to go into combat. Many raw recruits arrived in their first operational postings with barely a few hours of flying time in their logbooks and no real experience of air-to-air combat. This was another example of Darwin's thinking at work. Those that survived had the natural ability to become fighter pilots.

Pilot Officer Eric Lock was one of those who had those Darwinian qualities. He had not served with Fighter Command prior to the war. He joined 41 Squadron at the start of August 1940 just as the Battle of Britain was beginning. He had a few days to prepare before the Germans embarked upon a new phase of operations that has become known as *Adlertag* (Eagle Day). At the end of the Battle of Britain he had amassed twenty-six victories including fifteen Bf 109s. Sadly a year later on 3 August 1941 he was to be posted missing after he had participated in a fighter sweep over France.

Flight Lieutenant Brian Cadbury was one of a number of aces in the Battle of Britain. The high point of his flying career was on 31 August 1940. On that day he claimed to have shot down five Messerschmitt Bf 109s in the course of three sorties. This was a feat that was only repeated by one other Royal Air Force pilot, Sergeant Ronnie Hamlyn of 610 Squadron. The latter's reward of the Distinguished Flying Cross in September 1940 was a just recognition of his achievements to that point when he had claimed six combat victories. The Bar to the DFC that he was awarded in October 1940 was for a further eight Bf 109 combat victories.

German intelligence reports consistently overestimated the destruction they had wrought on the ground, at one point claiming that the Royal Air Force was down to its last few operational machines. It was therefore disheartening for the German bomber pilots to consistently see formations of Spitfires and Hurricanes mobilized to meet them every day.

When intelligence gets its assessments wrong those who self-evidently see the errors in the reporting are not quick to forgive. The simple fact is that without the incompetence of the leader of the Luftwaffe, a few days' additional pressure on the airfields may well have achieved the desired outcome. Herman Göring had a lot to answer for as he switched tactics at crucial points in the battle. All of his interventions proved helpful to the survival of the Royal Air Force.

The first non-German to appear in the list of fighter aces is at position 110. That is the Finnish pilot IImari Juutilainen with ninety-four victories. A few places below him is placed the highest Japanese fighter ace and another Finn. The first aces from the United States Air Force and the Royal Air Force do not appear until the totals fall below fifty. The appearance of several members of the Finnish Air Force in the list may be a surprise for some and is worth exploring in some detail.

The Winter War between Finland and Russia

At the start of the Second World War the Germans and Russians had signed a secret accord that created a number of areas of political influence. Finland fell under the Russian sphere and on 30 November 1939 after a period of increasing political pressure Russian military forces launched attacks into Finland across the full length of the border region.

At the outset of the campaign Finland's air force was tiny in comparison to the Soviet Air Force. An estimated 700 fighters and 800 bombers of the Soviet Air Force faced 114 serviceable aircraft deployed by the Finnish Air Force (FAF). While this ratio may look bad it was, in fact, even worse as when war broke out the FAF were only able to field seventeen bombers and thirty-one fighter aircraft. In an act of philanthropy a Swedish Count, Carl Gustav von Rosen, donated two Koolhoven F.K.52 two-seater fighter-reconnaissance aircraft that had been developed in the 1930s to the Finnish Air Force. The aircraft arrived in Finland on 18 January 1940. They had originally been part of an order for thirty-nine placed by the Dutch in 1939. Only six had been built by the time the Germans invaded The Netherlands.

The remaining aircraft in the force were only really suitable for carrying passengers and passing messages between units. By the end of the campaign a large number of Finnish aces had been awarded a range of medals for achievements that to this day highlight the nonsense of simply using numbers of aircraft as a measure of an air force's capability.

The leaders of the FAF decided to concentrate their limited forces in the south of the country in support of the ground defences that comprised the Mannerheim Line. This was Finland's main defensive position along the Karelian Peninsula. For the Russian forces that was the direct route to Helsinki.

The FAF leadership marshalled their limited forces carefully. The Bristol Blenheim bombers were deployed to attack Soviet rear echelons massing around Leningrad. The small number of Fokker CX and DXXI air interceptors were held back to attack Soviet SB-2 bombers attacking important lines of communications, such as railheads and the capital. The first attack on Helsinki had occurred within hours of the outbreak of war. The most intensive air-raids took place at the start of the war.

In the course of what turned out to be a relatively short military campaign the Russians bombed Helsinki on eight occasions. In total 350 bombs landed on the city causing largely superficial damage and claiming 97 lives and injuring just over 250. The Soviet inability to make progress on the ground against stubborn Finnish army resistance saw a stalemate unfold with trench warfare reminiscent of the First World War. Despite their numerical superiority the Russians were simply unable to make a decisive breakthrough on the ground. The war in effect petered out and an armistice was signed on 13 March 1940.

During the Winter War the FAF achieved many notable successes and achieved a combat victory ratio of 10:1. In March as the Soviets tried to use the frozen lakes to the south-east of Helsinki to by-pass the Mannerheim Line the head of the FAF declared that his air force had to throw everything that they had at the Soviets 'regardless of losses'. It was a desperate moment. Even the two Koolhoven F.K.52s were committed into the battle, flying fifteen sorties against the Russians at Virolahti.

The Finns held out and at the end of the Winter War over 600 Soviet aircraft had been lost. Sixty-two FAF aircraft had been lost and sixty-three air-crew killed. February had been a specifically bloody month for the Soviets as seventy of their aircraft were shot down. This was also the month when the FAF received thirty Moraine-Saulnier M.S.406 fighters that looked very similar to the Hawker Hurricane. The aircraft was a sturdy if underpowered fighter that had suffered badly in the Battle of France, losing 387 aircraft in return for 183 combat kills. Their arrival in February meant that they made no contribution to the Winter War.

The outcome of this initial conflict was inconclusive. It was only a matter of time before a new conflict would ignite. Realizing their perilous position at the outset of the Winter War the FAF had embarked upon a purchasing spree. They were literally seeking to buy any aircraft they could get their hands on. By the time the Continuation War as it is known started, German forces launched their surprise attack into Russia. The Russians used Operation Barbarossa as a pretext to invade Finland on 25 June 1941.

The FAF was able to field a very different capability at the start of this longer conflict which would end with the completion of the Second World War. In June 1941 the FAF could field 235 aircraft: a significant increase on the numbers it had available in 1939 including the Moraine-Saulnier M.S.406 which the Finns had spent time upgrading and taking a specific measure of replacing the engine.

The rest of the FAF was an eclectic mix of aircraft types mixing the procurement of Brewster B239 fighters and Fiat G.50s with a smattering of Hurricanes, Gloucester Gladiators and the survivors of the Winter War. In total at the start of the campaign the FAF fielded seventeen types of aircraft. Eight of these were primarily fighter aircraft: 192 of the total of 235 aircraft available to the FAF (80 per cent) at the start of the Continuation War were fighter aircraft. They were organized into thirteen squadrons which came under four air regiments. The main Fighter Squadrons were 24, which fielded thirty-four Brewster B239s, 26 Squadron with twenty-eight Fiat G.50s, 28 Squadron with thirty Moraine-Saulnier M.S.406s, 30 Squadron with twenty-two Fokker DXXIs and four Hawker Hurricanes, and 32 Squadron with thirty-five Fokker DXXIs.

The Winter War saw eighty-seven aces receive accolades for their combat fighting skills. This was out of a total strength of 191 airmen. This is an astonishing rate of 46 per cent. It would seem unlikely that this figure will ever be surpassed. Clearly in the Winter War the men of the FAF had overcome all sorts of adversity to achieve a staggeringly high level of combat kills. Pictures taken at the time show FAF aircraft operating from frozen dispersed airbases that had temporarily been created to avoid bombing attacks by the Russians.

Ingenious ways of keeping the engines warm were also devised as small burners were installed under the aircraft to help avoid engines being disabled by frozen lubricants. When Russian bombing missions were sighted messages were relayed by field telephone to the remote outposts allowing the fighters to be scrambled. From their dispersed airfields the combat veterans could quickly evaluate the best tactics to use to attack the incoming formations. This enabled the fighter pilots to gain an almost mythical status as flying aces. While some of that status was undoubtedly due, the dice were stacked in their favour in so many ways.

It may seem that some fighter aces rapidly gain a reputation for panache in air-to-air combat that makes them almost indestructible. In reality it is the combination of man and machine that makes the difference and in the First World War and the Second World War as fortunes favoured both sides for brief periods of time certain men made the most of it and enjoyed their associated status and rewards. In Finland this was the case as on several occasions even the small numbers of relatively old fighters were still able to outmanoeuvre the Soviet fighter escorts and bombers.

India-Pakistan Air War in 1965

Tensions between India and Pakistan have flared up occasionally resulting in the outbreak of hostilities. Aside from the clash in 1999 the conflicts took place when both countries were not armed with nuclear weapons. From an air-to-air viewpoint the air war in 1965 is the only example where a significant series of engagements took place.

Before the outbreak of the 1965 war the Pakistani Air Force (PAF) on paper was outnumbered by a ratio of 5:1. It could field twenty-four B-57

Canberra bombers alongside 102 F–86 Sabre and twelve F–104 Starfighter jets. In comparison the Indian Air Force (IAF) could count upon a number of Hawker Hunters, Folland Gnats, de Havilland Vampires and a squadron of MiG-21s. The Hawker Hunter aircraft had been supplied as part of a contract that saw 140 aircraft delivered to the IAF at about the same time as the PAF received its F-86 Sabres.

The IAF also purchased a number of twin-seat trainers for the Hawker Hunter. Shortly afterwards the PAF made informal approaches to the British government to see if they could buy up to forty Lightning aircraft. The enquiry was politely shunned by the British as they did not wish to upset the Indians.

The first time the IAF used the Hawker Hunters was in the Sino–Indian War of 1962. The Hunter proved to be more than a match for the MiGs operated by the Chinese. It helped deter the Chinese from attempting to use their Ilyushin II-4 bombers to conduct strategic raids over India. This was a case when air superiority clearly prevented an escalation of the conflict. Once the Chinese knew their MiG could not cope with the IAF Hunter, the scope for increasing the conflict disappeared.

The subsequent war between India and Pakistan in 1965 also saw the Hunter play an important role. As is often the case in warfare the claims of combat kills vary. In a wrangle over the outcome of the war the two protagonists posted differing claims of the outcome of the air-to-air battles. The PAF suggested that they had shot down 104 in return for losing nineteen of their own fighters. This was a combat kill ratio of 5.5:1.

The IAF, however, were less expansive in their claims stating that they had shot down seventy-three PAF planes and lost fifty-nine of their own, a kill ratio of close to 1:1. Immediately after the cessation of hostilities the PAF flew eighty-six F-86s, ten F104s and twenty B-57 Canberra aircraft in a military parade which very effectively demolished the IAF claim of having destroyed nearly all of the front-line fighter force of the PAF.

The parade suggested they had potentially lost sixteen F-86s, two F-104s and four Canberra bombers, a total of twenty-four aircraft. Reports emerging after the war suggested that in fact the PAF had lost twenty-five aircraft, eleven of which were shot down in air-to-air combat. The same sources suggested that the IAF had lost sixty aircraft, of which twenty-five were as a result of air-to-air engagements. This is a combat kill ratio of 2.4:1. However, while in headline terms that may look satisfactory, in practice the PAF needed to achieve a much higher rate to overcome the 5:1 numerical advantage enjoyed by the IAF at the start of the conflict.

In 1971 when the IAF and the PAF were to resume their air-to-air battles the IAF had six squadrons of Hawker Hunters available. The PAF claimed in the conflict to have destroyed thirty-two of these aircraft. While the Hawker Hunters were ostensibly a fighter jet, they were also used by the IAF for ground-attack operations. Overall across the two conflicts in 1965 and 1971 the IAF Hunters performed well and were seen to be superior in both power and speed to the F-86. The IAF also claimed that the F-86 was vulnerable to the Folland Gnat, which gained the nickname of the 'Sabre-Slayer'.

The PAF also made exaggerated claims about the effectiveness of their twelve F-104 Starfighters. At high altitudes the F-104 enjoyed an advantage that it lost as dogfights took place at low altitudes. The rather smaller Folland Gnat came into its own at lower altitudes, even though it had an obvious speed disadvantage. Despite the relative advantages enjoyed by some airframes over others the two wars between India and Pakistan in 1965 and 1971 saw neither side able to gain air superiority over the battlefield. This materially hampered both campaigns which ultimately became caught in a stalemate. The lesson that a clear numerical disadvantage did not immediately translate into an air campaign being lost applied here.

Confrontation with Libya 1981

The air-to-air battle over the Gulf of Sidra on 19 August 1981 where two Libyan Su-22 (NATO Code Name: Fitter) aircraft were shot down by two United States F-14 Tomcat aircraft had its roots in an incident that occurred eight years previously. In 1973 the Libyan regime of Colonel Gaddafi claimed the Gulf of Sidra as part of its territorial waters. The United States disputed this claim and carried out freedom of navigation operations in the area. This was not, and is unlikely to be, the last time the United States navy is involved in such activity.

These operations have been repeated by the United States navy more recently in the South China Sea. In the future a confrontation over Taiwan or the oil and gas reserves that are believed to lie beneath the Spratly and Paracel Islands may see the United States conducting similar operations to enforce its right to free passage as defined under the United Nations Convention on the Law of the Sea.

In August 1981 President Reagan authorized the deployment of a large naval task force into the Gulf of Sidra. On 18 August three MiG-25s (NATO Code Name: Foxbat) approached the carrier battle groups and were escorted away by F-4 Phantom and F-14 Tomcat aircraft. After this initial reconnaissance mission a much larger wave of Libyan aircraft approached the task force. This comprised thirty-five pairs of MiG-23 (NATO Code Name: Flogger), MiG-25, Su-20 (NATO Code Name: Fitter-C), Su-22M (NATO Code Name: Fitter-M) and Mirage F1 aircraft. This time seven pairs of F-4s and F-14s escorted the Libyan Air Force aircraft away from the area.

The next morning two F-14 aircraft flying Combat Air Patrol (CAP) detected two Libyan Su-22 Fitter aircraft taking off from their base at Ghardabiya near to the town of Sirte, the birthplace of the Libyan leader. As the two formations approached each other head-on at an estimated distance of 300m one of the Su-22s fired an Atoll missile at one of the F-14s, missing the target. As they passed the two Libyan jets split their formation; one heading north-west, the other south-west. Under their rules of engagement the F-14 pilots were allowed to engage the enemy. Each F-14 fired a single missile that shot down one Su-22. Both Libyan pilots ejected.

Within an hour, as the Libyans initiated combat search-and-rescue operations two MiG-25 aircraft sped towards the carrier battle group at Mach 1.5. They were confronted by two F-14 aircraft and the Libyans turned for home. The Libyans shortly returned and had to be confronted again by the F-14s. Once the Libyans were re-acquired by the radar systems on the F-14s they broke off the engagement. Later that day in another brief flurry of activity one more Libyan Air Force formation headed out towards the task force. The brief but conclusive air-to-air engagements were to inspire the combat sequence at the end of the film *Top Gun*.

This was not the last time that the United States navy would face off in air-to-air engagements in brief conflicts. In 1989 a similar incident occurred over the Gulf of Sidra when two F-14s confronted two Libyan MiG-23 aircraft. Initially four MiG-23s had been detected as they left the Al Bumbaw airbase in Libya. The United States navy F-14s turned towards the first formation of two MiG-23s and acquired them on the AWG-9 radar system. This would normally trigger an alert in the headset of the Libyan pilots and be sufficient to warn them to break the engagement.

On this occasion the MiG-23 pilots were not deterred. Over the following eight minutes in a series of aggressive manoeuvres the MiG-23s first approached and then broke away from the Americans. The brief battle was coordinated by a United States E-2C aircraft operating from the naval task force. Calling out the range, heading and altitude of the Libyan aircraft the radar operator in the E-2C positioned the F-14 for an engagement.

On the fifth manoeuvre, at a range of 20 nautical miles, the back-seat Radar Intercept Officer (RIO) in the lead F-14 declared the Libyan MiG as hostile and fired an initial AIM-7M Sparrow missile to the initial surprise of his pilot. Due to a switch setting being in the wrong position the missile failed to locate the target. At a range of 10 nautical miles the RIO fired a second AIM-7M. That too failed to operate.

The MiGs continued to approach the F-14 and the carrier and at 6 nautical miles the F-14 split. The MiGs followed the wingman. This allowed the lead F-14 to manoeuvre to get into a tail-on firing position. At 5 nautical miles the lead F-14 fired an AIM-7M. This destroyed one of the MiGs. The lead F-14 then manoeuvred to get a firing solution on the second MiG and at 1.5 nautical miles fired an AIM-9L Sidewinder missile that destroyed its target.

Both MiG pilots were seen to eject from their aircraft but neither was recovered by the Libyans. The regime in Tripoli issued a protest after the incident claiming that two unarmed reconnaissance planes had been shot down by the Americans. Subsequent footage capturing the engagement showed that both MiGs had in fact been armed with Russian-made AA-7 (NATO Code Name: Apex) missiles.

The two brief incidents in the Gulf of Sidra, while eight years apart from each other, came to epitomize the shadow-boxing that occurred throughout the Cold War as the Russians and the Americans used proxy wars to evaluate their respective military capabilities. For the Russians the majority of these engagements were to highlight the serious technological disadvantage that they held in combat aircraft and missile capabilities.

A Very Unusual Air Victory

Not all air-to-air victories are achieved by shooting down an adversary. Other techniques can apply. In 1991 EF-111A Raven aircraft participating in Operation Desert Storm brought down an Iraqi Mirage F1 through outmanoeuvring it on the battlefield. The story is one that is worth recounting as it illustrates that not all air-to-air combat is about homing missiles or getting into a position to bring guns to bear on an enemy.

On the first night of the air operation an unarmed EF-111A was to secure notoriety for achieving a combat victory over another aircraft. This is the only recorded occasion where an unarmed EF-111A achieved an aerial victory through manoeuvre alone.

At night as the first wave of attacking aircraft finally penetrated Iraqi airspace the EF-111A was flying at 5,000ft at the tip of a packet of twenty-two F15-E strike aircraft heading into western Iraq. Their mission was to bomb a number of key targets which lay between two key Iraqi airfields. As the EF-111A was jamming the Iraqi surveillance radars a warning tone in the ear of the EWO alerted them to the presence of an Iraqi Mirage F1EQ aircraft that had been scrambled from one of the airbases once the strike packet started its attacks. For the pilot and EWO of the EF-111A the warning tone of their radar warning receiver was not good news. On paper the unarmed EF-111A is no match for a Mirage. It was not intended to get into dogfights.

The Mirage was more than able to outmanoeuvre the EF-111A with its superior climb rate and it was equipped with 30mm cannon and the Magic 2 air-to-air missiles. The Iraqi Mirages also had the benefit of combat experience in the Iran-Iraq War.

The Mirage quickly got a lock on the EF-111A and launched a Magic 2 missile which was guided by a passive infrared guidance system. The EWO called 'break right' to close the distance with the Mirage and attempt to confuse the homing system on the Iraqi missile. Pulling a 5-G turn, which was the maximum limit for the aircraft, the captain also released chaff and quickly descended towards the ground. The Magic 2 missile flew past the EF-111A missing its target. As the two aircraft continued the dogfight an F-15C arrived to lock on to the tail of the Mirage. It would seem the presence of the F-15C disorientated the Mirage pilot who lost situational awareness at 400ft and plunged into the ground.

By flying fast and very low on its Terrain Following Radar system the EF-111A was able, with the help of the presence of the F-15C, to avoid an Iraqi Mirage F1 aircraft that was trying to manoeuvre into a firing position. By manoeuvring violently the EF-111A managed to avoid a piece of terrain in a valley that the pilot of the Mirage F1 was unable to miss.

The aircraft involved in this incident, EF-111A-66-0016, now occupies the position of Gate Guard outside Cannon Air Force Base in the United States. The only loss of an EF-111A in combat occurred a few nights later as serial number EF-111A-66-0023 crashed into the terrain in somewhat similar circumstances. Both crew members died in the crash. In the history of the EF-111A only four aircraft of the fleet of forty-two were lost.

Operation Mole Cricket 19

Headlines that appear in war often arise when a conflict lasts for many days, weeks and even months. When a battle is decided in two hours its significance can be lost. Over the Beqaa Valley in June 1982 the Israeli Air

Force conducted Operation Mole Cricket 19. Its outcome was to have a profound effect on the future of air-to-air warfare and on the international political landscape. It was quite literally two hours that changed the world.

The background to the operation lay in the problem of the security of people living in northern Israel. Even today the regular bombardment of rockets that occurs from locations inside the Lebanon is a cause of friction between the two countries. It has been an issue that has dogged the Israelis for a long time as they have resorted to military incursions into the south of the Lebanon to try to create a cordon sanitaire from which the rockets could not be fired.

To deter Israel from attacking southern Lebanon the Syrians moved a number of batteries of air defence missiles into the area. The combination of SA-2, SA-3 and SA-6 missiles had proven very effective nearly ten years previously at the start of the Yom Kippur War. In the first hours of that war the Israeli Air Force took what came close to crippling losses from the air defence missile shield that was placed over the invading Egyptian army in Sinai and the Syrian forces trying to recapture the strategically important Golan Heights.

As they deployed into the Beqaa Valley nearly ten years later the Syrian army and air force failed to appreciate the lessons the Israelis had learnt in the interval. This time the Israelis had come prepared. Within a matter of hours they would record a stunning victory that would see reports suggest at the end of the short conflict that eighty-two Syrian aircraft had been shot down with no losses recorded by the Israeli Air Force (IAF).

The most obvious initial difference from the disastrous first few hours of the Yom Kippur War was the level of careful intelligence collection that had been carried out beforehand. Unmanned Israeli drones had been flying over the Beqaa Valley for several weeks. They had already spotted the advanced deployment of three Surface-To-Air Missile (SAM) batteries by the Syrians. If Israel was to move its forces into southern Lebanon to counter the rocket attacks it would need to take measures to reduce the threat to its air force created by those missiles.

As the crisis developed the Syrians moved additional batteries into the area. Just before the outbreak of hostilities nineteen SAM batteries had been deployed into the Beqaa Valley and were operational. On 6 June 1982 the Israeli ground forces moved into the Lebanon. They did so confident in the knowledge that a great deal of effort had been expended over the previous years to find a solution to the SAM problem. One element of that would be to employ Suppression of Enemy Air Defence (SEAD) techniques. If the Syrian forces' communications were jammed, how could they direct any counter to the Israeli incursion?

Our focus in this chapter of the book is on the lessons that can be learnt in the application of air power in an air-to-air situation. We shall therefore confine our analysis of the battle over the Beqaa Valley to the air-to-air element.

Three days into the incursion the Israelis decided they had to deal with the problem of the SAM shield that had been deployed by the Syrians. This was a one-sided battle as the Israelis used a variety of techniques to entice the Syrian radar systems into action. The first wave of strike aircraft totalled ninety-six F-15s and F-16s and was launched early in the afternoon. The second wave, which was launched nearly two hours later, comprised ninety-two aircraft. Through a combination of measures the Israelis were able to destroy the Syrian SAM network, with seventeen of the nineteen SAM batteries deployed into the Beqaa Valley destroyed. A reported fifty-seven SA-6 SAM were fired at the attacking Israeli air formations to no effect.

In response to the destruction of the SAM network the Syrian Air Force, which had previously been held back from the conflict, was launched. The Syrians had presumably hoped that the SAM network would have had a similar impact on the IAF as it did in the first hours of the Yom Kippur War. Their hope must have been to reduce the imbalance in forces in their favour before their air force became involved. With the SAM network destroyed and Syrian ground units requesting air cover the Syrian Air Force (SAF) had little alternative but to engage in air-to-air combat.

The Syrian MiG-21 and MiG-23 relied upon communications with ground controllers to vector them onto the IAF. Early warning of the commitment of the SAF came from three drones that had been located over the Syrian airbases. As the MiGs scrambled the IAF knew they were on the way. Very quickly the IAF used its new SEAD systems to disrupt the communications between the MiGs and their ground controllers.

The Syrian MiGs also had a major disadvantage which was well-known to the IAF. The MiGs only had the capability to see radar-guided threats from the rear and front of the aircraft. Sideways-on and from above and below the SAF MiGs were blind. The combination of jamming the ground controllers and exploiting the weaknesses in the equipment fit of the MiG allowed the IAF to attack the MiGs at will. The IAF were directed into firing positions by the E-2C airborne early warning aircraft operating above the battlefield. The Sparrow missiles sped towards their targets and wreaked havoc among the MiGs. In the first two hours of the battle twenty-nine MiGs were shot down.

Such was the scale of the air-to-air victory that among the IAF the battle became known as the Beqaa Valley Turkey Shoot. It remains one of the most one-sided air-to-air battles in history. Taking place as it did at the height of the Cold War the outcome was a sober reminder to the Russians that the technological advantage enjoyed by the west at the time rebalanced what appeared to be a numerical advantage to the Warsaw Pact forces arrayed against NATO in Western Europe. The obvious lesson to learn from this was that as far as air-to-air warfare was concerned the west now enjoyed a qualitative advantage over the Russians.

By acting as a proxy force for the Cold War the IAF and SAF had helped dampen down any Russian sense of adventurism. Indeed, some commentators have even gone so far as to suggest that the outcome of the air war over the Beqaa Valley led to a fundamental reappraisal of the balance of forces in Europe by the Kremlin and was instrumental in the development of the new political approach called Glasnost. While that point of view might be slightly extreme, there is some credibility in its viewpoint. It provides an excellent example of how air power can influence the international security landscape.

Guns, Rockets and Missiles

The century of air power has been one in which advances in technology have had a material impact on the ways in which air power has been applied. This is particularly true in the air-to-air arena where the development of ever-more agile missiles has had a major impact on the ways in which wars are fought. For air power to mean anything aircraft had to be designed that could shoot down an adversary's air force if that was required.

Over the last century a number of solutions to this problem have been researched, designed, developed and fielded in operational theatres of war. They can be characterized into one of three broad groups of solutions based on guns, rockets and missiles.

At the outset some innovative ideas were implemented to try to use air-to-air rockets to bring down balloons being used by an adversary for reconnaissance purposes. Le Prieur rockets were attached to the struts of bi-planes. They were initiated electrically. Needless to say, with no homing capability they were largely ineffective. The first serious attempt to bring an air-to-air missile into service took place at the end of the Second World

War when Germany used its emerging rocket technologies to produce the R-4M.

This was an air-to-air rocket that was nicknamed the Hurricane (German: *Orkan*). It was seen to be a solution to the problem of the increasing weight of armaments being carried by German fighter aircraft. Anecdotal evidence from the time suggests that it took on average twenty hits from 20mm bullets from the standard MG 151/20 cannons to bring down an Allied bomber. The MK 103 calibre autocannon was the first 30mm gun to be introduced by the Germans with a dual air-to-air and air-to-ground capability.

Attempts to offset the weight problems that arose as more ammunition was carried were largely ineffective. It did offer a solution with a longer range and greater muzzle velocity, although its rate of fire was only 380–420 rounds per minute. As more effective 30mm armaments were introduced in the MK 108 cannon that were able to shoot down a bomber in less than three hits, the weight penalty began to create operational limitations. One of these, its wing-mounting position, affected the aerodynamic characteristics of the aircraft.

Its low muzzle velocity meant that as soon as the projectile was fired gravity took over and curved the trajectory by over 40m in a 1,000-yard engagement. To be certain of a combat kill the attacking aircraft, such as the Fokker Wolf Fw 190 fighter, had to get within the range of the bomber's defensive weapons. The R4-M was designed to be a solution to the problem. Its maximum range was 1,500yds although its effectiveness dropped markedly beyond 1,000yds.

The R-4M was usually fired in four salvoes of six missiles at intervals of 0.07 seconds. Engagement ranges would vary depending upon the combat situation but a typical range of around 500–600m was seen to provide a high probability of success, although this was inside the range of the target's defensive guns which had an effective range of between 500–1,000yds. At this point in the development of air-to-air combat weapon systems the shooter and target still had to get very close to each other to be certain of a combat victory.

One innovation that did appear towards the end of the Second World War that is still in wider use in missile technology today was the wire-guided Ruhrstahl X-4 missile. While its development came too late for it to be deployed operationally, the performance of the missile introduced a step-change into the air-to-air environment. Its catalyst came in the crucible of war when the United States Air Force daylight bombing raids over Nazi Germany were at their peak in 1943.

The aim was to develop a capability that could be fired outside the range of the defence guns on the Allied bombers and be guided with enough accuracy to ensure a successful engagement. The design envisaged a missile that could fly at 715 mph with an operational range of between 1.5km and 3.5km. Its liquid motor produced 140kg of thrust for the initial part of the seventeen-second burn before tapering off to 30kg.

This gave the missile an average speed of 325m per second, making a typical engagement last for between five and ten seconds. As the missile flew towards its target flares on the body helped the operator in the attacking aircraft keep it in sight and guide it, using a joystick, to its target. The missile's warhead had a lethal radius of around 8m and weighed 20kg.

The first test of the missile occurred on 11 August 1944 when an Fw 190 fighter was used as the launch platform. The plan had been to deploy the missile on single-seat fighters but the workload of flying the aircraft and trying to steer the missile proved too high. The plan was altered to place the X-4 on the multi-crewed Ju 88 fighters. The first test flight occurred two months after D-Day and nine months before the end of the war in Europe. The X-4 was never to enter service with the Luftwaffe.

This was the first generation of what would be known today as a stand-off missile. It was able to operate well outside the effective range of the defensive guns of the bombers. Had it ever been formally introduced into service in the Luftwaffe it could have had a dramatic effect on the strategic bombing campaign. Any increase to the already grievous losses being experienced by the United States Air Force and Royal Air Force crews in the middle of 1943 would have slowed the tempo of operations. While the debate about the effectiveness of the strategic bombing campaign is unlikely to ever reach a definitive conclusion, its impact on the German war machine was discernible. Had that been reduced the Nazis may well have been able to draw out the war over a longer period.

Air-to-ground rocket technology in the Second World War had also provided new capabilities. These advancements were to provide the basis of the air-to-air missile systems that are in service today. In a matter of sixty years missile technologies have come a very long way, mirroring the advancements in fighter technologies. While rocket motor designs have changed significantly it is in the area of the seeker-heads, guidance mechanisms and the associated aerodynamic capabilities of the missiles that the most important developments have been seen.

The first American derivatives of the various German missile systems used in the Second World War appeared in 1949. They had a very limited operational range over around 1.8km. After the war this became the basis of developments in the United States and the United Kingdom. These developments took time. It was not until the middle of the 1950s that the first real attempts to introduce air-to-air missiles brought the Fairey Fireflash into service with the Royal Air Force and the AIM-4 Falcon with the United States Air Force.

The Fairey Fireflash missile had started its life in 1949 under the project name Blue Sky. The missile was tested on a Gloster Meteor against a Hawker Tempest target drone. Videos taken at the time show the missile being launched from the wing-tip of the Meteor and spiralling towards the target. This was a beam-riding missile that followed a pathway from the launch platform to the target designated by the radar system on the attacking aircraft.

Concerns about the emissions from the missile attenuating the radar signal guiding it to the target led to some rather unusual features being incorporated into the design. Two solid rocket-boosters attached to the forward fuselage were quickly jettisoned after 1.5 seconds of flight, leaving the main body of the missile to coast to its target. The limitations of this in a dynamic air-to-air environment were apparent from the start. Destroying cooperative targets was one thing; doing the same to a target trying to avoid being hit was quite another.

Having bought around 300 missiles in the initial purchase, the Royal Air Force quickly saw the operational limitations in the design. It was briefly introduced into service in 1957 where it was seen to have a limited capability against slow-moving and unmanoeuvrable piston-engine bombers. In 1958 the Royal Air Force deployed the de Havilland Firestreak infrared missile. This was the first really operational air-to-air missile to enter service with the Royal Air Force. Operationally it was based on the notion of fire-and-forget. It could acquire its target in a field of view of ±20° of its boresight.

Its trademark image was its installation on the English Electric Lightning interceptor that was the backbone of the air defence of the Royal Air Force during the late 1950s and the 1960s. It also saw service with the Royal Navy flying on de Havilland Sea Vixen aircraft and the Gloster Javelin.

The seeker-head of the Firestreak missile was based upon an infrared seeker. Its operational range of between 6 to 8km allowed visual identification of the target before launch. However, it could only latch onto an enemy aircraft's jet exhaust in an arc of ±15° either side of the target. It would fly to its target at Mach 3 before a proximity infrared detonation system would initiate the 50lb annular blast fragmentation warhead. The one major operational limitation was that it could only be fired outside cloud, which over the United Kingdom in the winter and some days in the summer limited its operational ceiling. Its principal task would have been to engage and destroy Bison, Badger and Bear Russian strategic bombers operating from Murmansk.

The replacement for the Firestreak was the Red Top missile which entered service in 1964. It had a larger warhead and improved seeker-head technologies which were more sensitive and a changed booster rocket configuration. The Violet Banner seeker system provided the Royal Air Force with its first all-aspect weapon system. The missile's electronics were based on transistor technology and remained in service until the retirement of the Lightning in 1988 and it was faster and had a longer range than the Firestreak.

For the Royal Air Force these were essentially close-in weapon systems that would have been used against relatively slow-moving Russian bombers. In time, as the nature of the threat was to change, the range of the missiles had to be extended. A proposal to develop a variant of the Red Top missile that was based upon a semi-active radar homing technology that was eventually to be successfully deployed in the American AIM-7 Sparrow system was cancelled in 1958.

In the United States progress on air-to-air missile systems initially took a similar pathway but gained a huge impetus from the Korean War. The AIM-4 Falcon missile is widely regarded as the first to enter service with the United States Air Force. The original design concept for the missile was for it to serve as a self-defence weapon for bomber aircraft. The first variants of the AIM-4 were, like their United Kingdom counterparts, deployed in the mid-1950s. They saw service on the F-89 Scorpion, F-101B Voodoo and F-102 Dagger interceptors. Export orders were also received from Canada, Finland, Sweden and Switzerland.

It first saw operational service in 1967 when the missile was deployed on the F-4D Phantom aircraft in the Vietnam War. The missile's performance was poor as it took several seconds for the seeker-head to cool to obtain a lock on target. It was also only able to do this once. On release of the coolant to bring down the temperature of the seeker-head it would evaporate. In addition the AIM-4D variant also lacked a proximity fusing capability and only carried a small warhead. While that may have been acceptable against slow-moving bombers, it did not cater for air-to-air combat against manoeuvring fighters. As a result of these deficiencies only five combat victories were ever declared for the AIM-4D. The AIM-4 was removed from service in 1969. It was replaced with the AIM-9 Sidewinder missile system. Over forty years later this iconic missile system still remains in service.

Sidewinder: The Iconic Air-to-Air Missile

The development of the Sidewinder missile system was started by the United States navy in 1950. Its name was based on a venomous rattlesnake which uses infrared sensors to locate its warm-blooded prey. The Americans currently envisage it remaining in service until 2055 and possibly beyond. This is a remarkable testament to the design principles and ideas upon which the missile was first developed which have seen over 110,000 deployed by twenty-eight nations. Records show that about 1 per cent of the missiles have been used in combat, accounting for over 270 air-to-air victories.

Inter-service rivalry within the United States Air Force saw its capabilities tested against the AIM-4 Falcon system in 1956. In what turned out to be a one-sided contest the AIM-9 Sidewinder emerged as the clearly more capable missile system. Even in its earliest inception as the XAAM-N-7 (the AIM designation was to come later in 1963) its capabilities were impressive. During one test-firing the famous United States test pilot Wally Schirra, who later flew the Mercury spacecraft in the United States space programme, had to avoid a Sidewinder he had just launched as it doubled back on him. It would seem that even test trials can be exciting.

Throughout its in-service life the Sidewinder has been designated as a supersonic, heat-seeking, short-range, air-to-air missile which has been deployed on a huge number of aircraft types. Its main elements are the infrared homing guidance element, the active optical target-detector, the warhead and the rocket motor. Throughout its life each of these major subsections of the AIM-9 has been subjected to improvements. The missile is a within-visual-range system that is slaved to the target either manually by the pilot or by one of the host platform's sensor systems. It is a fire-and-forget missile.

The first generation of the Sidewinder became known as the AIM-9A and AIM-9B. It was designed with a 4.5kg blast-fragmentation warhead which was triggered by an infrared proximity or a contact fuse. The warhead had a kill radius of approximately 9m. The missile could pull 12G and propulsion was provided by a solid-fuel rocket motor that provided 17.8kN (4,000lb) for 2.2 seconds. This would accelerate the missile to a speed of Mach 1.7 above the launch speed.

The technology limitations of the early infrared seeker restricted pilots to tail-on engagements and to ranges of between 1km and 5km. The 4° angle of view of the sensor system increased the level of background noise against which the seeker had to try to detect targets. Its 11 degree per second angular tracking rate also limited the ability of the missile to acquire manoeuvring targets. However, despite these limitations, on 24 September 1958 an AIM-9B was the first missile to bring down a target in a guided air-to-air engagement when a Taiwanese F-86 Sabre gained a combat victory over a Communist Chinese MiG-15. The United States had conducted a clandestine programme to supply the Taiwanese with the AIM-9 missile. In total in the brief confrontation between the two sides the AIM-9 accounted for eleven MiG aircraft.

There was, however, one drawback to this deployment. In one engagement an AIM-9 hit a MiG and lodged itself in the airframe. By flying skilfully the Communist Chinese pilot was able to bring the AIM-9 back to China. Years later the Russians would admit that information supplied by the Chinese from this incident, combined with material supplied by a Swedish Colonel called Stig Wennerström allowed them to reverse-engineer their own equivalent of the AIM-9 called the K-19 (NATO designation AA-2 Atoll). Its introduction into service in the 1960s had a huge impact on United States Air Force bombing tactics. In 1972 the Finnish Air Force drew similar conclusions when they compared the AIM-9P which they had purchased with the Russian Atoll missile.

In the course of the Vietnam War the United States Air Force would achieve twenty-eight successful combat engagements with the AIM-9A and AIM-9B variants; a kill probability across the spectrum of engagements of 16 per cent. The United States Air Force most successful variants of the Sidewinder were the AIM-9D and AIM-9G which were attributed with achieving the highest air-to-air kill ratios in the conflict. In total the AIM-9 missile system is acknowledged to have achieved eighty-two combat victories in Vietnam.

The AIM-9L was the variant operated by the Royal Navy Harrier aircraft in the Falklands War. It had first seen operational service when two Libyan Su-22 Fitter aircraft were shot down in air-to-air combat over the Mediterranean Sea. In the Falklands War the AIM-9 Sidewinder achieved seventeen combat kills and a kill probability of 80 per cent. Over the Beqaa Valley in the Lebanon months later the AIM-9 operated by the Israeli Air Force accounted for the majority of the Syrian MiGs that were shot down.

As subsequent developments have shown, the basic design and superstructure of the AIM-9 has remained largely the same over the many variants that have entered service. The first two variants, the AIM-9C and the AIM-9D, were unable to provide the kind of improvements that were needed and only around 1,000 of these two versions were built. That was in marked contrast to the 8,000 AIM-9Bs that had been built up until the end of 1962. The next variant of the missile, the AIM-9E, was to produce a small step-change in capability and to foster three other improved variants. These were the AIM-9J, the AIM-9N and the AIM-9P.

The AIM-9E was the first variant of the Sidewinder specifically developed by the United States Air Force. A new seeker that was able to support a faster tracking rate of 16.5° per second was one of a number of improvements. The United States Air Force upgraded 5,000 AIM-9Bs to the AIM-9E configuration with a slighter larger nose section.

Summary

The analysis shows that the air-to-air element of air power remains a test of man and machine. What has changed is the speed with which the actors have to react and the range of measures that are available to them to provide an advantage in combat. Technological developments have had a major impact on the ways in which air-to-air engagements are conducted.

In Vietnam the arrival of the first operationally-effective air-to-air missile systems created a paradigm shift in air warfare. Until then missiles had largely proven to be relatively ineffective in dogfights in locations such as Korea. Since the Vietnam War the opportunities for air-to-air combat have been limited.

Wars, such as those over Iraq in 1991 and against the Serbians, brought brief periods when aircraft tussled in the skies before one side was able to establish air superiority. Over the Lebanon in 1983 the Israelis benefited a great deal from their ability to disrupt the communications systems upon which the Syrian fighters depended. In the future instead of targeting an enemy's bomber and fighter an adversary might go after the assets they see to be controlling the battle.

In recent conflicts the role of the AWACS aircraft has subtly shifted from being the asset that allocates fighters to incoming enemy formations to a role of battle management. This trend started over Kosovo and was crucial in helping establish air superiority over Libya in 2011. In that campaign the deployment of fifth-generation fighter systems such as the Typhoon and Rafale quickly ensured that members of the Libyan Air Force avoided conflict. The outcome would have been very one-sided.

For anyone tempted to think, based on the evidence presented in this chapter, that air-to-air combat is now a thing of the past they should take care before drawing too many conclusions. Of late many of the conflicts where air-to-air combat air power has been applied, the asymmetry in capability of the adversaries has often led to an inevitable outcome.

Developments in Russia and China of their equivalents of the fifth generation of fighter aircraft will enable them to provide a formidable adversary if future international tensions come to more than an exchange of rhetoric. Couple their manoeuvrability with the development of longer-range missile systems that can be fired at AWACS at ranges of over 150km and the nature of the air-to-air environment is likely to change significantly in the next decade. Such developments fundamentally change the nature of the dynamics of the air-to-air battle and will have to either lead to the development of platforms whose radar performance allows them to stay outside the Missile Engagement Zones (MEZ) of this advanced air-to-air missile, or for some other means of shooting them down to be developed. It may not be too long before the vulnerability of the AWACS in a major conflict means that the development of the RAP will fall to another platform tasked with integrating the data collected from fighter aircraft.

The FGR4 Phantom

Of all the fighter jets that have served in the inventory of NATO countries throughout the Cold War arguably the FGR4 Phantom is the most iconic aircraft. Ironically that is not because of its performance in combat; the demise of the Soviet Union ensured that the NATO operators of the FGR4 would never have to explore its capabilities in a shooting war.

Given the considerable investment made in the FGR4 across NATO, and its ultimate emergence as a ground-attack aircraft alongside its air-to-air mission, it was interesting for NATO when export variants of the aircraft became involved in so-called proxy wars where the United States and the Soviet Union equipped partners with variants of their latest high-technology fighter jets to settle their own disputes. For the FGR4 this was to come in two major confrontations. One of these occurred during the Yom Kippur War in 1973 and the other, ironically, during the eight-year war between Iran and Iraq.

The ability of the Iranian FGR4 to engage and secure combat victories over contemporary Russian fighter jets must have provided interesting reading material for NATOs defence analysts. Despite the obvious difficulties the Iranian air force experienced as a result of the hostage crisis and the overthrow of the Shah, the Phantom aircraft were able to be used throughout the war with Iraq. This was clearly an example where the highly-trained Iranian pilots, many of whom had benefited from deep ties that had been established with the United States air force, outclassed their Iraqi opponents.

It is true to say that the FGR4 excelled in its air-to-ground role in the war. That was where it made its major contribution. The F-14 Tomcat aircraft supplied by the United States during the reign of the Shah provided the primary air defence capability for the Iranian air force, but in an illustration of its flexibility the FGR4 made an important contribution to the air-to-air war. In purely statistical terms both types accounted for similar numbers of combat victories.

Incomplete records of the air war show F-4E variants securing over eighty combat victories over a range of Iraqi aircraft types such as variants of the MiG-21, MiG-23, the Su-20 and the Su-22. This mirrored the performance of the F-14, although unofficial records suggest that the F-14 may have also accounted for a further forty Iraqi aircraft.

Of all the combat victories the success rate against the MiG-21MF was the highest with the Iranians claiming over twenty combat kills by FGR4 pilots. The MiG-23MS and its MiG-23BN variant fared a little better with a smaller total of FGR4 victories. With that level of success it is not difficult to understand why the FGR4 still forms the backbone of the Iranian air force. At the start of the twenty-first century over 5,000 of the FGR4s remained in service in air forces all over the world.

Looking into the records the single victory of a FGR4 over a Tupolev Tu-22B bomber operated by the Iraqi air force is perhaps understandable. However, the victories against what were seen to be the latest Russian aircraft that would be launched against NATO were encouraging, especially as the vast majority of them were achieved using the AIM-9 missile system. Had those same reports been read in the Kremlin they would have made sober reading. Even the introduction of the formidable MiG-29 into the Iraqi air force towards the end of the war did not faze the Iranian FGR4 pilots who continued to penetrate the Iraqi air defence systems almost at will right up to the cease-fire on 19 July 1988. The MiG-29 also proved to be no match for the F-14 and the FGR4.

If any technological advantages enjoyed by the west are eventually evened out, the apparent similarity of aircraft performance will inevitably bring the outcome of future engagements down to one simple thing: the quality of the people placed in the cockpit and their training. While the language and flight dynamics of combat may have changed significantly, there are some perennial factors. In all forms of warfare, no matter where it is conducted, it is ultimately a test of the people involved. That is a conclusion on the air-to-air element of air power that remains unchallenged over the 100 years since its inception.

Chapter Four

Tactical and Strategic Heavy-Lifting

Context

In the twenty-first century air power manifests itself in many different ways. It is not always about applying kinetic effect. There is also a dimension of reach. Air power can be applied at a strategic, operational and tactical level, but it is important not to immediately equate the notion of strategic effect to range. That has been a stereotype in the past that has gained traction among those writing doctrine. In the highly-connected world of the twenty-first century distance no longer has the same impact upon people. That translates into a public expectation that things can be done on a worldwide scale quickly.

In days gone by a need to fly humanitarian relief aid halfway round the world was a big issue. The payload that aircraft could fly was severely limited and there was always a question of where the nearest airfield to a disaster zone was located. Today military planners do not regard distance as a challenge.

This is the world where physical manoeuvre is less difficult than cognitive manoeuvre, where the aim is to secure support from the population. Strategic effect occurs where an action has an impact upon the world stage and other countries take notice. Mobilizing strategic airlift capability can be a very important way of projecting air power in what is seen as a beneficial way.

With the advent of the Boeing C-17 strategic heavy-lifting aircraft and its worldwide support network many of the past challenges of moving emergency freight over large distances have been addressed. Countries that operate the C-17 such as America, the United Kingdom, Qatar and Australia are able to work together to create an international heavy-lifting capability.

NATO has also purchased three C-17 aircraft, operating them from the Pápa airbase in Hungary. In July 2009 the first NATO supply mission involving one of those three aircraft was mounted into Afghanistan. The first three years of operations have proved so successful that in October 2012 NATO announced its desire to obtain additional C-17s for its fleet despite the imminent draw-down of its forces from Afghanistan. NATO clearly envisages that it will be conducting out-of-area operations in the future, but perhaps not in support of upstream interventions such as the deployment of its forces into Afghanistan.

In the case of responding to natural and man-made disasters this often sees ad hoc alliances of countries coming together to respond in the immediate aftermath of an event when the air agencies are simply overwhelmed. The scale of the disaster is often framed through the lens of the media. In response to the scale of the humanitarian disaster in Haiti in the wake of the earthquake in 2010 NATO deployed its C-17 fleet on their first humanitarian relief operation in February. This was the first time the NATO airbase at Pápa had been used as a logistics hub for relief supplies. Supplies from Sweden, Estonia and Bulgaria were flown first into Hungary before being loaded onto the NATO C-17. Three support missions carrying relief supplies were mounted into Haiti.

When disasters strike, through the careful choice of words and images reporters can quite literally mobilize public support at home. Pressure builds for governments to act and help those in need. Where governments are seen to be slow to act public opinion and donations to various charities can compel political action.

Today once that pressure builds any government that is unable to respond quickly becomes rapidly labelled as being unresponsive. That is a label that can easily stick as President George W. Bush found out in the wake of Hurricane Katrina. While the situation in New Orleans deteriorated rapidly the inaction in Washington led to the perception that the leadership simply did not care.

This is where the military's ability to swiftly mobilize its resources to deliver medical supplies and other vital equipment to a place in the world in desperate need is a huge asset. It provides another insight into the application of air power and shows its ability to quickly mobilize urgent supplies over global distances in short periods of time. This is one that sometimes stereotypes of its use fail to fully appreciate. To explore this application of strategic and tactical airlift in greater detail a number of case studies are analysed from a range of viewpoints.

The Balkans

The conflicts in the Balkans in the 1990s provided an early portend of what was to follow once the stability of the Cold War had passed into history. In the Balkans old rivalries and ethnic tensions that had not been buried into the sands of time found new expression as the former Yugoslavia broke up into warring factions.

Throughout the mayhem of the conflicts whose axis seemed to shift almost on a daily basis some isolated communities got caught up as ethnic islands (or enclaves) in what was a sea of tensions and retribution. Local geography and highly variable weather conditions made maintaining supplies to these areas extraordinarily difficult. Of all the documented instances that emerged from the long series of wars in the region the siege of Sarajevo is one that is not readily forgotten. It still provides an important case study for future military commanders to examine.

When the last pallet of flour was carried away from a C-130 to a warehouse in Sarajevo airport on 13 February 1996 the longest-ever airlift operated in the world came to an end. The mission had commenced on 3 July 1992. It lasted for 1,321 days; far surpassing any other airlift recorded in history. It had run almost continuously over that period; only being suspended for a short time in 1993 when the aircraft were diverted to drop 20,000 metric tons of relief supplies into eastern Bosnia.

Operation Provide Promise had delivered 179,910 tons of food to Sarajevo in the course of 12,895 missions. On average ten flights a day brought 136 tons of relief supplies into Sarajevo. Most of the airlift capacity that achieved this feat was undertaken by five partners. USAF undertook 4,597 missions. Behind them their NATO allies Canada (1,860), France (2,133), Germany (1,279) and the United Kingdom (1,902) carried out the majority of the remaining missions.

Many of these involved flights into and out of Sarajevo under the threat of attack from ground fire and surface-to-air missiles. Many of the missions involved tactical transport aircraft such as the ubiquitous C-130. On one well-reported occasion twelve bullets destroyed the windscreen of a C-130 as it was attempting to land at the airport. For the crew on board that day, they had a lucky escape.

Fortunately, being fired upon when delivering humanitarian aid is a rarity. This also highlights an important point. Some missions flown into these operating environments have to be undertaken by military teams. The threat environment demands it. In permissive environments the role played by civilian cargo–carrying aircraft can be really important.

Worldwide Airlift

Across the world air forces are conscious of the need to play their part in delivering humanitarian relief to people in difficulties as a result of natural or man-made disasters. When Saddam Hussein turned on the Kurdish people, enclaves were established to try to protect them from his military forces. No-fly zones were created in which Iraqi airplanes would be engaged and shot down if they tried to attack the Kurdish people who were fighting for a separate homeland to respect their rights as an ethnic group. In the early stages of that campaign strategic heavy-lifting aircraft from the USAF were used to drop supplies to the people when a humanitarian disaster loomed.

In the immediate aftermath of the fighting that saw the Northern Alliance break out from their enclave in North Afghanistan and march on Kabul in the early part of 2002, a similar set of air-drop missions was conducted. This was all part of a plan to try to secure the hearts and minds of the local population.

When natural disasters strike air power is also readily mobilized to help bring in urgently needed food supplies and aid to people who are often in a desperate situation. In the wake of the tsunami that affected Japan and threatened a major environmental disaster as engineers fought for control of the Fukushima nuclear plant it was to strategic air power that the USAF turned to ensure that the urgent requests for help from the Japanese government did not go unanswered. With aircraft like the Boeing C-17 USAF was able to change its flying programme to accommodate the need to fly specialized fire-fighting equipment and other supplies into the disaster area.

Another tsunami that struck communities in the Pacific Ocean on 29 September 2009 saw USAF crews from Hickam Air Force Base in Hawaii fly eleven C-17 aircraft loaded with 157 passengers and 378.3 short tons of cargo to American Samoa which had been struck by 15-ft waves. The aircraft carried cargo vans, trailers, water, medical supplies and ready-to-eat meals. The speed of response was helped by the close proximity of the C-17 aircraft to the area affected by the disaster. Two civilian airliners were also used in the relief operations.

Other examples also exist where air power has been rapidly mobilized in the wake of a major natural disaster. In 2005 as the drama of Hurricane Katrina played out across the world's media an international relief effort was mobilized. Hurricane Katrina was the worst of its kind. The cost of damage exceeded $100 billion. This was four times the scale of any previous major natural disaster that had affected the United States. The response of the Bush Administration was slow and uncertain. The scale of the disaster seemed to overwhelm the authorities.

India, a country familiar with many disasters of its own, dispatched an IL-76 transport aircraft to deliver 25 tonnes of relief aid. Initially aid from Russia and France was politely turned down by the Bush Administration. Once the scale of the disaster became apparent those offers were quickly accepted. Even countries such as Sri Lanka, still recovering from the tsunami, offered help. When natural disaster strikes it appears the world community, no matter what their ethnicity or culture, is prepared to help.

After the terrible disaster in Haiti in January 2010 air power was at the focal point of the international community's response. The earthquake which had measured 7 on the Richter scale claimed over 300,000 lives. Some 250,000 houses and over 30,000 commercial buildings were also destroyed, making over 1 million people homeless.

Across the world military and civilian aircraft were mobilized to move aid into Haiti. In this case such was the scale of the disaster that the ability to handle the arrival of the aid became an immediate problem. Electrical supplies, communications equipment and other basic services and infrastructure had all been destroyed. Air power was available but the rate at which aircraft would arrive in the country was slowed by the lack of rudimentary air-traffic control systems.

For a while the international response went into meltdown. Once military expertise was applied to the problem, things improved. For some of the seriously injured people the destruction of hospitals in Haiti meant that evacuation to America was the only way in which their lives could be saved. Even then political issues arose as hospitals in Miami became swiftly overcrowded. Similar tales arise from other major disasters. When there is an immediate need to deliver relief supplies air power's unique qualities come to the fore.

The response of USAF to that sudden and unexpected disaster highlights one of the enduring qualities of air power. This is its ability to be versatile and flexible. In the United Kingdom the RAF shows similar qualities. The build-up of the RAF C-17 fleet from an initial leasing arrangement for four aircraft to a contract which saw a bigger fleet of eight mobilized provides a testament to the versatility of the platform.

Its range and payload capabilities are impressive and it has allowed RAF air-crews to mix the routine operations of the air-bridge into Afghanistan with some more diverse missions into places such as Pakistan, Columbia and Benghazi carrying disaster relief supplies to the first two countries and large amounts of cash into Libya to help maintain the viability of the banking system.

Air power can be applied in so many different ways to achieve effects. One other important mission, both for the RAF and USAF, is the return of injured personnel from theatre to specialized hospitals in the United Kingdom and the United States. Possibly the most difficult of all the missions flown by the C-17 are those that repatriate the bodies of servicemen killed in action. Those are very sombre affairs.

The cost of aircraft like the C-17 means that very few countries can afford to buy and operate their own fleets which can then be deployed in times of crisis. NATO has come up with one model where three C-17 aircraft have been bought as a result of twelve countries pooling resources. Ten members of NATO and two partner countries (Sweden and Finland) agreed to come together to purchase a strategic heavy-lifting capability that would be based in Hungary.

The first aircraft arrived in July 2009. By October all three aircraft had been delivered to their operating base at Pápa Air Base. In deciding where the air wing was to be located those involved had carefully looked at the potential expansion of the facility at the airbase and its geo-strategic location. Planners envisage that in time the airbase could become a strategic hub for humanitarian relief operations.

This relatively new capability was mobilized in January 2010 to provide assistance to the victims of the Haiti earthquake. On the third flight into Haiti NATO's Heavy Airlift Wing flew supplies and equipment donated by Estonia, Finland and Sweden to supply and construct a camp for aid workers at the airport at Port-au-Prince.

Berlin Airlift 1948

Of all the applications of tactical and strategic heavy-lifting capability the Berlin Airlift stands out as the leading example. As the Second World War had come to its inevitable conclusion once the German attack on Russia had so spectacularly failed, the race had been on between the Allies and the Russians to capture Berlin.

That was won by the Russians. However, because of the significance of Berlin as a political centre in Germany it was agreed that despite it being well inside what was now de facto occupied Russia, the city would be divided into four zones. These would be administered by the Russians, United States, France and the United Kingdom. At the time when the city was partitioned an agreement was signed that provided for road and rail links through the Russian-occupied territories to bring supplies into the city. To assert Soviet authority over the links they were subjected to periodic interruption. On 1 April 1948 the Soviets applied new rules over the movement of supplies by rail. No cargo was allowed to leave Berlin without permission of the Soviet commander in the city.

This caused the Americans to start a small airlift to supply their own forces in the city. This was nicknamed the 'little lift'. The Soviets responded, flying fighter jets to confront the transport aircraft. Sometimes this was deadly serious. One incident occurred as a result of direct harassment by a Soviet Yakolev Yak-3 fighter which collided with a British civilian aircraft on 5 April 1948. All of the people on both aircraft died. In total throughout the crisis USAF reports published at the time suggest that the Americans complained of interference in the flights on nearly 750 occasions. It seems in hindsight that this figure was probably an exaggeration.

Eventually the continued disruption of these links precipitated the crisis. It also stopped the 13,500 tons of food a day that routinely flowed into Berlin. Only the air corridors that were protected by an internationally-recognized treaty remained open.

From 24 June 1948 to 12 May 1949, a period of nearly a year, the combined efforts of the Allied air forces sustained a city under siege flying over 92 million miles in the process. This is almost the same distance as from the Earth to the sun. In the course of the airlift the Allies maintained air supplies to a population of just over 2 million people. In the early part of the response as the numbers of aircraft available were steadily ramped up, one flight took off every three minutes. That separation was maintained throughout the 270-km flight. It was like a conveyor belt of food in the sky.

The initial force of 100 C-47 'Gooney Bird' aircraft were just able to move enough supplies into Berlin to support United States forces based in the city. General Curtis LeMay who then commanded USAF in Europe was able to fine-tune this delivery a little, but he knew that to try to achieve the wider objective of feeding the population as a whole he would need additional aircraft.

To supplement the initial effort C-54 Skymasters were made available. They could carry a payload of 10 tons which was four times the capacity of the C-47. By the end of August 1948 225 C-54s were dedicated to the airlift. This was 40 per cent of the USAF total fleet.

By today's standards these are quite small loads. The C-130 tactical transport aircraft (Hercules) can carry a payload of 19 tons. The C-17 can carry up to 85 tons and the C-141 is able to lift 34 tons. The USAF C-5 can lift 145 tons. The air speeds are also appreciably faster. Had the Berlin Airlift to be repeated today, the same effect could be achieved with sixty C-17 flights per day.

In the course of the crisis 2.3 million tons of cargo had been moved into Berlin in nearly 280,000 flights; an average close to 1,000 a day. This is an average lift of 8.3 tons per flight. That meant that at least 600 flights a day had to land in Berlin to sustain the food flow. By contrast the lengthy effort to sustain the people of Sarajevo lifted about 8 per cent of the total supplies moved into Berlin.

The flight pattern was organized with military efficiency. Aircraft occupied five different flight levels separated by 500ft from a lowest level of 5,000ft. At each flight level aircraft were maintained at a distance of fifteen minutes' flight time. The net effect was to create a three-minute gap between each aircraft arriving in Berlin at the start of the operation.

Given that there are only 1,440 minutes in a day and at the start of the airlift aircraft were only landing once every three minutes, it is possible to see just how far the original effort ramped up. It also cost seventeen American and eight British planes that were lost due to crashes. This cost 101 airmen their lives, including forty Britons and thirty-one Americans. The total cost of the operation was put at just over $220 million. This is the equivalent of just over $2 billion today. Final figures show that the RAF carried nearly 550,000 tons of supplies and USAF 1,750,000 tons. The Royal Australian Air Force also delivered nearly 8,000 tons of freight and 7,000 passengers in just over 2,000 sorties.

To feed and keep warm the people of Berlin the initial estimates suggested that up to 5,000 tons of food and heating supplies would be needed to be flown into Berlin every day. This split as around 1,500 tons of food and 3,500 tons of coal and gasoline. The first calculations undertaken as the crisis deepened suggested that 2,000 tons a day was the bare minimum. This of course was a very low estimate.

In the course of the winter period this grew by an additional 6,000 tons a day. Coal was the most difficult substance to move into Berlin. It amounted to 65 per cent of the cargo carried into the city. Its dust got everywhere and helped corrode cables and flight controls. Crews also complained of breathing difficulties.

The American name for the airlift was Operation Vittles. The United Kingdom called it Operation Plainfare. At its peak one aircraft was arriving in Berlin every thirty seconds. Each captain was only allowed a single approach. If they missed the landing they went back to the airbase from which they had launched their sortie. It was quite simply an extraordinary achievement.

The crisis had blown up over a period of time as the Soviet Union tried to apply pressure on the west. Rail and motorway supplies into Berlin had been disrupted on some occasions previously as tensions waxed and waned, but to try to force the situation where Berlin became integrated into the Soviet Union these routes were suddenly cut off. The population of Berlin was being held to ransom. Soviet offers of free food for those that crossed the border in the city into the zones not controlled by the Allies were rebuffed by the population. Attempts to rig elections were also similarly defeated.

Throughout the crisis the Berliners maintained a steadfast approach. During the winter months fog proved to be a huge challenge. On 20 November forty-two aircraft had set out to fly into Berlin and only one aircraft landed. At one point the amount of coal left in the city was down to a level that could only sustain it for a week. With an improvement in the weather over 171,000 tons of food and fuel was supplied in January 1949. In February that fell back to 152,000 tons before increasing again in March to 196,000 tons. As the crisis came to a close the Allies mounted a huge effort over the Easter period. This became known as the 'Easter Parade'. On 16 April 1949 1,398 flights brought in 12,940 tons of supplies. At this point aircraft were arriving into Berlin at one every minute.

By this time the Soviets began to realize that the Allied effort had been sustained through the winter and that with the arrival of the spring and summer months a backlog of supplies could be built up ahead of the next winter. Soon after this point negotiations started to bring an end to the crisis. The west had been able to stop Berlin falling into the hands of the Soviet Union. It was now at that last moment that the Allies and the Soviet Union had a stand-off over Berlin. In 1961 another crisis blew up as the west confronted the Soviet Union over the future of Berlin.

Berlin Crisis 1961

In previously highly-classified documents recording the meeting in Washington on 5 April between the newly-installed Kennedy Administration and the United Kingdom's Prime Minister Harold Macmillan and senior members of his Cabinet the matter of just how far those contingency plans should go was debated. In the course of the meeting a specific agenda topic on Berlin was discussed.

Dean Acheson, acting in a personal capacity as an advisor to the President on the subject of Berlin, outlined his position on the current situation. He asserted that 'the Soviets would press the Berlin question in the course of 1961.' He went on to say that 'we should not wait for the crisis to come upon us. Berlin was the key to Germany and to Europe.' He also noted that political and economic measures taken against the Soviets if they decided to ratchet up the pressure on Berlin again would be insufficient to resolve any situation. The military instrument of power would also need to be engaged.

Acheson's predictions proved to be true. Within weeks of the meeting the building of the Berlin Wall had started. Towards the end of 1961 another confrontation developed over Berlin. This one saw over sixty American and Soviet tanks confront each other as the Berlin Wall was erected.

Acheson announced that he had initiated a number of studies looking into the ways in which the west might be able to confront any new move on Berlin by the Soviets. He opined that while those studies had not concluded anything yet, he foresaw difficulties if air power alone was to be used as the primary military instrument of power. His thinking clearly involved a fairly large-scale land component. He thought that surface-to-air missile systems had reduced the manoeuvre room in the air domain.

In his analysis Acheson would have been influenced by the shooting down of Gary Powers over Russia nearly a year earlier. That was quite a shock to the Americans. If the fast and high-flying U-2 could be shot down by a SAM, a slow transport aircraft flying into Berlin would be an easy target. In 1948 that had simply not been a threat that had to be considered.

Acheson went further in his analysis, looking at the possibility that fighter jets might escort transport aircraft on their re-supply mission. He ventured the view that the Soviets would simply pick off the transport aircraft and leave the fighter jets alone. He saw the solution in a large land-based formation heading up one of the main road links into Berlin. President Kennedy expressed doubts about this, noting that he thought the land-based element was 'not strong enough'.

The minutes of the meeting showed that Harold Macmillan was not enthusiastic about a land-based approach. He argued for a wait-and-see approach adjusting the reaction to the specifics of the situation. Reading between the lines Macmillan was not quite so ready to give up on the element of air power.

In the meeting President Kennedy was clear about the need to maintain the freedoms of the people of Berlin. In his election campaign he had suggested that Berlin be given the label of a free city, borrowing ideas that created special trading situations for some ports called Free Ports. It was a hugely significant moment. The Soviets rejected the idea out of hand. As the Cold War went into the freezer, with the creation of the Berlin Wall the threat to encircle and cut off Berlin raised its head again.

In his first meeting with the Soviet President Khrushchev in Geneva in June 1961 the Soviet leader had proposed that western military forces leave

Berlin. Using polite diplomatic language President Kennedy declined, highlighting the importance of the people of Berlin to the Americans.

Had that become yet another crisis air power would have undoubtedly played a role in trying to bring the situation back under control. In October 1961 as Soviet and American tanks were deployed on each side of the famous crossing known as 'Checkpoint Charlie', it appeared yet again that the world stood on the edge of another major war. A year later as the Cuban Missile Crisis developed Berlin was again at the centre of the wide-ranging considerations that were discussed. It was possible that the whole crisis in Cuba had been brought about simply to create another excuse to see Berlin integrated into the Soviet Union.

That crisis was narrowly averted. In November 1961 a US intelligence report classified as secret provided summary of the situation around Berlin. The Allies were clearly watching the Soviet Union military force readiness levels to try to obtain any indications or warnings of their intent. It was yet another moment in which the thermometer recording the temperature of the Cold War showed an increase in temperature.

To place his own views on the table President Kennedy quickly arranged a visit to Berlin. His remark in a speech given at the symbolically significant Brandenburg Gate 'Ich bin ein Berliner' ('I am a Berliner') was greeted with huge enthusiasm.

As the Cold War started to thaw it was the location where another American president was to issue a call to the Soviets to put actions behind their political détente. When Ronald Reagan called on the Soviet President to 'tear down this wall' he was using the historical context of President Kennedy's original speech. Throughout the Cold War Berliners were quite literally in the front line of the ideological fault line that existed between communism and capitalism.

Withdrawal East of Suez

As the sun started to set on the British Empire it became a political and economic imperative for the United Kingdom to pull out of its military bases in the Far East. That withdrawal from the strategic commitments in the Far East was facilitated by a combination of air and sea power. At the time, in the 1960s and early part of the 1970s, the RAF's strategic heavy-lifting capacity was provided by a fleet of ten Shorts Belfast aircraft. The largest of the operations conducted by the Belfast fleet took place in November 1967 as British forces left Aden. Two Belfast aircraft participated in an orderly evacuation from the area that saw over 6,000 troops and 400 tonnes of equipment moved to an initial staging-post at Bahrain or directly on to the United Kingdom.

The sheer size of the payload bay in the Belfast allowed it to carry a wide variety of loads. Its first mission saw three Westland Whirlwind helicopters and their support equipment rapidly mobilized from Guyana to Fairford, staging through Barbados and Lajes in the Azores. The distance travelled in the mission was 5,200 miles. On landing the aircraft was quickly turned around to deliver two larger Westland Wessex helicopters to RAF Akrotiri. Tensions in that area of South-East Asia had occasionally required the RAF to respond quickly, increasing the military resources in the region. The Belfast fleet was ideally suited to provide that kind of strategic heavy-lifting response.

In the early part of its career the Belfast fleet had distinguished itself in the role of delivering humanitarian relief aid. In March 1968 a Belfast airlifted what at the time was a record payload of 70,682lb (around 31 tons) of Red Cross medical supplies from Changi to Saigon. That record lasted just over a year before another Belfast moved a heavier load in the course of a NATO exercise, beating the previous record by 1,500lb (total of around 32 tons). In the coming months and years these records were also beaten on specific missions.

In 1970 another Belfast flew relief supplies into Romania which had been hit by torrential rain and subsequent flooding. In 1974 responding to yet another emergency relief operation in Africa four Belfast aircraft were deployed to Addis Ababa in Ethiopia.

In what would be a forerunner of the aero-medical evacuation missions now flown by the C-17, a Belfast was used to move a seriously ill small boy from RAF Akrotiri to the famous children's hospital at Great Ormond Street in London. The baby was accompanied by a medical team to provide care throughout the flight.

The Yom Kippur War 1973

The initial onslaught at the start of the Yom Kippur War caught the Israeli political and defence leaders off guard. Secret planning by the Egyptians and Syrians had maintained a blanket over their real intentions. In the days leading up to the outbreak of war the mobilization of the Egyptian ground forces had been touted as an exercise. For once, the famous Israeli intelligence services were surprised. Along the disputed territory of the Golan Heights the scale of the problem rapidly became apparent: 180

Israeli tanks faced 1,800 Syrian tanks. In the Sinai, due to the religious holiday in Israel, 436 soldiers faced 80,000 Egyptians.

The swift advance by the Egyptian forces into Sinai was supported by a shield of Russian-supplied mobile SAM systems. As Israel brought its tactical air power the mobile SAM systems took their toll. The Russian SA-6 (NATO Code Name: Gainful) was particularly effective. The signature of the guidance radar was not initially programmed into the radar warning receivers flown on the Israeli aircraft so the pilots had no idea they were being illuminated. While Israeli losses in the early stages remain the subject of historical debate, it is widely believed a total of around forty F-4 and A-4 aircraft were lost in the opening salvos of the campaign.

Over the first week of the war over 1,000 SAMs were fired by the Egyptians and Syrians. Syrian air power was also brought to bear with over 100 aircraft taking part in initial combat operations designed to neutralize Israeli command posts.

The Israelis desperately needed ways to counter the effects of the mobile missiles. Initially they mobilized their small military and civilian air fleet to bring in supplies from the United States. However, the capacity of El Al's 707 and 747 jets was far too small, given what was unfolding. The very future of Israel was at stake.

In what is a largely unheralded response the Americans quickly mobilized a huge airlift of advanced sophisticated counter-measures and new weaponry to help replenish war stocks that were becoming rapidly depleted. This massive airlift was mobilized within days and saw C-5 Galaxy and C-141 Starlifter aircraft flying over the Atlantic via the Azores into Israel. KC-135A tanker aircraft were also deployed to create an air-bridge from America to Israel. This facilitated around thirty strategic transport aircraft to fly the route each day. The KC-135s supported the movement of A-4 and F-4 aircraft directly from the factory in St Louis, Missouri to Ben Gurion Airport.

It was called Operation Nickel Grass. It saw over 22,000 tons of military aid flown into Israel by C-5 Galaxy and C-141 Starlifter aircraft, and lasted for a month from 14 October 1973. By sea the Americans also delivered an additional 33,000 tons of supplies. In parallel the Soviet Union undertook its own re-supply mission to assist Egypt and Syria.

The scale of the support task was also huge. As the vulnerable transport aircraft flew along the Mediterranean Sea into Israel they were escorted by fighter jets from the United States navy provided by the 6th Fleet. As the transport aircraft got to within 150 nautical miles from the coast, Israeli fighter jets mobilized to escort them into Ben Gurion International

Airport. To provide protection to the air-bridge an American warship was located every 300 miles along the Mediterranean to provide radar coverage of the area. These were backed up by aircraft carriers.

In addition to equipment that would be flown on the strategic heavy-lifting fleet the Israelis also requested new aircraft to replace those lost in the early hours of the campaign. Within hours two F-4 Phantom jets a day began arriving in Israel, having flown non-stop from the United States. In total forty F-4 Phantom aircraft were delivered directly into Israel. As the American pilots landed, Israelis took their place in the cockpit and started flying missions. Thirty-six A-4 Skyhawk jets were also flown in via Lajes and were refuelled by tanker aircraft operating from the aircraft carrier the USS *John Kennedy*. In addition, twelve C-130E Hercules aircraft were provided to the Israeli Air Force.

History will show that Operation Nickel Grass saved the Israelis from a dire situation that was getting more difficult by the hour. In 1973 the application of strategic air power helped Israel initially to stabilize the situation before being able within a matter of hours to go onto the offensive. Since then nothing of a similar ilk has occurred. The airlift of French forces into Mali in January 2013 was supported by the United States and the United Kingdom with small numbers of C-17 aircraft. In the future similar deployments may well occur. While warfare is always unpredictable, an airlift the size of Operation Nickel Grass is unlikely ever to be repeated.

However, in such an uncertain world that may be a foolish assessment. With China increasingly asserting what it believes to be its territorial rights over the vast reaches of the South China Sea it is conceivable that the security situation in South-East Asia could quickly deteriorate. This time the strategic airlift could well be mounted across the Pacific, staging through Hawaii and Andersen Air Force Base into Taiwan, Korea or Japan. However unlikely that may seem, if it were to occur it would again be an opportunity for those who advocate the merits of air power to demonstrate just what can be achieved in a short period of time. For any planners involved, a good look at Operation Nickel Grass would be an excellent case study.

Operation Desert Shield 1991

When Iraqi tanks mounted their surprise attack in 1991 on what they regarded as territory that was rightfully theirs the potential for that invasion to go beyond the border of Kuwait into Saudi Arabia was very real. This was an international crisis that had simmered for a period but few analysts thought Saddam Hussein would actually dare to invade Kuwait. Iraq was only just starting to recover from its debilitating war against Iran. Iraq's dire economic situation, however, and a long-standing dispute with the Kuwaitis over oil rights in the region were enough to tip the balance.

On 2 August 1991 Iraqi forces crossed the border into Kuwait. Within a matter of hours the Kuwaiti armed forces had been overwhelmed. At that moment a shocked international community went into political meltdown. They had never expected this to occur. Despite the usual political and diplomatic problems that surround such situations that inevitably result in procrastination and obfuscation, a United Nations Resolution was quickly passed. The international community decided that this act of war would not stand.

That Saddam Hussein's forces stopped on the border allowed the Americans time to assemble an international coalition that would ultimately see the Iraqis ejected from Kuwait. The political and diplomatic signals emerging from Baghdad at the time were mixed. It appeared that Saddam Hussein, having secured his objective, was prepared to discuss withdrawal. Pictures emerging from Kuwait, however, suggested that the Iraqis were brutalizing the Kuwaiti people who were mounting resistance to the occupation.

History shows that Saddam Hussein was in fact cleverly playing for time in the hope that international efforts to remove his forces from Kuwait would fail. In such situations air power offers an immediate demonstration of resolve providing a defensive screen. It also carries the threat of offensive action.

In halting at the border Saddam Hussein must have concluded that the international community would not bother to come to the aid of Kuwait or would be unable to bridge the obvious fault lines that appear in such situations. He must have reasoned that to have gone further into Saudi Arabia would have caused international consternation. He recognized that red line and chose not to force the issue. It is highly likely that Saddam Hussein believed that the Americans would be incapable of creating an international coalition to oppose him. That President Bush was able to achieve that, skilfully balancing the mix of nations participating in that ad hoc coalition of the willing, must have come as a huge surprise in Baghdad.

Assembling a coalition of the willing takes time. With Iraqi tanks poised on the border with Saudi Arabia and specifically within a short distance of the major oil fields in the north-east of the country a pre-emptive attack aimed at annexing the oil fields could not be ruled out. While diplomats played their cards at the United Nations the American military went into action to place a red line opposing Saddam's forces. Air power was to be the military instrument that would provide the first line of defence of Saudi Arabia.

Once the immediate threat of an invasion of Saudi Arabia was removed the international community could then turn to the diplomatic and political instruments of power to establish a plan for restoring the government of Kuwait. First things first: the 900-km border between Iraq and Saudi Arabia had to be defended.

To mobilize troops, tanks and equipment into a country such as Saudi Arabia takes time. When coalitions get involved it becomes even more difficult. United States military doctrine is based upon the availability of a Time-Phased Force Deployment List (TPFDL). Despite the United States military having a draft plan for such an emergency as an invasion of Kuwait (Contingency Plan 1002-90), no TPFDL existed. It took until the end of September to build up a balanced capability in theatre that would have been able to mount an operation to remove Saddam's forces from Kuwait.

In launching Operation Desert Shield the United States military had to start to move a range of equipment quickly into Saudi Arabia. Permission to start moving equipment was sought and quickly granted. The Saudis were fearful of Saddam Hussein's intentions. The deployment order for Operation Desert Shield was transmitted on 7 August at 0050Z.

The first USAF units had been mobilized into the Area of Responsibility (AOR) within twenty-four hours of the signing of the order to deploy. This was a squadron of the versatile F-15C air superiority fighter. They landed at the Dhahran Airbase in Saudi Arabia. By the end of the first week five fighter squadrons of 112 fighter aircraft (comprising a mix of F-15E, F-16, F-117A, A-10 and F-4G) and fourteen B-52G conventional bombers, seventy tanker aircraft and the first elements of the command and control systems had arrived in the region. Of itself, that was a huge effort. In such chaotic situations everyone believes their piece of equipment has priority on the next strategic transport aircraft flying over the air-bridge. It is understandably a logistical nightmare. However, that was simply the start of a major airlift into the AOR.

To support these initial forces an air-bridge had to be created from the United States into Saudi Arabia. A number of options were looked at in the first few days before the signing of the deployment order. In the immediate aftermath of the war the think-tank RAND (Research and Development) was asked to look at the initial deployment and develop some recommendations for any future operation of this type. Their report documents the planning options being considered at the time. One envisaged sending either eight F-15Cs or twelve F-16Cs to the AOR. Airborne Early Warning and Control Systems (AWACS) were also a priority, along with a Rivet Joint ELINT platform. This would have required the USAF Military Airlift Command (MAC) to mount the equivalent of 395 C-141 Starlifter sorties to deploy those assets into the AOR.

An air-bridge of this size and undertaking will naturally suffer from bottlenecks that constrain its throughput. In-flight refuelling provides a minimum capability to move some equipment directly into the AOR, but that can only be sustained for a short period of time.

To create a flow of equipment into an AOR requires the air-bridge to overcome limitations such as ramp space in transit airfields, fuel availability, cargo-handling equipment and capacity on runways. These are all obvious operational limitations that political leaders may overlook when it comes to ordering the military to undertake a specific tasking.

Manpower is also important and quickly President Bush invoked the call-up of 200,000 reservists. This enabled the constraint on the numbers of air-crew to be quickly solved. Inevitably, as defence spending comes under pressure in the western world, this model of having trained reservists ready to go into action when crisis situations develop is going to become more attractive. The United States has this built into its war-planning. Other countries are likely to follow this approach.

The airlift to support Operation Desert Storm (as 'Desert Shield' became) surpassed the sortie generation rate for the Berlin Airlift. By the end of September over 3,800 missions had been flown by both military and civilian aircraft over a fifty-five-day window. This is an average sortie generation rate of sixty-nine aircraft a day. Over 130,000 passengers had been moved into the AOR. That was also accompanied by 124,000 tons of cargo. This is an average daily movement rate of 2,486 passengers and 2,285 tons of cargo. In this period the RAND analysis suggests that the airlift moved 17 Million-Ton-Miles per day (MTM/d) on average. This did not fulfil the figure of 23 MTM/d mandated by Congress.

The main burden of the airlift fell to the C-141 Starlifter and the C-5. Throughout August the C-141 maintained an average of forty sorties a day. Its peak of sixty sorties in a day occurred in the middle of September. By contrast the C-5 averaged fifteen sorties a day with a peak of twenty-five in the very earliest part of the operation. By the end of the first sixty days RAND reports that 3,839 strategic airlift sorties had been undertaken. This had shifted 124,000 short tons of cargo and 134,215 passengers. At the sixty-day point USAF had fielded eighteen tactical fighter squadrons, twenty B-52Gs, ninety-nine KC-135 tankers and ninety-six C-130 tactical transports plus a range of other air capabilities.

In contrast the daily airlift into Berlin during the summer months of 1948 was around 5,000 tons of cargo. In terms of aircraft involved, the arrival rate of aircraft into Berlin was sustained at over 1,400 sorties a day for a long period of time. The payload-carrying capacity of the aircraft involved, however, was far less than their contemporaries. Counting the mission generation rate as a comparator the Berlin Airlift easily surpasses the effort to build up forces in Saudi Arabia.

Air-Bridge Afghanistan

When a country, such as the United Kingdom, commits nearly 10,000 members of its armed forces to a war in a country many thousands of miles away from home it inevitably has knock-on effects. The air-bridge into Afghanistan is flown by a variety of aircraft that perform slightly different roles. The Tristar provides the trooping flights. That enables force rotations to occur, moving significant numbers of people into theatre and returning others home at the end of their tours or returning them home briefly at the mid-point of their tours of duty. Staging through the airfield in Cyprus the outbound and homebound flights last between ten and twelve hours.

To back up the trooping capability the RAF operates the C-17. Its main role is to move equipment into theatre over the air-bridge. A simple testament to the workload placed on the C-17 is that any visit to RAF Brize Norton, the United Kingdom airhead, rarely finds a C-17 on the ground for very long. These are the workhorses of the air-bridge as far as the movement of equipment is concerned. To maintain a force in Afghanistan the C-17s are operated at a very high mission generation rate. Its other less well-known task includes the medical evacuation of injured service personnel.

As far as the air-bridge into Afghanistan is concerned, the importance of the operation is often misunderstood. With overland routes into Afghanistan from various parts of Pakistan under almost daily attack from insurgents, the air-bridge has provided the only reliable way of resupplying the troops operating in theatre. The logistical support operation in Afghanistan mounted by the Royal Air Force and the United States Air Force has quite literally redefined the notion of airborne re-supply operations. The fleet of eight C-17 Galaxy aircraft operated by the RAF continues to perform an outstanding role supporting the members of the armed forces based in Afghanistan.

Chapter Five

Maritime Air Power

Nascent Beginnings

Not long after the Wright brothers took their first tentative steps into the air the potential for air power to contribute to the maritime domain started to be taken seriously. Initially that potential was explored by the Royal Navy in 1909 when it purchased an airship. That proved to be a false dawn and it would be a few years before the value of air power in a naval environment was really appreciated.

In France, however, the potential for maritime air power was quickly recognized. They, after all, had seen the invention of the first seaplane (*Le Canard*) in March 1910. It had been four years in design and development. This was a strange-looking contraption with its wings and fragile body seemingly precariously balanced on three floats. The pilot sat atop the superstructure. All in all the seaplane did not look much like a war machine. Its wingspan of 14m added to its sense of being unwieldy to control. Its maximum speed was just less than 90 km per hour (55 mph).

It first flew on 28 March 1910, recording a total distance of 457m or approximately 1,500ft at Martigues, a few miles from the French port of Marseille. Photographs at the time show the aircraft moving slowly away from the shoreline on a dead flat calm sea.

The pilot, Henri Fabre, was typical of many of those pioneers involved in aviation at the time, seemingly oblivious to the risks. The first flight of the seaplane was also Fabre's. He was to take the seaplane on three more trips on the same day. Within a week he had extended the range to over 5,600m (3.5 miles). Other developers were hard on his heels and the floats designed by Fabre were soon in demand. Initially these were little more than experimental aircraft. The idea of these machines carrying a payload other than the pilot to deliver some kind of effect in warfare was still firmly on the drawing board.

In time seaplanes were to prove how maritime air power can provide a significant contribution to a battle. The role of the Sunderland in the Second World War in the Battle of the Atlantic is one of many examples. Its ability to engage and destroy U-boats on the surface was crucial in helping turn the tide of the very serious situation that faced the United Kingdom at the time.

In 1910, however, it was the French who were quick to spot the potential of the seaplane. A former torpedo boat tender called *Foudre* was converted into a seaplane carrier. The ship was equipped with a flat surface at the stern and a crane to retrieve the seaplane once it had completed its mission.

In July 1912 operational trials started with the *Foudre* during naval exercises in the Mediterranean Sea. The seaplanes used for the trials were the *Canard Voisin* (a derivative of the original *Le Canard*) and a specially adapted Nieuport. These aircraft proved their value on several different occasions in the exercises warning of the approach of a previously undetected naval formation. By 1913 the French navy had eleven trained naval aviators.

The role of aircraft to help fleets see over the horizon was now understood, even if weather limitations could restrict their use. If the weather was good having an eye in the sky prevented naval commanders being surprised. It also meant that they could concentrate their force. In the past destroyer screens and cruisers had been used as ISTAR outposts operating on the edge of the fleet, diluting the ability to mass fire-power.

The First World War, however, provided a catalyst from which maritime air power was to build. The special view from the air over a naval battle was to become one that contributed notably to a number of major sea battles. The application of air power in these cases varied from using the platform to conduct reconnaissance activities to either sanitize an area or to detect possible targets for strike missions, either as a single aircraft or as part of a formal attack package.

A striking example of the initial limitations of air power in the maritime domain at this time emerges from the Battle of Jutland. Initial intelligence warnings had seen the Royal Navy sortie from Scapa Flow and the Firth of Forth. The German High Seas Fleet had been making short-notice sorties to sea from the Jade to raid the east coast of England. By the time the Royal Navy was able to sail from its northern bases in Scotland and the Orkney Isles the German navy had retreated through the German Bight back into the Jade. On the eve of the Battle of Jutland some wireless intercepts had enabled the Royal Navy to make steam and get under way.

What then followed is a classic example of an intelligence failure. The German High Seas Fleet did put to sea but for a variety of reasons errors were made over their location. As the Royal Navy sailed southwards in an attempt to get into the German Bight and attack the German High Seas Fleet as it emerged, the two battle fleets passed within just over 20 miles of each other without realizing they were so close. The absence of air power to extend the visual range of the fleet was sorely felt.

The contribution of air power to the Battle of Jutland was minimal. One out of a possible four Shorts 184 seaplanes was launched from HMS *Engadine* in the course of the confrontation to conduct surveillance of the German High Seas Fleet. The flight had been personally ordered by Admiral Beatty at 14:47. It took twenty-one minutes to open the doors on the hangar and get the machine ready to fly. The aircraft had been launched at just after 15:05. It had to fly at low level around 90ft as by this time a combination of poor weather conditions and the residual smoke from the battle had hampered visibility.

In the course of a relatively short mission, after being airborne for just over twenty minutes they spotted four cruisers of the German High Seas Fleet and reported these back to HMS *Engadine* by wireless. With a temporary clearance in the weather the pilot Flight Lieutenant Rutland was able to climb and see the panoply of the battle in front of him. Shortly afterwards a problem with the aircraft's carburettor caused the aircraft to land on the sea.

Before he could get airborne again Rutland was ordered back aboard HMS *Engadine*. A quickly deteriorating weather situation started to increase the swell. This prevented any aircraft playing a further role in the battle. The first mission had barely lasted forty minutes. The lack of a major contribution did cause some soul-searching at the Admiralty at the end of the First World War. However, despite the emerging debate which saw all sorts of issues discussed it seemed to many that the current limitations on the application of air power, such as the time to deploy it over the side of the tender and the impact of the weather, would be overcome in time. From that point onwards naval doctrine would have to be rewritten. Maritime air power was very quickly coming of age.

Geoffrey Bennett in his detailed account of the events that transpired that day, *The Battle of Jutland*, notes that after the battle Flight Lieutenant Rutland observed that 'the picture from the air of the battlecruisers and of the "Queen Elizabeth" battleships, with their attendant light cruiser screen and destroyers, all rushing forward to cut off the enemy is [one] that can never be forgotten.' It was the first time an aircraft had played a role in a major fleet action. It was not to be the last. From his vantage point over the battle Rutland and his observer Assistant-Paymaster Trewin had not just seen the choreography of the battle of Jutland: they had also taken a glimpse into the future.

If the Short seaplane had been able to rejoin the battle, who knows what role it might have played? It could have provided value insights on the direction and intent of the German High Seas Fleet as it withdrew. The Germans took the opportunity of the worsening visibility to withdraw. The Admiralty's appreciation of the situation was rapidly thrown into confusion. Further intelligence failures compounded the problems as intercepts were incorrectly interpreted. For the naval commanders at sea this was the final straw. It completely removed any trust that they could place in wireless intercepts as a means of helping situational awareness. Admiral Jellicoe made his own appreciation of the situation which turned out to be incorrect. Had an airborne platform been available the outcome might have been very different. Many naval historians lament the failure of the Royal Navy to press home another attack in the aftermath of the Battle of Jutland.

Arguments have been voiced suggesting that a decisive outcome to the battle could have had a foreshortening effect on the First World War. As ever when historians argue over potential outcomes of warfare it is very hard to prove if one interpretation or another would have been right. If the German High Seas Fleet had been decisively defeated at Jutland it is possible that the German high command could have sensed that the time was right to try to conclude a peace treaty based on the current situation on the land. The stalemate was to go on for over two years and cost countless thousands of lives. For some historians that alone would have made it all worthwhile. Sadly at that point maritime air power was in its early stages and the arguments involved can remain little more than an interesting intellectual aside.

The Shorts 184 is the same type of seaplane that had first sunk an enemy warship. Its first engagement against a warship saw an uncertain outcome as the vessel had already been crippled by a torpedo fired from a submarine. The second attack on 17 August 1915 was more conclusive when a Turkish warship was sunk by a torpedo launched from a Shorts 184. This was a time when history could quite literally be written, as a seemingly endless list of 'firsts' were recorded for maritime air power. In a very short window of time the application of maritime air power started to take shape. From these nascent beginnings air power would become embedded into the wider military instrument of power.

One early example of the use of air power in a naval context was the Cuxhaven Raid. This is recorded as the first ship-based air-raid on an enemy harbour. It was carried out on Christmas Day 1914. Three seaplane tenders (HMS *Engadine*, HMS *Riviera* and HMS *Empress*) supported by the Harwich force of a group of cruisers, destroyers and submarines set sail to position the tenders just off the island of Heligoland in the German Bight.

The target of the raid was the Zeppelin sheds at Cuxhaven from which raids had been mounted on the east coast of England and London. Nine aircraft were scheduled to take part in the raid. They were lowered into the water from the tenders. In an indication of just how difficult the situation was two of the aircraft could not start their engines and were recovered onto the tenders. The weather conditions were also challenging with fog hampering visibility. This prevented the raid from being able to press home its attack fully. The mission lasted three hours and saw all seven airmen involved return successfully. Only three of the aircraft were able to be recovered to the tenders.

With that kind of loss rate for aircraft it is possible to question the utility of the raid. The Zeppelin raids on London were little more than nuisance value from a military viewpoint. However, the fact that they could fly over the United Kingdom seemingly with impunity did have a psychological effect on the population. For that reason alone the raid on Cuxhaven was important. It showed the Zeppelins could be attacked on their own territory. A few follow-up raids were also conducted but again these had little military value.

An artist's impression of the raid that was published shortly afterwards captured the drama of the attack. Its depiction seems slightly unreal with aircraft seen to be attacking two airships that are flying. The seven aircraft are seen to be attacking the airships from above and also smoke is pouring from a number of warships in the harbour.

It is a chaotic scene in which the artist has clearly and somewhat liberally interpreted the real-life version of events. The reality of the mission was slightly more mundane and saw the aircraft drop bombs on shore-based installations in what can be described as an opportunistic attack. One aircraft tried to attack the German cruiser *Graudenz* without success. For the German navy, however, the mere fact that someone tried to apply maritime air power in such a situation provided a wake-up call. The sheer audacity of the attack was to call the entire disposition of the High Seas Fleet into question.

From a propaganda viewpoint, however, the story made good reading for a public concerned by the attacks from the Zeppelins. A detailed account of the raid is provided in David Wragg's *A Century of British Naval Aviation* in which he also recounts the story of a short retaliatory raid mounted by the Germans against the Royal Navy force involved in the raid. Wragg's account of the attack on HMS *Empress* by two German seaplanes shows how the Germans had also started to recognize the utility of air power in the maritime domain.

In those days intelligence collection using photographs was in its earliest stages and it is unlikely that any material of any great value about the nature of the specific aims points would have been available prior to take-off for the pilots of the seaplanes. Hence it is highly likely that the pilots attacked what they perceived to be targets of value. However, while the damage was slight and had a minimal impact on the operations of the Zeppelins, the strategic consequences were quite dramatic.

The German navy saw the raid as a precursor of more attempts to bomb its surface fleet and quickly took the decision to move it away from the area to locations on the Kiel Canal which it assessed to be beyond the range of the Royal Navy seaplanes. This decision became known to the Admiralty through an intercepted cable. Nearly four years later that assessment was to be found wanting as the Royal Navy launched a raid on a German airship base at Tondern, just a few miles to the north of the Kiel Canal.

The first aircraft-carrier strike that was undertaken from a flight deck on a warship was carried out from HMS *Furious* in July 1918. It was launched over an eight-minute window starting at 03:13 in the morning. The aircraft formed up after take-off into two flights. One of the seven aircraft ran into trouble with an engine problem and was forced to ditch before being recovered safely. The other six pressed on in two waves to the target.

Understandably, given the immaturity of carrier-based operations at the time, the arrival of seven naval variants of the Sopwith Camel (2F.1) over Tondern was a complete surprise. The aircraft had been modified in several ways to operate from what in those days was called an 'airplane carrier'.

The dark and overcast weather conditions added to the sense of shock as bombs started to fall on the hangars. One detonated an ammunition dump creating what a reporter for the *New York Times* in a dispatch filed several days later from London described as a conflagration. This was a lucky hit but the scale of the blast that ensued showed the pilots what they could achieve if they only had better intelligence information. It is trite to suggest that warfare is often punctuated by such events but there is some veracity in the argument that says military tactics can suddenly evolve on the basis of the unexpected. The report also showed the degree to which the Royal Navy had tried to conceal its work on the development of the 'airplane carrier', describing its role as shrouded in 'mystery'.

To locate the target the leader of the attack had descended to around 50ft to get below the cloud ceiling. As he flew overhead he passed a farm cart whose occupant happily waved to him, totally unaware that he was a British bomber on what in those days can be classed as a daring mission. One of the aircraft involved failed to return and the pilot was presumed to have been lost at sea when he did not return from the mission.

The mission to bomb the hangars had been tried several weeks earlier in June. The limited range of the Sopwith Camels meant that the base at Tondern was one of a small number that were within reach of a carrier-borne strike group. On 27 June HMS *Furious* had put to sea from the Royal Navy base at Rosyth escorted by the First Light Cruiser Squadron and eight destroyers from the 13th Flotilla. Arriving at the launch point on 29 June the weather conditions were extremely difficult with winds blowing between 25–30 miles per hour (Force 6). Given the difficulty of flying in such conditions the attempt to attack Tondern was called off.

On 17 July HMS *Furious* returned to sea to repeat the attempt. Initially really bad weather conditions prevented the attempt. Rather than disengage, HMS *Furious* withdrew from the launch-point to await a clearing in the weather. In the early hours of 19 July, having postponed the launch for twenty-four hours the seven aircraft took off just before dawn.

The transit from the launch-point just off the Danish coast took just over an hour before the attack was pressed home just after 0430 hours in the morning. The German navy lost two airships in the attack which were used for reconnaissance purposes when the German High Seas Fleet sortied into the North Sea from its base in the Jade at Wilhelmshaven. The base, which was then in Germany, was perfectly located to allow airships to patrol the area in the vicinity of Heligoland Island to ensure the Royal Navy was not waiting outside the Jade to spring a trap.

Given the time of day, only four Germans were injured in the attack. Given the weather conditions, the flimsy nature of the aircraft and the need to fly over enemy territory to locate the base and then return and land at sea, this was a remarkable operation. From the launch-point the aircraft had to fly a heading that was almost due east at around 100 knots over a range of around 100 miles before crossing over the peninsula of Sylt before making landfall 10 miles (15km) away from the target.

The Sopwith Camel had a maximum range of 300 miles when flying on a ferry mission. The launch-point for the raid would therefore have been around 80 miles from the Danish coastline. This was a good point for HMS *Furious* not to be accidentally detected by an airship operating from Tondern.

The success of the raid was to herald a new dawn in air power. It could now be projected against the land from the sea. The ranges over which it was possible to do that were obviously limited. Weather conditions could also hamper the use of air power. The fire-power that could be carried against targets was very restricted; a very small number of bombs. However, the simple fact was that through the application of maritime air power, targets that were once thought to be out of reach of air power suddenly had to take a new view of their vulnerabilities. In the overall development of military history it was a profound moment.

Between the World Wars

The end of the First World War provided a period for assessment and reflection on the contribution made by air power to the maritime environment. Initially that did not halt military operations. While the individual actions themselves could hardly be heralded as a great success, the potential of air power in this domain was increasingly being recognized. The issue was the operational constraints which often hampered its use.

In efforts to support the White Russians who opposed the revolution the seaplane tender HMS *Vindictive* saw action in August 1919 bombing the newly-formed Bolshevik or Red Fleet in Kronstadt harbour in the Baltic Sea. The naval vessels had previously formed part of the Russian Baltic Fleet. This location was deemed to be important for the protection of Petrograd. This was the latest in a series of operations mounted in the area to try to stabilize the Baltic States after the First World War. Several earlier raids had been mounted by the Royal Navy. The summer of 1919 had seen the Royal Navy attempting to blockade the Red Fleet in Kronstadt.

Slowly but surely, however, additional operations were undertaken that saw maritime air power become increasingly integrated into naval operations. That also meant recognizing that the improvised nature of maritime air power that emerged from the First World War needed to change. Rather than cannibalized merchant ships being adapted to carry aircraft, dedicated warships needed to emerge as a whole new class. The 1920s saw the first important steps taken to develop and build the second generation of aircraft carriers.

The first generation of aircraft carriers had provided some solutions to these issues but the aircraft themselves were still quite flimsy-looking machines. Operating in the rigours of the maritime environment surely required most robust airframes and engines to be developed. The irony is that one of the most successful aircraft to emerge from the Second World War was to be the Fairey Swordfish which at a superficial glance seemed to have inherited that air of vulnerability that was associated with the first generation of maritime aircraft.

In 1924 the Fleet Air Arm was created initially as part of the Royal Air Force. It took over responsibility for the aviation assets that were operating from aircraft carriers. The formation of the Fleet Air Arm appeared to recognize the unique operating environment of the global commons of the sea. Aircraft operating in a maritime environment needed to be thought of differently. In 1937 the responsibility for the Fleet Air Arm passed to the Admiralty.

In this period of time political moves designed to consign warfare to the history books took place. International conferences attempted to limit the size of warships and aircraft carriers. Targets for the overall tonnage of naval vessels were set. These had a temporary effect on the development of the Royal Navy but its increasing interest in maritime air power did not dwindle.

Japan also increased its efforts to build aircraft carriers. David Wragg's work highlights the development of vessels with both starboard and port-based islands to allow aircraft to be recovered more quickly to be refuelled and rearmed. Clearly the Japanese navy, fresh from its success at Tsushima, was moving on and adding aircraft carriers to its fleet of battleships. At this point three countries were moving quickly to integrate air power into their maritime operations: these were Japan, the United States and the United Kingdom. France, which in December 1911 had led the way with the development of the first seaplane carrier, had to focus its energies elsewhere. The clouds of war were gathering again over Europe and France had to focus on opposing the German build-up in the land and air environments.

The debate and arguments over the need for a separate Fleet Air Arm still occur today. As technologies have converged some commentators would argue that the specific issues of operating aircraft in the marine environment have all but gone away. Others counter that despite these developments flying over the sea is very different. That argument is likely to continue for some time yet.

Looking back on the First World War some states took the view that maritime air power was now an essential component of any form of military force. Germany and Italy were not so sure. For the Royal Navy the responsibilities of safeguarding the sea lanes of communications to the Empire meant that it had developed what might at the turn of the century be regarded as an almost unique viewpoint on the importance of maritime power. For it, adding capability that manifestly could help its situational awareness and ability to reach out and strike an enemy's maritime infrastructure was a natural evolution of power projection. The old days of sailing a gunboat into a harbour under sail and fire from shore batteries to attack an enemy fleet were over. Air power could now project power over the horizon.

For Germany and Italy, however, maritime air power had less attraction due to a number of factors. For Germany its geo-strategic situation meant that in the inter-war years it had to focus its resources on the development of the army and air force arms of its military forces. The navy, with the exception of the investment in battleships and submarines, was to play a limited role in any future war.

In Germany in the inter-war years the need for an aircraft carrier was rarely debated. To a great extent this was a legacy from the First World War, during which the German High Seas Fleet had largely been what is known in naval circles as a 'Fleet-in-being'. It had not stamped itself on the psyche of the nation except for a notable defeat of the Royal Navy at Coronel in November 1914.

The way in which this battle evolved was also to highlight the issues that arise when either side has limited intelligence information on the disposition of the other. That the Royal Navy knew of Admiral Spee's intention to conduct commerce raiding along the west coast of South America is a matter of history. Just where he intended to operate was a very different question. The huge German victory at Coronel was to be followed quickly by an equally resounding defeat at the Falkland Islands as the Royal Navy gained quick retribution for the disaster at Coronel. With maritime air power playing no role in either of these two major sea actions and the indecisive outcome of the Battle of Jutland it is hardly surprising that maritime air power did not feature highly in the Nazi military equipment plans.

Other countries, however, had appreciated the kind of vision expressed after Jutland by a young naval officer. The Japanese and Americans who both saw maritime power as a seriously important part of their overall capability pressed ahead with the development of maritime air power capabilities.

Ironically, in a foretaste of what was to come, the Japanese bombed and strafed the USS *Panay* in Nanking on 12 December 1937 as they pursued their campaign against the Chinese. The vessel sank at 15:54 with three people dead and twelve injured. The Japanese apologized for what they described as an accident. The Americans, however, were not convinced. Almost four years later to the day Japan attacked Pearl Harbor. The USS *Panay* was the first American warship to be sunk by air power alone.

Russia was, like Germany, preoccupied with its land-based situation and had suffered a major defeat at the hands of the Japanese at the Battle of Tsushima. It too was not to take an interest in the potential of aircraft carriers for many years to come.

Maritime Air Power in the Second World War

In the Battle of the River Plate the launch of the Fairey Seafox spotter aircraft from HMS *Ajax* during the battle helped gunnery officers correct for their fall of shot. While the *Graf Spee* was hardly damaged by the shells fired from the Royal Navy cruisers, the fact that it sustained some hits did force the captain to rethink. His run into Montevideo and the speed with which the Uruguayans made sure the pocket battleship departed all left him with little option but to scuttle the vessel.

During its own campaign before its demise at the River Plate the *Graf Spee* had also used its Arado 196 floatplane as a means of spotting vulnerable merchant vessels that would be useful targets. On 30 September 1939 that commerce raider had discovered the SS *Clements* and launched the Arado 196 to strafe the bridge in an attempt to prevent the crew from sending any signal to indicate they were under attack. In this case the Arado had no impact as the ship's crew did manage to send the 'RRR' signal.

The strategy employed by Captain Langsdorff also helped as he sought his prey in known shipping lanes, reducing the area of search required. The Arado was also launched as a self-protection measure when the *Graf Spee* met with its tanker the *Altmark* to replenish its fuel and food supplies. On at least one occasion the second airman on the Arado warned Captain Langsdorff of a Royal Navy cruiser in the area (in fact it was HMS *Cumberland*).

As the economic pressures caused by the presence of surface raiders in the Atlantic were compounded by the start of the U-boat attacks, the use of long-range Fokker Wolf reconnaissance aircraft to detect the convoys closing on the Western Approaches helped direct U-boat captains to their targets. One counter-measure to this was to deploy fighter aircraft on specially equipped merchant ships to fly single-launch missions to try to shoot down the reconnaissance planes.

Many examples emerge from the Second World War that illustrate the increasing contribution being made by air power in shaping the maritime environment, such as the attack conducted by the Swordfish aircraft from HMS *Ark Royal* on the battleship *Bismarck* or the strike by the Royal Navy Fleet Air Arm on the Italian Fleet at Taranto. History shows that this single action had a major effect on Japanese naval planners and led to the pre-emptive attack on Pearl Harbor. The loss of HMS *Prince of Wales* and HMS *Warspite* off the coast of Malaya to Japanese strike aircraft also showed how quickly the value of air power to destroy capital ships at sea was being recognized. Later on in the Second World War in the Pacific theatre of operations air power was to be used with decisive effect in the Battle of Midway.

The Falklands War

To say that the outcome of the Falklands War in 1982 depended upon maritime air power is to make a serious understatement. Unless another conflict breaks out between Argentina and the United Kingdom, which seems unlikely in the immediate future, the specific geo-strategic context in which air power played its role in that conflict will perhaps never occur again. The Falklands War provides the ultimate example of the application of maritime air power. Operating 8,000 miles from home with no overt local political support is arguably the ultimate challenge for maritime air power.

To project military power against an island in the South Atlantic that had been captured by an overwhelming military force whose homeland was barely a couple of hundred miles away and eject that occupying force against a backdrop of severely testing weather conditions was an amazing feat. This was also done under constant air attack. The loss of life and of Royal Navy warships meant that as ever in warfare the outcome was, to quote the task force commander Rear Admiral Sir Sandy Woodward, 'a close-run thing'. In a world where the use of language often tends to overstate the importance of an issue, this is a remarkable understatement.

To recapture the islands the task force had literally been thrown together in short order. The media coverage as key units departed from Portsmouth cast a shadow over the United Kingdom. This was not a task force deploying for a military exercise. The nation knew its servicemen and women were going to war.

Even a simplistic analysis of the problems facing the task force commander would have thrown up the problems of air attack. The geo-strategic context favoured the Argentinians. They also started to play the political instrument of power. When the meteorological extremes of the South Atlantic winter are just around the corner, prevarication is a good political and military tactic. To survive in such a harsh environment against a threat that might also employ stand-off missiles is a challenge.

Maritime air power arguably played a crucial role in the Falkland Islands campaign. The much-lamented Harrier force on board the two aircraft carriers deployed at the heart of the task force was able to perform two vital roles. These were ground-attack initially against fixed Argentinian positions, and after the landings at San Carlos Water in the close air-support role against fixed and mobile positions.

The Harriers also undertook the air defence role to help protect the fleet. In addition to the air threat the Argentinians did possess a small number of submarines. One feature of the campaign was the round-the-clock operations of Sea King helicopters pinging away with their sonar systems. This was not a covert mission. The threat from submarines to surface ships was amply illustrated by the sinking of the ARA *General Belgrano*.

Air power was also to play an important role in maintaining the supply lines to the task force as C-130 Hercules transport aircraft flew thousands of miles to drop vital equipment and people into the swells of the South Atlantic Ocean. A look down from underneath the canopy of a parachute to the freezing waters of the ocean below cannot have been an inviting sight. To place a Hercules into that area of the South Atlantic Ocean had involved undertaking a precarious in-flight refuelling operation with a Victor tanker that involved an unusual manoeuvre called tobogganing. This involved both aircraft flying at 230 knots and descending at a rate of 500ft per minute. On several occasions the manoeuvre was completed with barely 2,000 feet to spare before they ditched.

This was a manoeuvre developed in the cauldron of war when it became an operational imperative to deliver some cargos directly by air to the South Atlantic Ocean over a distance of around 4,000 miles. Due to the speed constraints on the Hercules each mission would last a day and involve three or four Victor aircraft and was fraught with danger. That no aircraft were lost in the course of Operation Corporate undertaking this re-supply mission is nothing short of miraculous.

It provides another in a seemingly never-ending list of examples of the flexibility of air power. The Hercules was bought as a tactical aircraft to operate in the confines of a land battle in Europe. With the end of the Cold War the aircraft have completed operations in many areas of the world, but it was never envisaged being flown over such strategic ranges for up to twenty-eight hours at a time.

With the sudden demise of the Nimrod fleet the C-130 is filling-in in the role of a maritime surveillance platform for the Royal Air Force while decisions on a future maritime patrol capability are discussed. The need for a Maritime Wide Area Surveillance (MWAS) capability may seem obvious to anyone who has studied the nascent beginnings of maritime air power. That rich history was overlooked as the SDSR (Strategic Defence and Security Review) was completed. The axing of the Nimrod makes no sense whatsoever in military terms, given the fantastic service it gave during its service life. It seems almost assured that common sense will prevail and the British armed forces will regain some form of MWAS capability. Some of that may come from unmanned aircraft and some from those that are manned, such as the Boeing P-8I.

Consolidating Air Power

In the 1990s and the first decade of the twenty-first century the way maritime air power has been applied has subtly shifted. In the effort against pirates off the coast of Somalia the helicopter has become the main means by which air power has been deployed. The helicopter provides the fast response required when vessels without security guards on board are under attack. Even then pirates adopting swarming tactics could overwhelm an on-board security team. The helicopter hovering nearby can provide the eyes on the target situation and help naval commanders shape an appropriate response. Experiments with unmanned aircraft and helicopter platforms may see the use of helicopters reduced at some point in the future.

Helicopters have also been a traditional platform for the prosecution of anti-submarine warfare. Their on-board sensor systems allow the detection of periscopes, and sonobuoys allow maritime air power to address an underwater threat. In the North Atlantic the Cold War envisaged air power being used to counter the activity of Soviet submarines trying to break out into the North Atlantic from their base in Murmansk. Military planners were prepared for a repeat of the Second World War Battle of the Atlantic as supply vessels bringing reinforcements from the United States would be attacked as they crossed the ocean.

To ensure the Soviet submarines were tracked and if necessary attacked as they tried to pass through the Iceland-Greenland Gap and the Iceland-Faroes Gap the Royal Navy was to deploy its anti-submarine-warfare ships, such as HMS *Illustrious* and her two sister vessels, to allow their helicopters to provide a means to detect, track and attack Soviet vessels. The Royal Air Force also had its Nimrod force of anti-submarine-warfare aircraft with nuclear-armed torpedoes ready to provide another means of deploying air power in the North Atlantic. It was all very reminiscent of the Sunderland flying boats attacking German U-boats, except that the types of weapons involved were somewhat different.

The Royal Navy played a huge part in projecting air power over the Balkans from warships such as HMS *Ark Royal* during the 1990s. Strike missions were called in against defined targets during the campaign to eject Serbian forces from Kosovo. This application of air power struggled against well dug-in Serbian positions. The much-heralded Revolution in Military Affairs found its nemesis in Kosovo. When an enemy decides to dig in and not move it removes 'emergent' targets from the battlefield. This has an impact on air power, whether it comes from the sea or from land bases, and is particularly important for maritime air power which often needs land-based air-to-air refuelling to support over-the-horizon strike missions. This was vital in the early days of the campaign in Afghanistan when ground bases had not been developed to a point where they were secure.

By the relatively simple application of camouflage techniques the Serbian military forces were able to deceive ISTAR assets. Similar results had been obtained by the Iraqis in the First Gulf War as they produced simple ways of mimicking the signature of a Scud Missile System, drawing expensive missile systems onto oil cans that had been set alight to look like the rocket motor of a Scud. Contacts between the Iraqis and the Serbians helped some of the ways of defeating ISTAR assets to be passed on, making the application of air power difficult.

One of the subtle changes that occurred was in the way maritime air power had to be applied. Instead of being launched to attack a specific target, aircraft took off to patrol a box. If targets emerged in that box, either detected by their on-board sensor systems or where threats were handed off by a dedicated ISTAR platform, it was their task to engage. This could be directly through the employment of a weapon or through a high-speed pass over the target to forewarn the enemy of what might happen if he were not to withdraw from a current engagement. This coercive effect of air power is often little appreciated. Its modern-day incarnation in the form of unmanned aircraft that persist over the battlefield is already showing specific effects upon enemy combatants.

In the early days over Afghanistan the sheer distances involved in flying maritime air power to a patrol box meant that aircraft were having to be refuelled several times to remain on station. The classic mission duration of the maritime strike aircraft operating in support of combat troops in the littoral changed dramatically. Instead of strike missions lasting up to two hours, pilots would be airborne for six to eight hours. As ground facilities became available in Afghanistan, the need for maritime air-strike diminished.

Over Libya in 2011 similar issues emerged but again with their own subtle overtones. Aircraft launched from airbases in Southern Europe again used airborne refuelling to remain for longer times on station. This was termed 'armed reconnaissance'. Unlike Afghanistan the jets did not have specific boxes to patrol. The situation on the ground was simply too fluid. The areas they patrolled were larger than the size of box defined in Afghanistan.

Over Libya aircraft on task could literally end up starting their mission at one end of the country and several hours later drop a weapon in a completely different area. One pilot likened the experience to flying halfway across Europe in the course of a flight while waiting for a target to emerge. Sometimes the need to refuel intervened and aircraft had to spend some time away from their designated patrol areas.

Given the fluidity of the battlefield it is hard not to conclude that the rather limited fleet of aircraft made available to the mission should have been reinforced earlier in the campaign. Belatedly, as the momentum stalled, additional aircraft were deployed. Even then, historians seeking to dissect the development of the campaign as the United States increasingly took a back seat after the initial two-week surge may find it hard not to conclude that European political leaders need to do far more to make sure that they have the resources available to properly conduct military missions on its periphery. Another important point also has to be borne in mind. While the United States stood back in Libya and Mali, it did provide important sources of intelligence to both operations, notably from space and air-based platforms. Even though the French operate their own constellation of Helios satellites to enable them to analyse potential targets on the ground, the United States Keyhole satellites still offer vital insights.

While the numbers of aircraft deployed to the UN-sanctioned mission looked reasonable on paper, political constraints on their operations significantly affected the air pace of the campaign. In the future if missions of that type are ever to be conducted again those restrictions will have to be removed. A small subset of countries cannot continue to bear the burden of delivering hard power while others join in the mission but end up contributing little of any military value.

Once the fixed assets on the ground in Libya had been removed from the target list the priority was to detect and target mobile threats in what was often a dynamic and highly confused situation. There were occasions where rebel forces and pro-regime elements were located in close proximity to each other. Applying air power in those situations where the threat of Man Portable Air Defence Systems (MANPADS) was always in the forefront of the minds of the pilots was difficult. Over the Balkans on a number of occasions bombing what were thought to be targets had tragic outcomes.

Air power in the form of strike capability appeared over Libya in two ways. One was provided by the fast jets such as the French Rafale and the Royal Air Force Tornado and Typhoon. The other came from the Tiger and Apache helicopters that flew from platforms such as HMS *Ocean*. They were able to engage both fixed and moving targets.

For the fast jets the situation placed a huge emphasis on their ability to network ISTAR assets and for on-board sensor systems to be capable of detecting and verifying potential targets. Maritime air power came from the French Rafales. Their location on board the French aircraft carrier *Charles de Gaulle* allowed them to be responsive. As threats were detected they could get airborne quickly. This highlighted a tactical deficiency in the maritime air power that the United Kingdom could bring to bear. It could not hold Harrier aircraft on station at sea ready to respond to emergent targets.

The swift retirement of HMS *Ark Royal* and the Harrier fleet as a result of the SDSR became the subject of a hotly-contested debate. The loss of its capabilities had an impact on the campaign. The five Apache helicopters deployed aboard HMS *Ocean* helped address some of the shortfall in capability that could have been available from HMS *Ark Royal*. Given the prominent role that the United Kingdom's aircraft carrier had undertaken off the coast of Kosovo, many siren voices took the opportunity to decry the outcome of the SDSR.

In practice the decision to retire the Harrier force came after detailed comparisons were undertaken by the United Kingdom Ministry of Defence into the utility of it versus the Tornado. Continuing investment in what was a difficult financial climate had allowed the Tornado fleet to be upgraded giving it greater military utility. The lack of investment in the Harrier meant that the outcome of the SDSR was inevitable. The Tornado was much better equipped to deliver precision strike. To give that capability to the Harrier would have required significant new investment in the aircraft and its weapons systems capabilities. It is therefore a moot point as to whether in practice the loss of HMS *Ark Royal* had an impact on the Libyan campaign. Indeed, the deployment of the Apache helicopters, while not acting as a replacement for the Harrier, certainly offered tactical air support to the operation under quite strict controls.

The use of the Tiger and Apache helicopters brought a new dimension to maritime strike. While their range restricted their operations to the first 100km of the coastline, their weapons-fit provided the capability to employ power in a measured way. The language of proportionate use of force is now something the military have to consider very carefully.

In a world where it would be very easy to portray some countries as being all too ready to throw their military weight around to achieve effect, air power has to be applied with increasing surgical precision. Images of dead children do not play well in the global media for a coalition trying to enact a United Nations Resolution. It gives those opposed to applying power in such ways verbal and visual ammunition.

One aspect of the Libyan campaign was the ability of the supporters of the regime in Tripoli to maintain a semblance of command and control. Mobile command and control nodes became a feature of the campaign, helping to extend its duration with clear political implications. Political leaders had gambled that the military intervention in Libya would be over quite quickly. As the campaign passed the significant milestone of 100 days all sorts of questions started to be raised about its efficacy. What had been trailed as a swift military intervention suddenly started to look like it was bogged down.

The word stalemate is one that must haunt every political leader's worst nightmares. At the beginning of June 2011 the global media was using that word almost hourly. Something needed to be done to break out. The answer came in deploying more assets into the campaign. This was something that political leaders had tried to avoid as it brought into direct scrutiny the consequences of recent austerity measures.

The Libyan campaign can be said to have been the first time that the proponents of the revolution in military affairs got it right. This was because of the military naivety of the pro-regime leaders and their commanders. They chose to ignore the superiority afforded by NATO's ISTAR capability and place their assets in harm's way.

The outcome, while it took time, was inevitable. The erosion of the military capability of the Libyan armed forces created an inevitable tipping-point. The seizure of the capital Tripoli in what was a brilliantly-executed manoeuvre with minimal bloodshed provided a model for how to topple a regime. That the fighting continued until the end of October simply highlighted the complex nature of the societal landscape against which the war was fought. Pro-regime strongholds, such as Sirte, were bound to try to hold out for as long as possible.

At the turn of the second decade of the twenty-first century the Royal Air Force, the Royal Navy and its counterpart in America will receive the F-35B Lightning aircraft. Its suite of on-board sensor systems will give it a new capability to provide close air support to friendly ground forces whatever their origin. The F–35B will be able to launch against emergent targets from one of the two aircraft carriers that the Royal Navy will be able to field at that point. Operating in tandem with the ISTAR platforms available from the Royal Air Force the F–35B will be capable of targeting an adversary's military equipment in the kind of fast-moving environment that emerged in Libya.

However, as everyone is well aware, it is not good to prepare to fight the last war. If any lessons are to be drawn from the thirty years of military operations from the Falklands to Libya, one would be to ensure that whatever military Order of Battle (ORBAT) that is developed needs to be flexible, agile and responsive. Once purchased, the military planners have obtained a capability. How that gets applied to address the specifics of a particular geo-strategic environment is crucial.

Throughout the SDSR process in the United Kingdom and similar austerity-driven measures across other European capitals and in Washington the elephants in the room were Iran and China. In a decade the geo-strategic picture may have started to come full circle. Military forces may no longer be required to operate against or in support of insurgents attempting to depose a regime. State-on-state warfare may re-emerge caused by conflicts over natural resources. The Arctic Sea, the Falkland Islands and the South China Sea are all locations where tensions over natural resources are growing almost daily. Any military confrontation in these areas will inevitably see maritime air power play a significant role.

Chapter Six

Air Power and Strategic Effect

The Zeppelin Campaign over Britain 1915–18

Of all the ways in which air power has been applied it is possible to argue that its strategic application has varied the most in its first century of use. History shows that the first recorded strategic use of a bomber was in fact a Zeppelin raid on Antwerp in August 1914. On this occasion eight bombs were dropped. The choice of Antwerp as the objective for such a mission reveals the importance of major harbours as possible targets.

The first time bombing from the air was used as part of a campaign to shape the resolve of the population occurred in the First World War. The sight of the huge Zeppelin airships floating over London was in itself quite frightening, but when the bombs also started to fall it is not difficult to imagine how that must have made the people under attack feel quite vulnerable. The airships were also well-equipped with machine guns to protect themselves from air attack. It took the invention of incendiary ammunition to tilt the balance away from the Zeppelins to the air defence fighters.

The strategic bombing role adopted by the Zeppelins was not their primary mission. The focus of most of their military activities in the First World War was on reconnaissance duties over the North Sea. When the German High Seas Fleet undertook its brief sorties into the North Sea to bombard a few coastal towns in East Anglia such as Lowestoft the Zeppelins would conduct a sweep of the southern regions of the North Sea to ensure the Royal Navy was not lying in wait.

In the war over 1,000 such patrols were undertaken, including a sweep prior to the departure of the German High Seas Fleet before the Battle of Jutland in 1916. With fifteen Zeppelins available the Germans were nearly able to maintain a constant patrol over the southern North Sea even in quite difficult weather conditions. The observers on board the Zeppelins became particularly adroit at detecting minefields that had been laid by the Royal Navy. They would then direct minesweepers into those areas to clear out the danger.

This was the genesis of the long-range maritime patrol mission conducted by aircraft such as the Catalina flying boat, the Sunderland, Shackleton, P3-C and Nimrod. From a strategic viewpoint its tasking was hugely important. Had the Royal Navy tried to carry out an ambush on the German High Seas Fleet the outcome could have been catastrophic.

In the First World War the impact of the Zeppelin attacks on London was minimal from a physical viewpoint. The Kaiser approved the first bombing of the United Kingdom on 19 January 1915. He specifically instructed that London should not be targeted. By the end of the war fifty-one raids had been conducted upon the United Kingdom by Zeppelin airships. This is a very low count as far as attacks are concerned. Due to operational limitations a number of planned raids by Zeppelins were cancelled or aborted before they reached their targets. High winds were a particular problem, as were cloud effects.

The initial focus was on military installations and port facilities. The first successful raid mounted by two Zeppelins was initially directed to attack the Humber. High winds diverted the attack to the south and bombs were dropped on Great Yarmouth, Sheringham and King's Lynn on the coast of East Anglia. The rapid introduction of the blackout soon reduced the effectiveness of such raids. This limited the areas in which Zeppelins could drop their bombs.

During the war the restrictions were gradually loosened allowing a greater diversity of targets to be engaged. In February 1915 the Kaiser permitted attacks on the docklands area of London. Attacks planned in March and April ran into problems with the weather. The Zeppelins also suffered some losses as airships crashed, depleting the fleet. It took the introduction of the new P-class Zeppelins in May 1915 to allow the attacks to be carried out on London.

The P-class Zeppelins were able to fly 2,760nm at an average cruising speed of close to 60 mph. They were driven by four engines in contrast to the three of the pre-war M-class variants. The P-class was designed to operate over twice the distance of the M-class and to carry a greater payload at 1,600kg of bombs. They also had two gondolas. The control cabin was at the front which also had a single engine. The rear gondola housed the remaining three engines. Their operating ceiling was close to 10,000ft which allowed the air-crew of eighteen to avoid having to specifically breathe oxygen. Their length of 163.5m and diameter of 18.7m made them an awesome sight.

The first P-class Zeppelin to fly was given a constructor's designation of LZ 54. When it went into service it was given the designation L 19. It was operated by the Imperial German Navy. Initially the L 19 was deployed in a reconnaissance role over the North Sea. On 31 January 1916 the L 19 took part in a large-scale raid on various targets in the United Kingdom. Nine Zeppelins were allocated to the raid in total.

On the German side hopes were high that this new type of Zeppelin would prove a most effective platform from which to bring the war to the heart of England. It is important to recall that in those days the British press were often less than candid about the difficulties being experienced by the troops on the Western Front. Casualties were often brought back in secret to military hospitals and kept away from prying eyes. By using the Zeppelin the Germans hoped to bring the reality of war home to the British public. The outcome of this raid, however, was to divide British public opinion for a very different reason and was to leave a legacy that the German propaganda machine could exploit for many years to come.

After take-off from their base in Tondern the Zeppelins quickly encountered a huge fog bank over the North Sea. Thick snow and rain over the English coast separated the force. The L 19 reached Burton upon Trent and dropped some of her payload over the city before heading south to Birmingham to release the remaining bombs. In total the nine Zeppelins killed sixty-one people and injured a further 101.

As the L 19 tried to return to Germany the aircraft experienced multiple engine failures. The last signal sent by the L 19 confirmed that only one of the four engines was functioning. The L 19 was not alone in this predicament. Four of the nine P-class Zeppelins had experienced engine failures on the raid.

On the return leg L 19 flew low over The Netherlands where ground troops fired upon the airship. It then drifted out to sea where it ditched with the loss of all the crew. The incident became famous as after the airship had gone into the water a lone British trawler called the *King Stephen* fishing illegally in the area came across the crew and refused to save them.

When the incident was eventually reported in the press it created a huge schism in public opinion. Some argued that the captain of the vessel was obliged to save the German crew. Others took a different view, praising the actions of the captain in making the safety of his crew his primary concern. The incident was used by the German propaganda machine to good effect. It was one of the first examples of a tactical situation developing into an outcome with strategic consequences. It was to resurface again in a similar vein as the Nazis used the event for their own propaganda in the Second World War.

The problem for the Zeppelins was always that of the accuracy with which they could drop their bombs. Cloud cover over the target was a frequent issue. If the Zeppelins flew in low they were vulnerable to attack by ground-based anti-aircraft guns. As the capabilities of British fighters improved after 1915, so the Zeppelins had to fly higher. This had a knock-on effect on the accuracy with which they could deliver their weapons. Over the Balkans eighty years later NATO aircraft operating at 15,000ft to stay outside the engagement zones of the Serbian Surface-to-Air Missiles experienced exactly the same problems.

The First Iteration: The Gotha Attacks

By the end of the First World War the impact of the Zeppelins had been minimal. While the death toll was small, it was nonetheless visible. By 1916 it was realized that the Zeppelins were not having a great deal of impact. The Germans embarked upon the development of what was initially called the 'K' or *Kampfflugzeug* aircraft. This was to be a bomber. In this role it was to be renamed the 'G' or *Großflugzeug*. This was to be used over the United Kingdom in 1917 as part of Operation Turkenkreuz (Turkish Cross).

The Gotha G.IV bomber became available in March 1917. It was a huge biplane with a wingspan of 78ft. It was driven by two 260hp Mercedes D IV engines and could fly to a range of 500 miles carrying a bomb load of up to 1,000lb. It was manned by three airmen. It was to be the forerunner of an even larger plane called the R-plane, prototypes of which had already been used over the Eastern Front in 1915. The R-planes were, however, to take some time to develop.

To carry out operations over the United Kingdom thirty Gotha G.IV bombers were based at airfields in Belgium as part of *Kampfgeschwader 3* located at Ghistelles after British air-raids had disrupted operations at other airbases in the area. The first attack mounted by the Gotha G.IV occurred on 25 May 1917. Twenty-three bombers departed to attack London. Over the North Sea two were forced to return due to mechanical problems.

Weather over London prevented the attack being driven home and the formation attacked the secondary target at Folkestone and the army camp at Shorncliffe. A total of 113 people were killed at the two sites and nearly 300 injured. As the bombers returned to Belgium, they were engaged by nine Sopwith Pups from the Royal Navy Air Service (RNAS). One bomber was shot down. Two weeks later the Gothas returned to attack Sheerness. They had to wait until the third attack before they could bomb London on

13 June. In that daylight air-raid on London 162 people died and 432 were injured.

For some historians this raid marked a turning-point in the application of air power. Eighteen schoolchildren died when their primary school was demolished by a single bomb. No Gothas were shot down during this raid. There must have been those at the time who had thought that the end of the Zeppelin raids meant that death and destruction would no longer be visited upon the streets of London. Sadly that view was unrealistic.

Attempted intercepts of the raids by the Royal Flying Corps had largely been unsuccessful as the Gotha's ceiling was above that of the ninety-two fighters launched to counter the raid. The idea that the bomber would 'always get through' would have started to gain some traction at this point.

However, for a while air defence tactics developed in their capabilities and as a result the Gothas did suffer losses. On 19 May 1918 a raid of thirty-eight Gothas saw six shot down. Many also suffered major damage on landing due to being tail-heavy. The loss rates were unsustainable. An initial switch to night-time bombing raids occurred. The first night raid involved four Gothas in an attack upon Chatham. This saw 132 naval recruits killed and ninety-six injured. It was a devastating blow.

However, mercifully, that was to be an unusual event. Most attacks suffered from navigation issues. Locating the target accurately to bomb it successfully also proved difficult at night, even when flying at lower altitudes. The German high command realized the impact of the Gotha attacks was minimal and they were withdrawn. The bombers were assigned to tactical duties along the Western Front. In total in twenty-two raids the Germans lost sixty-one Gotha G.IV aircraft while dropping 84,730kg of bombs.

The stage had been set for a more serious development of strategic air power. The idea of using bombers as a terror weapon to coerce a population into surrender had been born. In Guernica in the Spanish Civil War it was to see its first serious incarnation. From an historical viewpoint this marked the point at which air power took its first tentative steps to becoming an integrated part of a state's ability to project power militarily. In Poland a small matter of months later the lessons learnt from the Spanish Civil War were to be applied with ruthless efficiency.

The Origins of Terror Bombing

Without resorting to precise semantic definitions it is possible to offer the view that the first serious application of air power in a strategic context was over London when the Zeppelins appeared in 1915. Their limited bomb–carrying capabilities meant that their achievements, if indeed they can be accorded any military value, were extremely limited. Paradoxically their impact was primarily psychological and indeed it can be argued led to fierce debates in the post–war period when many commentators believed that the bomber would become the most important weapon of war.

In the early 1930s the prevailing view was that the bomber would 'always get through'. These were exactly the words used by the British Prime Minister Stanley Baldwin in a speech he made on 9 November 1932. Indeed, he went further, saying that 'I think it is well for the man in the street to realise that there is no power on earth that can protect him.' In the early 1930s as the inevitability of a second conflagration with Germany had yet to dawn on many in the United Kingdom it was a viewpoint that at the time went virtually unreported.

The speech marked a turning-point in his views on the likelihood of a coming war with Germany. His new-found enthusiasm for the bomber had been down in part to some serious lobbying by the head of the Royal Air Force, Sir Hugh Trenchard. He had advocated that the way to win wars in the future was to invest in bombers and not fighters. The debates in the United Kingdom had, however, found their genesis in the writings of an Italian.

It was a time when the ideas developed in 1921 by the Italian General Giulio Douhet in his book *Command of the Air* were in vogue. His thinking was also supported by Air Marshal, and soon to be Secretary of Air, Italo Balbo. He masterminded the development of the Italian Air Force in the 1920s. Support was also forthcoming from Benito Mussolini, Italy's fascist dictator. He had seen at first hand how the British had used air power in Mesopotamia in the early part of the 1920s. In 1929 the Italian Air Force applied some of these ideas when they swiftly overwhelmed the defences of Emperor Haile Selassie of Abyssinia.

The nascent Ethiopian Air Force had been a specific pet project of the Emperor after he had witnessed a demonstration of British air power in Aden in 1922. At the Battle of Anchem in March 1930 the Emperor was to unleash his small aircraft against his own people as two rival factions of the Ethiopian royal family battled for control of the country. This was one of the first recorded military actions where air power was used to have a psychological effect on the population.

As the small Potez 25 aircraft of the Ethiopian Air Force flew low over the battlefield they were to release bombs and not leaflets. Two days earlier they had dropped a number of specially-prepared leaflets warning the rebels of the consequences of their actions. The swift change from leaflet to bombs had the desired effect. Douhet's ideas were being confirmed in battle.

The aviator Billy Mitchell was also enamoured by Douhet's thinking, often writing and speaking in the United States of the invulnerability of the bomber. For writers like Mitchell the bomber took warfare to a new level enabling populations en masse to be terrorized from the air. Their eventual part in urging their national governments to capitulate was all but guaranteed.

In Germany Douhet's thinking was also advocated by the Chief of the Luftwaffe General Staff, Walther Wever. He was instrumental in shaping Nazi Germany's development of the Junkers 89 and the Dornier 19. In his writings Wever outlined his five key points about air strategy. They were:

- To destroy the enemy air force by bombing its bases and aircraft factories and defeating any enemy aircraft that were engaged in attacking German targets
- To prevent the movement of large numbers of enemy forces to what he called 'decisive areas' by destroying communications links such as roads and railways, with a specific emphasis on bridges and tunnels
- To support army operations through participating in air-to-ground operations
- To support naval operations by attacking an enemy's naval bases
- To paralyse the enemy by stopping production in armament factories.

Wever's ideas were not to survive his death in an air accident in 1936 at the age of 48. His plans to build a strategic air force were quickly consigned to the rubbish bin as other strategists like Ernst Udet and Hans Jeschonnek advocated a different approach based on smaller aircraft. The resulting development of the Heinkel He 111, Dornier Do 17 and Junkers Ju 88 provided a far less capable bomber force. The Junkers Ju 52 transports did, however, provide a hugely important strategic airlift during a critical period for the Nationalists.

Over the period from July to October 1936 the impact of flying 13,000 troops and over 50,000lb of equipment over the narrow Straits of Gibraltar had a huge strategic impact. It literally ensured that the Nationalist revolution did not collapse. This intervention was the first time in history that a complete army was moved by air into a war zone. That scale of air-drop was only matched five years later over Crete when the Germans conducted one of the largest airborne parachute drops. That operation, of course, was only possible because the Germans had first and foremost established air superiority over the area.

While in the Spanish Civil War and the early days of the Second World War the Luftwaffe proved more than adequate for the task, once they faced the Royal Air Force in the Battle of Britain their limitations became apparent. Had Wever been alive to put into action his plans, the conduct of the strategic bombing campaign against the United Kingdom during the Blitz may have been very different. Its outcome could also quite possibly have resulted in the prolonging of the war. While Wever subscribed to Douhet's thinking on the power of the bomber, he did not accept the idea that the population should be the target. Wever's focus was on the facilities by which an enemy could wage war.

At the height of the Battle of Britain the shift of focus from bombing the RAF airfields to the start of the Blitz was decisive. This was a departure from Douhet's teachings. One of his overriding concerns was that in conflict air superiority should be established by first bombing an adversary's airbases. It was something the Israeli Air Force did not forget in 1967.

The novelist H.G. Wells who made his name in writing science fiction also delved into the issues associated with air power. The film entitled *Things to Come* which he produced in 1936 provided a highly prescient view of a war which involved devastating air attacks on a place called 'Anytown'. His implication that the population would be the 'centre of gravity' of any forthcoming war was to cross the bridge from fiction to reality in a matter of five years.

Shooting down bombers seemed an almost impossible task. Operational analysis gurus looked into the issues and concluded that the rate of fire of any air interceptor had to be at a level beyond that which was available. The move to equip the Spitfires and Hurricanes that took part in the Battle of Britain with guns in their wings was crucial. Parallel operation of the guns was sufficient to have the desired impact on the Luftwaffe bombers. Their installation and subsequent use was crucial to the final outcome.

Analysis conducted after the war essentially showed that Baldwin's ideas were right. By and large during the Blitz and Bomber Command's efforts against Germany the bombers did get through. Bomber Command losses on average were 2 per cent per mission. Of itself that was not unsustainable. Douhet's thinking was right on one count, but he and those who supported his apocalyptic view of the impact of bombing were wrong when it came to the resilience of populations.

Since then, only disrupted in a single brief moment during the Cuban Missile Crisis when the world stood on the edge of a nuclear abyss, the potential strategic application of air power has declined. While in the Cold War bombers such as the British V–Force and the United States Strategic Air Command had an ability to deploy air power to have strategic effect, mercifully that was never employed.

This prevailing view on the invulnerability of the bomber was finally laid to rest after Gary Powers, flying a U–2 photographic intelligence mission over Russia, was shot down and captured. While the precise events that led to Powers being intercepted were in some ways fortunate, the Russians had been gradually developing their air defence systems capability. On that day those who advocated the bomber as the principal weapon of war had to take stock. As the Russian air defence systems improved, so the nuclear-armed V–Force operated by Bomber Command became increasingly vulnerable.

A report published at the time suggested that each V–Bomber trying to enter Russian airspace in a time of conflict would encounter at least six possible engagements with air defence missiles. Each engagement had a 75 per cent probability that the bomber would be destroyed.

For a while the solution was to employ the stand-off weapon system called Blue Steel. It would penetrate the final air defence rings around the major targets once the V–Force had got through the first layers of the defence system. Blue Steel only remained in service for seven years. Its withdrawal and replacement by the submarine-based nuclear ballistic missile Polaris put the last nail in the coffin of the idea that the bomber would always get through.

As Liberal-minded populations throughout the western world argued there must be a better way, so the manoeuvre room in which strategic air power can be applied has become constrained. It was only against the backdrop of total industrial warfare that strategic air power could be applied. This was a war without limits.

The Bomber Will 'Always Get Through'

They are one of a range of possible targets that could be regarded as strategic in nature. In simple terms a strategic target is anything that once destroyed has an impact on the campaign that is felt at the highest levels of a warring state. In simple terms their loss is so serious as to threaten the ability of the state to continue to conduct its military operations. In the Second World War strategic bombing was one of the crucial ways in which warfare was conducted, even though its effectiveness as an instrument of war is still a matter for debate.

In Spain in the 1930s the application of air power was still in its nascent stages, albeit that the Spanish Civil War did allow the Nazis to test out some of their emerging doctrine and concepts. Of all the events in the Spanish Civil War the attack on the small town of Guernica provided the most graphic evidence of what was to follow.

In January 1937 Lieutenant Colonel Wolfram von Richthofen, a distant cousin of the famous 'Red Baron' of First World War fame was appointed Chief of Staff to the Condor Legion that Nazi Germany had sent to Spain to assist the Nationalists. Von Richthofen was an avid believer in the power of aerial bombardment. He was specifically enthusiastic about its application in close conjunction with infantry and artillery.

His ruthless application of these ideas was encapsulated in what he called his 'golden rule' of bombing. Far from having due regard for the civilian population and avoiding collateral damage, his view was that even if cloud cover prevented the careful identification of the target, the bomber crews should drop their weapons anyway. If civilian casualties occurred that was simply a by-product of war.

Von Richthofen's view was simple: for every bomb dropped on the civilian population or military forces, the campaign would move closer to a positive outcome. He even developed the idea of a racetrack system where wave after wave of bombers would hit the same target relentlessly. Those that had dropped their payload would be returning to base to refuel and rearm while the next wave was inbound to the target. This tactic was simply designed to wear down the will of the defenders and to give them no respite.

It is a measure of the ad hoc nature of the approach that little thought was ever given to fitting the Ju 52 transports that were used as bombers with a bomb-aiming system. Once over the target area the air-crew were to release their bombs and then fly back to their bases to rearm. This was not in any way a sophisticated application of air power. What took place on 26 April 1937 at Guernica was to send a warning to anyone harbouring any doubts about what was to happen on the mainland of Europe.

The attack on Guernica was ordered by Von Richthofen. It was to be called Operation Rügen. The raid would be led by four He 111 aircraft supported by all three squadrons of Ju 52s, a total of twenty-three bombers. The bombers would be armed with a mix of high explosives and incendiaries. The total payload carried was 50 tons. They would be supported by Bf 109 aircraft which would also conduct strafing runs over the target area. After the raid Von Richthofen visited the town and noted that the bridge which had been the target for the raid remained intact. The rest of the town of Guernica, however, lay in ruins. The picture of the same name painted at the time by Pablo Picasso still conveys the horrors of what happened inside the town.

While Von Richthofen regarded the attack as a success, many media outlets quickly portrayed it as something very different. This was something akin to genocide. The newspapers were quick to highlight the importance of Guernica from a historical viewpoint to the Basque nation. It was the home of the 'Holy Oak', a symbol of the Basque nation. The town, the media ventured, had been singled out because of its importance to the Basques. Eye-witnesses at the time noted the indiscriminate nature of the attacks. Von Richthofen's 'golden rule' was applied to the letter.

The strafing attacks that followed up the bombing were equally indiscriminate, killing women and children in the market place. Sadly the day selected for the attack was market day. While initial estimates of the dead ranged from 500 to over 1,600, subsequent analysis showed that 300 had died on that fateful day. This, however, was only the starter. The main course was yet to come.

When blitzkrieg was unleashed on the ill-prepared people and military of Poland in 1939 it followed the same genre of applying air power which had occurred in the Spanish Civil War. And on 14 May 1940, a little over three years after Guernica, the Luftwaffe carried out a major attack on the port of Rotterdam. This had by now been labelled by some military writers as terror-bombing; for the German high command it was a strategic target that needed to be seized.

Pictures published after the raid show the scale of destruction. Only the St Lawrence Church remains standing in an area flattened by the bombing. It remained as the only surviving building that was reminiscent of Rotterdam's medieval architecture. The attack had been personally authorized by Adolf Hitler in his directive 'Weisung Nr. 11'. Impatient at the lack of military progress his directive called for the Luftwaffe to 'facilitate the rapid fall of the Fortress Holland'.

General Schmidt was tasked with achieving this success and planned a combined assault on the area on 14 May. He requested air support to his scheme of ground manoeuvre. His request for a precise attack was changed by the Luftwaffe high command in Luftflotte 2. Instead of getting a *Gruppe* of twenty-five aircraft he was allocated Heinkel He 111 bombers which conducted carpet bombing raids over the target area. Realizing the situation, General Schmidt tried to persuade the Dutch commander of the city, Colonel Scharroo, to surrender. He felt that a raid of this size may persuade the Dutch to stand aside. Scharroo refused the offer and tried to draw out negotiations.

The time for the air-raid had originally been set for just after 13:00 Dutch time. Sensing the Dutch would soon capitulate, General Schmidt agreed to postpone the ultimatum until 16:20. That decision, however, was not immediately relayed to the air command. At the allocated time ninety bombers from *Kampfgeschwader 54* arrived over the city and started their bombing runs. Just too late to stop the first bombs landing on the city, a radio message got through to the flight leader who called off the attack.

However, another formation that had arrived over the city a few moments later did not receive the abort signal. Due to poor visibility over the target, flares launched by German forces on the ground to warn off the bombers were also not observed. A total of 1,150 50kg bombs and 158 250kg bombs were dropped on the residential part of the city. The uncontrollable fires created a firestorm that consumed the city.

Although detailed casualty figures have never been established it is generally agreed that 1,000 people died and 85,000 were made homeless. The situation was made worse by the nature of the buildings in the area which burned easily. In total 2.6 sq km of the city was laid waste and nearly 25,000 homes destroyed. In addition sixty-two schools, nearly 800 warehouses and twenty-four churches were also completely destroyed. For the people of the city on the verge of surrender this was a terrible price to pay for delaying tactics and poor communications in the German high command.

Prior to the outbreak of the Second World War the British had developed elements of air power to enable them to maintain their Empire but it would be difficult to describe much of what went on in the 1920s and 1930s as strategic in terms of the application of air power. Certainly maintaining the Empire was a strategic necessity at the time, but that was done using many instruments of power. Air power played a really small part. This led to a weak initial response by the British at the outbreak of war in 1939, and directly bombing citizens was simply not authorized. Target sets would remain military and industrial complexes linked to the Nazi war machine.

Within twenty-four hours of the bombing of Rotterdam all that changed. The first RAF raid on the interior of Germany took place on the night of 15–16 May 1940. This was to be the first step in what would be a long effort to demoralize and eventually defeat Nazi Germany using strategic bombing.

As the war came to a close the Americans were to try to use similar tactics over Tokyo. Aside from the famous 'Doolittle Raid' in retaliation for the attack on Pearl Harbor, Japan's geographic dominance of its region was so complete that the Americans had no foothold from which to launch any air attacks.

As the war in the Pacific turned against Japan and the Americans seized bases such as the Mariana Islands, their ability to bring the war to the people of Japan changed. Strategic bombing of Japan started in 1944. The first attacks on Tokyo began in November. The initial results appeared to have little impact. The raids conducted at altitudes of around 30,000ft did not seem to have any military value.

General Curtis LeMay changed the tactics and ordered the bombers to carry out their raids at altitudes between 4,500 and 8,000ft. He also directed that more incendiary devices should be used to take advantage of the predominantly wooden construction of Japanese homes.

As the war against mainland Japan was stepped up, LeMay received a list of thirty-three Japanese cities that needed to be attacked in order to pave the way for an invasion of Japan. In looking through the list and realizing the magnitude of the task, LeMay is reported to have observed that he thought that 'for the first time strategic air bombardment faces a situation where its strength is proportionate to the magnitude of its task.'

He went on to say that 'I feel that the destruction of Japan's ability to wage war lies within the capacity of this command, provided its maximum effort is exerted unstintingly during the next six months.' Comments like this from a senior advocate of air power are rare. LeMay understood the magnitude of the task he was being asked to fulfil. Putting thirty-three cities out of action using conventional bombing techniques is not easy. Over the coming months 6,690 B-29 sorties dropped 41,592 bombs on some of Japan's major cities. They also conducted psychological operations, dropping millions of leaflets trying to persuade the Japanese to surrender. In total 94 sq miles of cities were flattened; fifty-six of these in Tokyo. LeMay lost 136 of his aircraft; an overall loss rate of 2 per cent.

Such was the effort put into that achievement by LeMay's air force that one of its commands, XXI Bomber Command, ran out of incendiaries. Other issues were to dog the campaign against the cities which involved assets being taken away for other more important short-term tasking.

The first raid to follow this new focus on attacking centres of population took place in February 1945 and comprised 174 B-29 bombers. This destroyed around 1 sq mile of Tokyo. Given that today Tokyo occupies an area of over 5,000 sq miles, even this new tactic was going to take time to have an effect. A follow-up raid took place on the night of 9–10 March in what was known as Operation Meetinghouse. Of the 334 B-29s in the attack, 279 released approximately 1,700 tons of bombs resulting in the destruction of 16 sq miles of the city.

Over 100,000 people are thought to have died in the firestorm that followed. This was later revised downwards by a United States bombing survey to 88,000. This is a greater casualty level than either of the atomic bomb attacks that were to follow in August 1945. To this day the final death toll in the Tokyo firestorm is the subject of debate.

One historian, Richard Rhodes, has suggested that the death toll was close to 100,000 people but that nearly a million were injured and made homeless. Other commentators, such as Mark Selden, have suggested the actual figures could be much higher. In an article in *Japan Focus* Selden posits that with an average of 103,000 citizens per square mile, an estimated 1.5 million citizens could have been directly affected by the raid.

The situation was also compounded by the prevailing weather conditions which created walls of fire to block the escape of those who were fleeing the area. Its place at the top of the list of those killed in attacks on urban and built-up areas makes it the single deadliest air-raid of the Second World War. By the end of the war 50 per cent of Tokyo had been reduced to rubble.

After this attack the United States Air Force switched to raids against mainly industrial targets. On 2 April 1945 100 B-29 aircraft bombed the Nakajima aircraft factory. A day later 68 B-29s bombed the Koizumi aircraft factory, and 101 B-29 bombers returned to the Nakajima facility on 7 April.

Arguably the two nuclear attacks represent the pinnacle of the application of strategic bombing as a means of influencing the population. Within days the Japanese leadership agreed to the end of the Second World War. What had started in Rotterdam in May 1940 came to a close over Tokyo nearly five years later. In that time countless thousands of people had died. It is unlikely that any time soon historians will stop the debate on the morality of such attacks or their military effectiveness.

Fire-Bombings

The bombing of Dresden and Hamburg in Germany and Coventry, the major dock areas of Liverpool, Bristol and Southampton, and the blitz over London were all elements of possibly the most comprehensive strategic air campaign in history. The aim was both to target the population directly and through death and destruction reduce their will to fight, and by targeting the dock areas restrict the flow of vitally-needed food supplies into the United Kingdom. This was designed to have a strategic effect. But what does that actually mean in practice?

German target selection for their use of air power in the Second World War saw bombs falling across the United Kingdom. The bombing of RAF airfields in southern England during the Battle of Britain was a tactical application of air power. The aim was to put those airfields out of action. They were in effect point targets. With them disabled, the effectiveness of the RAF in mounting operations against the Luftwaffe would inevitably decrease.

That was a tactical effect that also had an operational significance. Even today a grey area exists between the tactical and operational application of air power. In Afghanistan during the years when countering the insurgency was the priority there is no clear distinction between the two.

Over London and other major United Kingdom cities in the Second World War the strategic application had one motivation: to force or coerce the population into telling the political leaders to sue for peace. Due to what has been described as the indomitable spirit of the population of Great Britain and Northern Ireland, the desired strategic effect was never achieved. If anything most historians suggest it hardened the resolve of the people. This was not a factor that seemed to be grasped by many of those who advocated the use of strategic bombing campaigns.

Ironically perhaps the low point came as the end game for the Second World War seemed to be in everyone's grasp. The development and use of the V-1 and the V-2 weapons did have an impact upon the populations which could be regarded as strategic, but that was more about timing and the people's desire to see the end of the war.

While Bomber Command's reaction in attacking German cities was an understandable tit-for-tat, there is little evidence that they also sought to attack the docks and allied infrastructure in Germany. Their reliance on imported food was, of course, very different from the case in the United Kingdom. Bomber Command's target base inside Germany focused on the Ruhr as the industrial heartland of the country as well as a number of major cities.

Bomber Command's efforts over Germany have been extensively researched and written about. There is little that can be added to the literature base that already exists over the scale of losses and the evaluation of its impact. There are, however, two areas worthy of note. Harris was keen on Operational Analysis (OA). Indeed, his use of data collected from the missions pioneered a lot of what is routinely viewed as statistical analysis over trends in contemporary military campaigns. OA is now a given in places like Afghanistan.

For Harris, however, the analysis of the losses was to provide important insights. It allowed him to conduct exercises that looked at how best bombers should fly in formation to provide defence against the Luftwaffe. The arcs of fire of the various gunners on bombers could be factored into how that formation could best operate to provide self-defence. Before the introduction of the long-range fighters like the P-51 the bombers lost their fighter protection when they were engaged on long-range missions. Self-defence therefore became an important consideration. That was not the only way in which ideas were applied. There were others.

One of these occurred when it became apparent that a radar system installed on the Lancaster bombers to detect Luftwaffe night-fighters was actually being used to home in on the aircraft. This was the first of a series of steps taken in the electronic warfare field that would provide the basis for modern-day efforts at suppressing the effectiveness of enemy air defence systems. Harris and Bomber Command were to prove that despite their focus on the application of air power, they could adapt their tactics.

The use of jamming aircraft to accompany raids was another innovation, as was the introduction of chaff or window to confuse German radar systems. These measures started what today is known as the measure-counter-measure cycle where one innovation is countered by another in a never-ending battle for supremacy of the electronic spectrum.

Perhaps of all the raids conducted in the Second World War for strategic effect the Dambusters raid on 16–17 May 1943 is the most famous. The aim of trying to destroy three of the largest dams supplying water to the Ruhr Valley was novel. It was not a direct attack on the industry itself but an oblique or indirect attack against one of its major resources. Industry needed water to operate. If the dams could be breached then German industrial output must surely be affected.

Historians may still debate the efficacy of the arguments over the raid by 617 Squadron which cost eight air-crews their lives, but one point is difficult to deny. At a time when arguments raged over the effectiveness of the strategic bombing due to the obvious poor accuracies that were being achieved, the precision and daring with which 617 Squadron pressed home their attack could not be faulted.

The fact that to this day they still create highly-polarized reactions among historians suggests that the specific application of strategic air power in the Second World War did not have the effect that some of its strongest proponents might suggest. It is therefore worth exploring some of the history of what we might now refer to as strategic air power, even though at the time some might argue it was applied at either the operational or tactical level.

Of all the raids mounted by Bomber Command the attack on Dresden on the night of 13–14 February 1945 ranks as one of the most controversial. Dresden was a cultural centre in Germany that had first been established in 1458. On the day of the attack its population of 642,000 had been swelled by an additional 200,000 refugees and injured servicemen. Children who had initially been sent away from the city to its outskirts in case of bombing had only recently returned.

The general sense of the people in Dresden was that it was unlikely the city would be attacked. They of course could not know that at the Yalta Conference the three Allied leaders had agreed it would be the subject of a major raid. Stalin had been quite insistent that Dresden should be a target.

The first wave appeared over Dresden at 10.15 pm. The city was cloud-free and seemingly unaware of what was about to unfold. It was followed by a second attack that started at 1.21 am. The air-crews involved reported that anti-aircraft fire from the defences around the city was largely ineffective. Such was the intensity of the firestorm that engulfed the city that at one point temperatures at its heart rose to 1,500°C.

On the night 796 Lancaster bombers and nine Mosquito Pathfinders dropped a total of 1,478 tons of high explosive and 1,182 incendiaries. The next day the United States Air Force returned to follow up the previous night's attack, dropping 771 tons of high explosives.

The pictures taken of Dresden after the attack showed the scale of destruction of the city. From the images alone the echoes of Coventry in the Blitz are easily recalled. In total and unrestricted warfare only the people suffer. When human beings witness events of such fury, even hardened wartime leaders can be affected. Even Churchill was moved to express his regret at the scale of the devastation in an internal memorandum which he wrote days after the attack. Even he in his private moments must have questioned the military utility of the raid on Dresden. He was not alone in holding those views.

After the end of the Second World War the idea of terror-bombing took on a very different hue. The atomic bomb attacks in Japan had been clearly used as a weapon of coercion. The Japanese surrender in the aftermath of the second attack on Nagasaki showed just what the power of nuclear weapons could achieve. Atomic bombs, however, were not to be the last stage in the development of nuclear weapons.

The development and testing of the H-Bomb was to increase the destructive power that could be unleashed by such weapons to unimaginable levels. With the Russians conducting a test of what was labelled a 'Doomsday Weapon' that yielded the equivalent of 50 megatons of explosives, the idea of strategic bombing took on a whole new meaning. With weapons of that destructive power, whole cities could be obliterated in an instant.

This was a truly terrifying situation. No longer would bombers return night after night to a target to try to level an area of a city. In one single raid hundreds of thousands of people could die. Such atomic weapons brought a whole new meaning to the notion of a terror-bombing. This required some new thinking and doctrine writers had to retire to their desks to think through the implications of such weapons being available. The result, possibly ironically, was to reduce the likelihood of war. It now became unthinkable. Or did it?

For those who were happy to rest on their doctrinal laurels over the emergence of the idea of Mutual Assured Destruction (MAD), the Cuban Missile Crisis probably gave them a harsh reminder of the reality of the world's political landscape. Capitalism and communism faced off over a small island a few miles off the coast of the United States. In the end the Soviet leadership blinked.

A solution was found and the United States and the Soviet Union came to a sensible compromise that avoided a nuclear confrontation. That the Soviets blinked first was to rankle with some of their leadership. Some commentators suggested that at the time the Soviets were unsure of their ability to emerge from such a nuclear exchange as victors, whatever that would actually mean in practice.

What followed from the events in October 1962 was a massive build-up in Soviet nuclear capabilities. If the world returned to another nuclear precipice, next time the Soviets would be better equipped. Paradoxically that simply embedded the reliance upon MAD to safeguard the security of the world. Historians will no doubt debate the efficacy of such an approach for many years to come.

As the world's security landscape became more dominated by MAD a change of emphasis occurred in the ways in which air power was seen. Tactical applications of air power in many far-off parts of the world such as Oman became the main focus. In the 1960s against the backdrop of the Cold War the only notable use of air power using the same strategic bombing model that had been applied in the Second World War came when the Americans decided to bomb North Vietnam.

In what some commentators may regard as a repeat of the mistakes of the Second World War the bombing of Hanoi is often suggested by some historians as having little material impact upon the North Vietnamese leadership. In fact on the ground the bombing did create problems and was largely attributed to being the single factor that drove the North Vietnamese leadership to attend peace talks in Paris. There were also phases in the campaign where American losses to surface-to-air missiles were unsustainable. Conventional bombing again was shown to have its limitations when applied against a determined population. The lesson from the first sixty years of air power at that point was that if you want to terrify a population and subjugate them you would need to use nuclear weapons. That, of course, in Vietnam was never really an option although some military commanders did advocate their limited use on several notable occasions.

In the Korean War similar debates had occurred as the Chinese and North Korean armies swept through South Korea towards Pusan. The problem with MAD, as faced by all political leaders in making any decision to use nuclear weapons in a tactical situation, was that the following escalation that might occur was hugely difficult to predict and possibly control.

Into the Cold War

During the Tet Offensive in Vietnam the impact of the North Vietnamese attacks was so devastating that the Americans had to call in air power to try to regain the initiative. The battle for the ancient city of Hue was particularly savage and despite initial reluctance to use air power the situation for the United States forces on the ground became so severe that eventually air power was used. It had a decisive effect.

However, the images of the American forces battling to save Hue had a short-term strategic impact back at home. The American people finally realized what the war in Vietnam was costing in lives and material. While air power in Hue was used to create a tactical effect upon the battlefield, its strategic impact at home was to be a turning-point in the war.

For the Egyptian Air Force the impact of the pre-emptive attacks by the Israeli Air Force (IAF) ahead of the start of the Six-Day War in 1967 was strategic. It reduced its fighting capability significantly. It was a crucial application of air power in the opening exchanges of what was to be a brief and yet fierce war.

Six years later in the Yom Kippur War Israeli air power over Sinai was initially cancelled out by the deployment of Russian air defence missile systems. This reduced the contribution made by the IAF to a tactical level. As the IAF became equipped with better countermeasures as a result of direct American involvement in the war, the tide turned and the IAF started to play an increasingly effective role, but at no point could the IAF's targeting be described as strategic. The same can also be said for Russian air power over Afghanistan in the years in which they became increasingly bogged down in an occupation that was eventually to see the Russians withdraw ignominiously.

The IAF did use air power to achieve one notable strategic effect when they bombed the Iraqi nuclear reactor at Osirak in June 1981. The attack lasted about two minutes after the F-16A had flown a distance of 970km from Israel to the target, most of which involved low-level flying. Operation Opera as it was known was completely successful and completely destroyed the Iraqi nuclear facility. Years later the IAF was to complete a similar mission over Syria when it destroyed a nuclear reactor that was being supplied by the North Koreans. Given the potential for these reactors to produce the material required for Iraq or Syria to produce a nuclear weapon that would have inevitably been targeted on Israel, the destruction of these two targets did have a strategic effect.

As the IAF plans for any attack that might be required against Iranian nuclear facilities, the task of applying air power to neutralize what is a strategic target has become far more difficult. The hardening and geographic distribution of the facilities and the sheer scale of the distances involved makes attacking the Iranian nuclear establishments a much harder task. If the IAF is to succeed in destroying Iran's nuclear facilities it will require a great deal of precision, the application of some new weapons and a degree of luck in executing the mission. That such a raid would be designed to have a strategic impact is beyond doubt.

Post-Cold War

Once the Cold War ended and the former states of Yugoslavia quickly fragmented along ethnic lines, military forces were employed by NATO to try to stabilize the situation. Throughout the various campaigns that occurred in the coming years the strategic application of air power was limited to a few targeted strikes against the Serbian electricity system and their media centres. Novel weapons were used in these attacks.

Whereas once strategic air power meant unrestricted bombing of targets, now the concern was to leave infrastructure in place so that once the conflict was over the recovery could begin quickly. During the conflicts in the Balkans the Chinese Embassy in Belgrade was accidentally attacked. While not a strategic target in itself (the attack was a mistake as a result of an intelligence failure), the impact did have a brief strategic effect.

The comparatively recent air campaigns in Iraq as a result of Saddam Hussein's invasion of Kuwait and the 2003 military campaign dubbed the Second Gulf War all featured major bombing campaigns. However, very few of the missions flown by the B-2, B-52, B-1 and other bomber aircraft could be said to have been strategic in nature.

Today drone operations targeting the hierarchy of Al Qaeda in the remote areas of Pakistan or in Yemen or Somalia are hardly strategic in nature. It is possible to argue that if a drone were to be successful in killing the leader of Al Qaeda, Dr Ayman al-Zawahiri, that its impact would have a strategic effect upon Al Qaeda. Sadly, the speed with which the organization is able to promote new people into the key leadership positions means that any impact is likely to be short-lived.

Chapter Seven

Air Power and Tactical Effect

Overview

The term tactical air power is one that brings certain images into the minds of those who either use the term or hear others speak of its role. It does, however, suggest that the effect that air power has in this context is purely at a local level. In fact tactical air power, like the other forms that have been described, can have effects across the spectrum of strategic, operational and tactical levels of command. In particular, no matter where women and children die, the images of the bodies can have a huge strategic impact.

Tactical air power had a limited impact upon the First World War. In the immediate aftermath as the conflict continued against the Bolsheviks and in Macedonia air power did start to have more of an effect on the ground. Gradually, in this short period which many military historians ignore, the ways of using air power to support ground troops and to make forays across enemy lines were consolidated into emergent military planning and doctrine.

In Somaliland in 1919 air power achieved its first example of 'air control': a form of local policing of the population using air power. The basic idea was that if a local tribe became restive, leaflets would be dropped explaining in their local language what was expected of them by the local military commanders. If they continued to misbehave they would be warned that they would be bombed.

This was a different form of asymmetric warfare; a very one-sided affair where those enforcing the governance of the Empire used air power to ruthlessly suppress any dissident voices. For nomadic tribesmen in these areas the ability of air power to locate and attack them was very different from dealing with ground forces.

Needing to restore some semblance of government to Somaliland which had been beset by an insurgency since 1899, Air Marshal Trenchard sought to apply air power at a time when a 'boots on the ground' deployment was not practical. Using leaflet drops the RAF gave the head of the insurgency an ultimatum. His inevitable rejection of the demand was the catalyst for a three-week campaign to unfold in which air power was used to aid a small ground force to overcome the insurgency. Cost comparisons published at the time put a gloss on the achievement of air power suggesting that the air campaign had cost considerably less (£77k) than a conventional approach (circa £5M). Historians note the timely death of the insurgent leader and the lack of collateral damage as being important factors that saw a positive outcome. In 1921 the British sought to apply air power in Mesopotamia. Other campaigns were to follow across the Empire.

It may be fanciful to suggest that sometimes the most lasting of developments in military power occur in conflicts which are not widely viewed as significant but it is a point worthy of reflection. Often the collective psyche on military history subconsciously dismisses any confrontation or battle that has low levels of casualties. Somehow only new developments in war are forged in the heat of battle.

The Malthusian notion that 'necessity is the mother of invention' is somehow taken to be a panacea that suggests military commanders are only able to innovate in conflict. There is evidence that suggests that would be a very narrow viewpoint. Sometimes in what some may be keen to label as 'military sideshows' gradual developments take place in the application of military power that set new refined operational concepts develop that can then form the baseline for future major military confrontations.

One example springs to mind: the Spanish Civil War. While this was a terrible conflict for the people of Spain drawing in people from across the world to support either side in what was seen as a fundamental clash between vastly different ideologies, a new tactical evolution of air power arose. This theatre of war was where the famous Stuka dive-bomber was to get its first and defining operational experience. While the number of Stukas committed to the *Legion Condor* was small and their military impact virtually insignificant, the pilots and operators of the aircraft had learnt some important lessons that would carry them into the Second World War.

While some writers suggest that the Spanish Civil War was a testing ground for the Second World War, their comments are sometimes too general. The essential elements of blitzkrieg were developed in German doctrinal thinking more than fieldwork in Spain. Besides, the nature of the engagements in Spain was not in the classic sense frontal. The battlefield in Spain was quite fragmented. Often the demarcation of where the opposing sides had secured land was unclear. Blitzkrieg was arguably at its most effective when two forces opposed each other along a distinct front.

Blitzkrieg was the result of a major tactical innovation drawing close air-support fighters, the Stuka bombers. In the Second World War aircraft like the Typhoon would swoop down from the skies over Normandy in the run up to D-Day or its aftermath and attack logistic supply lines trying to bring supplies forward to the front line. Attacking the enemy in the rear was important to relieve the pressure on the front line. In the desert Montgomery had applied similar tactics to disrupt Rommel's supply lines before the Battle of El Alamein.

In the desert in the Second World War tactical air power was applied with little accuracy. It was carpet-bombing at a local level. One thing had an overriding effect on the application of tactical air power: the desire to avoid dropping bombs on one's own side. In seeking to avoid that on what could often be dynamic and fast-moving battlefields, air power was often constrained to operating against fixed formations.

Problems also arose has to who owned the air power. Army commanders wanted air power to be available under their direction. Air force officers, however, had often been indoctrinated into the strategic role of air power. Its tactical application was something they did not fully appreciate. If army commanders saw a target that they thought air power could attack, they wanted control of the assets to make that happen. Limitations on the way air power could be used in the tactical domain arising from endurance and tasking issues associated with communications issues often added further restrictions on its application in a ground-attack role.

Doctrine writers had also stressed the application of air power to prevent hostile reconnaissance. Air power was about air superiority and making sure the enemy could not see army formations on the ground. The ground-attack mission was seen to be a far less urgent requirement.

In recent campaigns the availability of in-flight refuelling has transformed the application of tactical air power. Missions now last many hours as pilots fly over areas waiting to be called into a strike. Over the desert in 1942 that luxury of in-flight refuelling was not available. When missions were developed they often had an operational focus, working to interdict enemy supply lines and rear bases.

Ironically it was in the crucible of the initial forays into Normandy after D-Day that the shape for future applications of tactical air power developed. Interestingly its foremost advocate was General Patton. He was to acknowledge that it played a pivotal role as his army drove across Europe after its break-out from the Cherbourg Peninsula.

The author David Spires writing in 2002 documented the ways in which General Patton working alongside his tactical air commander Brigadier General Otto Weyland pioneered air operations at the tactical level. The success attributed to Patton in taking his Third Army across Europe owed a lot to the relationship he forged with Weyland. The two could be described as the 'odd couple'. But together their blend of skills and understanding has seen some historians suggest that they were the supreme practitioners of tactical air power.

Over the period from the point the Third Army became operational on 1 August 1944 until the end of the war Patton's troops covered more ground, took more enemy prisoners and suffered more casualties than any other army operating in North-West Europe. While other tactical air commanders were also to help re-write the doctrine manuals, it was Weyland working with Patton that really helped provide the foundations for future uses of tactical air power. Today in Afghanistan the role of the Forward Air Controller (FAC) is built upon the ideas applied by Weyland and Patton.

It was not until the dawn of the missile age that an era of more precise application of air power can be detected. As the first century of air power moved close to the end of its first fifty years it was the Israeli Air Force that became one of its foremost practitioners.

Israeli Air Power

Of all the advocates of air power the Israeli Air Force is one of the most important to examine. For a country that has spent a significant period of its short life surrounded by hostile states and groups acting as proxies for states, such as Hezbollah, the Israeli Air Force has traditionally relied on its tactical air power to provide an advantage on the battlefield.

Israel's pre-emptive attack on the Egyptian Air Force, called Operation Focus (*Moked*), at the start of the Six-Day War in 1967 can rightly be argued as one of the most decisive applications of tactical air power that had a strategic effect. This was not the indiscriminate application of inaccurate bombers targeting Egyptian cities to strike fear into the local population. This was an accurate application of tactical air power at the outset of a brief campaign. The destruction of most of the Egyptian Air Force on the ground, a viewpoint still challenged by Egypt today, saw the most powerful Arab air force effectively removed from the forthcoming war in a matter of hours. It was a body blow to the Egyptians and their allies from which they did not recover. The whole venture undertaken by the Israeli Air Force was also risky as virtually every plane that could fly was involved in the initial strikes.

A combination of things ensured Israel would achieve tactical surprise. The Israeli intelligence agency Mossad had used high-level agents placed in the high command of the Egyptian armed forces to monitor their preparations for war. A crucial double-agent also played his role in deceiving the Egyptians. The preparations for the initial attack had been exhaustive. Israeli pilots had been involved in a wide range of mission rehearsals. They had memorized each target. Ground crews were also well trained to ensure that a high sorties rate could be generated. Historical reports of Operation Focus suggest that the Israeli Air Force achieved a mission generation rate of four flights per day from its strike aircraft.

The Egyptian Air Force operated at a tempo of around half that figure. This provided some compensation for the imbalances that existed in combat aircraft. Before the war Egypt had an air force that was estimated to consist of around 450 aircraft. The balance of Tu-16s (NATO Code Name: Badger), forty IL-28s and a number of MiG-17, MiG-19 and MiG-21 fighters provided the Egyptian Air Force with what in 1967 was a formidable capability.

For Israel to survive the impending war it simply had to neutralize the Egyptian Air Force on the ground in the opening hours of the war. By any account, no matter how disputed the claims and counter-claims may still be, the pre-emptive attack helped Israel secure a notable military victory in the Six-Day War. They had seen the spectre of war rising over the region and had decided to act first.

That was the prelude to a phase of the confrontation between Israel and its neighbours that is often referred to as the War of Attrition. This is a part of history that again is often forgotten by amateur and professional historians. This was a period of eighteen months in which the Egyptians embarked upon a campaign on the ground and in the air that was designed to test the Israelis' resolve and ability to hold on to the ground they had seized in the Six-Day War. The campaign made sense.

For the Israelis the strategic landscape had significantly changed. They had moved from defending a number of rather small border areas with fractious neighbours into encroaching upon and seizing their land. While the borders with Lebanon, Syria and Jordan largely remained unchanged in terms of their length, the effect of capturing Sinai had significantly altered the length of the border. Of all the gains the vast swathes of the Sinai Desert were both a benefit and disadvantage. On the one hand it provided a buffer zone to which any future Egyptian incursion would have to travel to reach the old Israeli border. On the other it was a large area to defend. For the Egyptian military to embark upon a series of raids and military incursions designed to exhaust the Israelis was a sound military approach.

For the Israelis the War of Attrition was now becoming serious. It was becoming clear the Egyptians had embarked upon a strategy to gradually erode the Israelis' military capability. Where that would lead was anyone's guess. This was not the short game of a swift military campaign. This was the long game. To counter this approach the Israelis needed to move from being reactive to proactive. The shift in emphasis is initially barely discernible but it is significant and tactical air power provides one instrument by which that increased effort is employed.

The War of Attrition was to receive little press coverage in the west. In part that can be explained by the rather intermittent nature of the clashes that occurred. In July 1967 in the immediate aftermath of the Six-Day War the Egyptians embarked upon a number of artillery and air-raids against Israeli positions in Sinai. On 14 July in one notable exchange seven Egyptian fighter aircraft were shot down. A period of relative calm then ensued before the Egyptians managed to sink the Israeli destroyer INS *Eilat* with the cost of forty-seven sailors in October. That provoked a serious reaction from the Israelis with attacks mounted against oil refineries and depots near Suez. All the time the threshold for all-out war was being tested.

Another period of low-level military activity then followed before the Israelis unleashed Operation Boxer on 20 July. In this eight-day mini-campaign nearly the entire Israeli Air Force was employed on raids on the northern sector of the Suez Canal. Eight Egyptian aircraft were shot down and over 300 Egyptian soldiers were killed. A month later in August 1969 the Israeli Air Force conducted over 1,000 sorties destroying SAM sites and shooting down twenty-one Egyptian aircraft for the loss of three Israeli jets.

On 11 September the Egyptians launched a large package of sixteen aircraft to attack Israeli positions. They lost eight MiGs in air-to-air combat with Israeli Mirage jets and three Su-7 ground-attack aircraft to Israeli anti-aircraft and SAM batteries. In what was a rare air-to-air victory an Egyptian fighter achieved the first combat kill of an Israeli F-4 Phantom in December. Newly-delivered Russian P-15 radar systems, operated and manned by a small detachment of the Red Army operating in Egypt, helped the Egyptian pilot to secure the air-to-air victory. While it was a small event, it was to presage much bigger changes in the balance of power between the two countries as they vied for position along the Suez Canal.

Such was the scale of losses suffered by the Egyptians in this period that President Nasser flew secretly to Moscow in January 1970 to appeal for more military aid in what was tantamount to a request for the Red Army to intervene in the confrontation. His initial approach was dismissed out of hand by the Kremlin. At that moment the Soviet bloc did not wish to be drawn into a war with the Americans.

After further discussions the Russians reluctantly agreed to deploying 'observers' into Egypt. This was to alter the dynamics on the battlefield and lead to a very different security situation. New SAM and radar equipment was also quickly deployed into Egypt. As the new equipment came into service Israeli aircraft routinely conducted operations against the sites where they were housed.

In April 1970 a more sinister development was detected as evidence appeared from intercepted radio transmissions that the Russians had now deployed fighter pilots into the conflict. To avoid any danger of escalation Israeli commanders ordered their air force to withdraw from any confrontation if Russian pilots were thought to be flying Egyptian aircraft.

These rules of engagement, however, fell apart on 30 July 1970. On that day Israeli and Russian pilots became engaged in a massive dogfight to the west of the Suez Canal. Between twelve and twenty-four MiGs confronted twelve Israeli Mirage III and four F-4 Phantom jets. In a well-executed ambush the Israeli pilots managed to shoot down four of the Russian-piloted MiGs. A fifth was also later reported as missing. Four Soviet pilots died and no Israeli combat losses were recorded.

The manner in which Israel accomplished its military goals in the Six-Day War perhaps led to a sense of superiority in the IDF. The War of Attrition also helped enforce a sense of complacency. That was to be rudely shattered in October 1973.

The Egyptians and Syrians had learnt their lessons from the Six-Day War. The boot was literally on the other foot. The planning for the attack over the Jewish religious holiday of Yom Kippur had been closely-held with only a very small number of senior officers being aware of the decision to go to war. The military manoeuvres conducted in the build-up to the campaign were given a cover story of being a major exercise. When those exercises quickly turned into a crossing of the Suez Canal under the mobile umbrella of a Russian-supplied Surface-to-Air Missile system the situation dramatically changed. The Egyptians and Syrians achieved total surprise.

To reduce the effectiveness of the now-fabled Israeli Air Force the Egyptians moved forward under the cover of a mobile surface-to-air missile shield. These missiles were to shoot down a large number of Israeli ground-attack aircraft. One aircraft that bore the brunt of this was the A-4 Skyhawk. During the Yom Kippur War the IDF lost fifty-three Skyhawks out of total losses of 102 aircraft. By any standards of military attrition this was significant. If those levels had continued the Israeli Air Force would have been destroyed. Within hours, realizing the perilous state that the Israelis were in, the United States mounted a massive strategic airlift to supply new weapons and equipment to their embattled friend.

For those observers thinking about a Cold War scenario with a similar surprise attack being launched by the Warsaw Pact into Germany, the events at the start of the Yom Kippur War made sober reading. The outcome of the first few days of the war was to form a major point of study for defence analysts in NATO. Here was a case study that needed to be fully appreciated. The attrition rate initially sustained by the IDF could not have been sustained, had the Americans not intervened.

During its service with the IDF the Skyhawk gained an enviable reputation for its manoeuvrability and its ability to keep flying even when it had sustained significant battle damage. Its air-to-air capability was also sometimes underestimated. Its choice as the enemy fighter at *Top Gun* was not by accident. While the F-5 was to take over that role, the Skyhawks flown by highly-experienced combat pilots gave many United States navy pilots a good test of air-to-air engagements.

In one engagement in the Yom Kippur War an A-4 managed to shoot down two Egyptian MiG-21s and was about to get into a firing position on a third when an IDF Mirage IIIC intervened and shot the remaining MiG-21 out of the sky. Many of the A-4 Skyhawks that served in the IDF are now part of the Indonesian Air Force. Their longevity in service is a testament to their versatility as warplanes.

Since the Yom Kippur War the security landscape in the Middle East has profoundly changed. While Israel's political ties with Egypt can best be described as strained, the chances of another war erupting are minimal. Despite the clear shift in power that has happened in Egypt in the wake of the Arab Spring, the Egyptians are focused on internal matters.

In August 2012 Islamic extremists operating in the Sinai attacked both Israeli and Egyptian outposts in the Sinai Desert. The attacks appeared opportunistic. Whether that was a crude attempt to re-start a war between the two former adversaries is unclear, but the unequivocal reaction of the Egyptian military to the threat sent a positive message to the Israelis. Under its new government Egypt was having no truck with any nomads in the desert who wished to take advantage of a period of uncertainty in the relationship between Israel and Egypt. As Egyptian military forces embarked on operations in the Sinai to locate and destroy the Islamist camps the Israelis cautiously looked on. This was not to be a prelude for another war.

The relative stability in the state-on-state relationships that evolved in the wake of the Yom Kippur War were not reflected in what became a more complex security landscape. Israel found itself increasingly dealing with non-state actors. Hamas and Hezbollah were difficult adversaries who had learnt how to fight asymmetrically. On several occasions the IDF has been called into action in Lebanon. Persistent threats from Katyusha rockets falling randomly in northern areas of Israel have resulted in IDF incursions into southern Lebanon. These have had mixed results.

In the first of the campaigns the IDF was able to use tactical air power to good effect. The firing-points used by Hezbollah were readily spotted by Israeli ISTAR and air strikes were quickly called. Hezbollah underestimated the Israelis' ability to find, fix and destroy a target. Hezbollah learnt from this campaign and spent a great deal of time and effort hardening their missile firing-points. The Israelis had again underestimated their opponents. Air power alone was not going to grant the kind of security craved by its population that had to endure almost daily rocket attacks. A ground invasion of southern Lebanon became necessary. While this was initially limited in scope, mission creep set in and the Israeli Air Force was drawn into attacking targets over a wide area of Lebanon. The international outcry that resulted saw the campaign quickly concluded. For the Israelis this was not a satisfactory outcome.

For the IDF, used to applying air power in a dominant way over the battlefield to achieve the desired effect, the outcome was a salutary one. It was even suggested by some commentators that this was the first time the IDF had been defeated.

The outcome was to cost a number of senior figures in the IDF their reputations and jobs. It was also to set the baseline for a very difficult period in the Middle East. From now on, rather than having to live with fractious state-based neighbours, Israel would have to come to terms with living under the constant threat of attack. The conditions that applied in the War of Attrition had returned, only this time the enemy was elusive and quite prepared to use human shields.

Against Hamas, however, Operation Cast Lead was a very different and more difficult situation. This was the first time that contemporary tactical air power had been applied in the full glare of the media in densely-populated areas of the Gaza Strip. Israeli sensitivity to the pictures that would inevitably emerge led them to veto any media presence on the ground in Gaza.

Instead foreign journalists were confined to reporting from remote vantage points in Israel. Ironically the pictures of smoke and dust arising from bomb explosions in the centre of Gaza had more impact on the world's population as they simply instilled images of what was likely to be happening in reality.

Wider Viewpoints

In Korea tactical air power was also hugely important in trying to counteract the sheer size of the North Korean and Chinese military forces. The images of jets dropping down out of the skies over Vietnam in support of ground troops to deliver a variety of ordnance on the ground is one that remains vivid. Air-to-ground missile systems were used to attack targets alongside a range of what euphemistically may be described as conventional weapons.

Fragmentation, napalm and cluster bombs have a quite specific effect on the ground over a large area. In Poland in 1939 the German fragmentation bombs had proven particularly effective against troops on the ground. On one occasion six Polish divisions were literally bombed into surrender by Stuka bombers.

Today the use of those weapons has been banned by international law. This is understandable but there may yet be an attempt to reverse this position. As western defence budgets continue their apparent inexorable decline the need to re-visit the use of area weapons may return to address specific military missions. While that is a view on the future, for the moment the emphasis from the employment of area-based weapons to those that are more discrete in their targeting capabilities is clear. Today, as far as the application of air power at the tactical level is concerned, the focus is all about precision.

In the Cold War with Europe facing the might of the Warsaw Pact cluster bombs and any other area munitions were seen as a counterweight to the imbalances that existed in conventional forces. Tactical air power was defined by the need for it to destroy as many Warsaw Pact armoured vehicles as possible. These were in close proximity to the Forward Edge of the Battlefield Area (FEBA) and in the areas where second-echelon troops would be assembling.

To force a military stalemate the front-line and second-echelon forces had to be attacked by tactical air power. This was the best NATO could hope for at the time. Through the employment of tactical air power any incursion into Western Europe would be halted in its tracks. On paper that sounded like a sensible strategy, but the stark reality was that conventionally-armed tactical air power was the last line of escalation before the nuclear option. If conventional tactical air could not blunt the attack then small nuclear warheads would be selectively employed to disrupt the advance of the Warsaw Pact forces.

Contemporary Air Power in COIN Operations

On 10 June 2012 the Commander of NATO forces in Afghanistan General John Allen made a statement that said 'NATO will no longer bombard residential areas and people's homes in Afghanistan.' This was a quite profound moment for the advocates of air power. It showed its contemporary limitations. Despite the developments in ISTAR and the ability to look at targets from a range of sensor systems, the potential for mistakes to be made and for collateral damage to occur will arise. It is a facet of warfare that is uniquely difficult to completely remove.

The decision to withdraw air power from that specific part of the battlefield is one that has been a long time coming in Afghanistan. Importantly General Allen's remarks did not rule out the use of air power in support of ground forces on operations in non-built-up areas. The problem, of course, is where does a built-up area start and finish?

This is the latest in a series of alterations to the rules of engagement in Afghanistan that have progressively reduced the manoeuvre-room of the military commanders. In a situation where military forces are trying to maintain the support of the local population it seems that pictures of dead women and children have a dramatic political effect. The decision came several days after the Afghan President Hamid Karzai met with relatives of those who died at a wedding ceremony in the village of Sajawand in the Baraki Barak District of Kandahar Province where eighteen people had been killed in an air strike on 6 June 2012. He had returned home quickly after the incident from a major regional conference he was attending in Beijing to discuss security issues.

It was the latest in a number of such incidences where the Afghan president had clearly sought to build his own political capital when tragic events occurred. Throughout his tenure as commander of the NATO forces in Afghanistan General David Petraeus had to deal with the fall-out from many similar incidents. It could be said that the issue of collateral damage was the single thing that increased toxicity in the relationship between NATO and the Afghan president and sections of his people.

For then-proponents of air power the signs emerging from thirty years of war from the First Gulf War, through the Balkans campaigns and into the aftermath of the Second Gulf War and Afghanistan were not good. Where the world's media is happy to act as a proxy judge and jury, bringing the harsh realities of war into the living rooms of an increasingly concerned domestic population that has grown tired of war, political ramifications were inevitable. Somehow a disconnection had developed between those who saw that the revolution in military affairs would consign the equally toxic blue-on-blue attacks and civilian collateral damage to history and the reality on the ground. In the course of those thirty years warfare changed.

The state-on-state symmetrical world of 1991 morphed into the multi-national effort against groups of insurgents using a variety of very different tactics based on what has been called asymmetric warfare. Military purists argue that this term is wrong because warfare is always asymmetric. That is how one power defeats another, by creating an imbalance of forces at a crucial point in a campaign that enables a military and consequential political tipping-point to be reached.

Their discussions on the nature of exactly what type of warfare was being fought in Iraq in 2005 and Afghanistan from 2006 onwards led to the reincarnation of the term 'irregular warfare'. Seeking to avoid the semantic arguments that can sometimes surround such debates a simple and yet profound observation can be made. In symmetrical warfare often the military forces and civilian populations on both sides of the campaign suffer losses. In irregular warfare losses are borne by the military on one side and a combination of insurgents and the civilian population on the other. Little wonder then that the insurgents find those among the civilian population who will offer them sanctuary.

At the start of the First Gulf War air power had been used to prepare the way for the launch of a land campaign. That after such intense bombing many Iraqis chose to surrender and not fight is hardly surprising. Air power was applied in line with the Powell Doctrine named after General Colin Powell, the former Chief of the Joint Staff in the United States and then Secretary of State in the Bush Administration.

He advocated a simple principle when it came to warfare. When it was conducted it should be a national effort and not done half-heartedly. The build-up of forces prior to the First Gulf War and the extensive air campaign that preceded the launch of the incursion into Iraq adhered to this doctrine. It was one that tried to deal with the lasting impact of the Vietnam War on the American psyche.

Twenty years later the Vietnam War has been replaced by the years of deployments in Iraq and Afghanistan. Once again in the aftermath of war people debate its value. The perennial question of 'Was it all worth it?' haunts politicians. The language of the 'exit strategy' now occupies endless debates before military forces are even engaged on the ground. Superficially it would be easy to conclude that in the aftermath of those twenty years of operations political leaders might want to allow their national exchequers to take a rest from funding overseas adventures.

The Arab Spring lit a brief light on the Middle East. Optimism flowed from many commentators, some clutching at these developments in the hope of avoiding future military conflicts. Political leaders in some countries, notably the United Kingdom, started to justify switching spending from the employment of military weapons to those that provide proactive support to states ahead of them becoming embroiled in conflict. Developing indicators of states that were at risk became a new focus for political leaders. At long last it would seem the political landscape is realizing that prevention is better than intervention.

Sadly, all too predictably, the Arab Spring will soon prove to be a false dawn. In Syria the international community has failed to find a formula for action despite the relatively successful campaign in Libya. In the Yemen international terrorist groups have gained an advantage from the political turmoil that affected the country as the Arab Spring spread its tentacles across the Middle East. The much-hoped-for democracy in Iraq is stalled by political in-fighting. Iran sits on the sidelines of the Arab Spring, seeding chaos wherever it can to ensure the ideals expressed by those who started it in Tunisia do not reach Tehran.

The Limitations of Contemporary Tactical Air Power

When it agreed to the imposition of United Nations Resolution 1972 to protect the people of Benghazi Russia did not envisage that the outcome of that would see one of its few friends in the Middle East deposed and be killed. Mission creep that saw tactical air power applied across Libya was not part of the original deal as far as the Russians were concerned. The aim was to protect the people of Benghazi from what was likely to be mass slaughter or genocide on a very large scale.

In the aftermath of NATO's successful prosecution of the mission the Russians made it abundantly clear that this will not be an option they will consider over Syria. Russian rhetoric on this has pursued two quite distinct lines. The first is to call for independent investigation of a number of alleged occasions when NATO's air power is alleged to have caused civilian casualties. The second is to make it very clear that they will not see NATO impose regime change on Syria.

In the immediate aftermath of the campaign over Libya there were a number of commentators who were anxious to herald this as a new dawn in the precise application of air power. While it is true that the French Air Force and Royal Air Force pilots who conducted strike missions against pro-regime elements in Libya did everything they possibly could to avoid civilian casualties, some were bound to occur. That is the nature of warfare. No ISTAR assets, no matter if they are located on the platform delivering the strike or handing off a target from another dedicated suite of sensors, can completely lift the fog of war.

The situation on the ground in Libya was verging on the chaotic. Once the main air defence systems operated by the regime had been quickly neutralized, the targeting cell in NATO had to move on to a wider range of fixed and mobile targets. Some fixed targets were located in the course of the battle. It took time to develop the intelligence on ammunition dumps. Some vehicle assembly-points where pro-regime forces gathered to refuel and re-arm were fixed on a temporary basis.

The time from detecting where such activity was being undertaken to the point at which a strike could be called in was short. The inevitable delays in processing ISTAR data saw several tactical innovations as operators who traditionally work in the non-real-time environment of the ground were flown on ISTAR platforms. Their real-time assessments enabled the time delays associated with ground-processing to be significantly reduced. This allowed even temporary vehicle assembly-points to be targeted.

The pro-regime forces, however, were quick to adapt to the changing situation. Their adaptation of their mobile command and control facilities tested NATO right up until the end of the campaign. In the last month attacks had to focus on such mobile nodes as by then many tanks and armoured personnel carriers operated by pro-regime elements had been systematically destroyed. That the armed resistance lasted right up until the end of October is a testament to the ability of the pro-regime forces to outmanoeuvre NATO using relatively simple measures to maintain command over forces whose position was increasingly precarious.

Attacking command and control nodes using air power is specifically problematic. On several occasions it was clear that the pro-regime forces were deliberately placing their remaining nodes in places where if they were attacked civilians would be killed. The Israelis have seen this tactic employed by Hezbollah in the Lebanon and in operations in the Gaza Strip. The tactic of dropping a smaller bomb that did not detonate to warn the occupants of buildings to evacuate before lethal force was applied was one that evolved in the cauldron of war. This was nicknamed 'knocking' as it was likened by some to be a knock on the door before an armed weapon was deployed to destroy the target. To counteract this, the Israelis produced photographic evidence to show how Hezbollah followers had coerced people into remaining in the building.

It would seem that no matter how great the effort made, any conflict that relies on air power is bound to see a level of civilian casualties. Sadly it is a by-product of conflict that to date ISTAR technologies are unable to completely prevent. This is especially true when it comes to attacking underground and hardened command bunkers; a point illustrated by the international reaction to the destruction of such a bunker in Baghdad in the First Gulf War that had been thought to be a command centre. The actual role of that facility remains unclear even today, as competing claims of its role have never been fully resolved.

In December 2011 the prestigious *New York Times* released a detailed analysis of thirteen case studies it had considered in some detail where civilian casualties had occurred. The *Times* concluded that they had found what it termed 'credible accounts of dozens of civilians killed in several distinct attacks'.

The problem when civilian casualties occur is particularly acute when the aim of a military mission is to protect people. Any collateral event causes acute and emotional responses. Time will tell if the Russian accusations of NATO involvement in killing civilians in Libya prove to be correct. A United Nations report that tried to find evidence of the deaths of civilians did praise NATO for its efforts to reduce civilian casualties. Several non-governmental organizations have remained sceptical of the report, implying that it was biased. As ever in these situations some things are very difficult to verify.

Giving itself some political wriggle-room, the United Nations did observe that several examples of the military documentation associated with attacks on a small number of targets appeared to be incomplete and called for an internal enquiry to be conducted by NATO. The accusations have moved a number of political leaders, such as the Danish defence minister Nick Hækkerup, to express regret for the deaths of civilians caught up in the war.

In his remarks Nick Hækkerup sought to lessen the impact of the report by noting that the alleged deaths of sixty people in NATO air strikes were small by comparison with what the pro-regime followers could have achieved had NATO not intervened. His concluding remark that when warfare occurs we have to 'clearly and unequivocally state that there is a risk of civilian casualties' and that political leaders need to be 'frank about that risk' shows the increasing pressure that exists today when images of dead women and children can be beamed around the world in a matter of seconds.

In the aftermath of the Libyan campaign the ongoing violence in Syria saw a number of political and military commentators call for a similar intervention. Steadfastly the Russians have resisted these calls. Their position has been reinforced by China which has expressed similar concerns about the outcome should NATO be called into action again.

Noting the Russian concerns as to how the definition of a no-fly zone over Benghazi developed into a series of air strikes all over Libya that saw a pro-Russian regime fall, diplomatic and political leaders sought to change the language. All mention of a no-fly zone over Libya was removed from the table. It was as if the term had been wiped from the lexicon of military options at a stroke. As one term left the military lexicon, another emerged. This was 'safe corridors'.

Understandably given their vehement opposition to any form of intervention in Syria the Russians were quick to reject the notion. They saw the idea as being a no-fly zone by any other name. Any attempts to broker a new United Nations resolution to gain a diplomatic way to move forward using this idea was dismissed out of hand. In its view Russia had been duped over Libya and was not about to allow itself to be drawn into seeing its last regional ally deposed.

Of late that stance has moderated as the Assad regime has seemed to exploit what it believes to be fulsome Russian support. President Milosevic made a similar mistake over Kosovo. Even the Russians, it would seem, have a bottom line. If Assad has to step down to allow free elections to occur, then the recent noises emerging from Moscow may find some traction in the international community.

While the threat of using air power was never on the table politically, it may just have created the conditions in which the Russians have been forced to give up on President Assad. The talk in Moscow is of a Yemeni solution. This is where power was transferred from a long-standing and hated dictator to a temporarily-installed leadership while national elections were planned and carried out. In Syria it might just work.

If President Assad was to resist the calls for change, the clamour for international action would continue. Despite restrictions on the internet and other media reporting, the rebels have shown themselves as being adept at keeping the scale of the onslaught being unleashed on the civilians in some cities in the eye of the international media.

With military solutions involving any form of boots-on-the-ground approach being something that NATO leaders would be very reluctant to employ given they are within sight of extracting themselves from Afghanistan, the only options appear to be to apply air and maritime power.

This inevitably raises comparisons again with events in Libya as these were the two instruments of military power that were applied.

If NATO planners had to revisit the use of air power, what options could be on the table? Airbases in Syria's northerly neighbour Turkey would be an obvious consideration. Turkey, however, may not wish to become politically involved, fearing a backlash from Islamists who would use any intervention to step up their terrorist activity in the country.

The Royal Air Force base at Akrotiri in Cyprus would be an obvious location for flight refuelling tankers that would have to fly to support missions being flown over Syria. For the air-crews involved the dangers would be appreciably different. In 2011 in Libya the pro-regime air force remained firmly grounded once NATO imposed the no-fly zone. It is very debatable whether the Syrian Air Force would adopt similar tactics.

Attacks against the AWACS and air-to-air refuelling capabilities employed in conjunction with the fast jets would rapidly see an escalation in the situation. Images of the wreckage of a VC-10 or NATO E-3 would not play well at home in NATO. The Syrian Air Force might just conduct an attack to test the resolve of any international coalition that had been formed to implement a United Nations resolution.

Over Libya the non-appearance of the Libyan Air Force helped the ad hoc coalition of countries involved. Those assigned to the air-to-air mission were not seriously tested. For countries like Sweden the Libyan campaign was pain-free apart from the expenditure on maintaining a force on operations. If a similar situation developed over Syria the loss of a Swedish pilot may quickly provide an acid test of the degree of political commitment.

Carrier-based air power would naturally become part of a solution if the United States was able to dedicate the 6th Fleet to the task. The arrival of the USS *George Bush* off the coast of Syria in November 2011 just ahead of the pre-planned arrival of a Russian naval task force led by the aircraft carrier *Admiral Kuznetsov* provided a stark indication of the juxtaposition of political views over Syria.

One of the obvious issues with the definition of a safe corridor is what it precisely means. Does it infer that what is in fact created is a protected zone in which civilians can live without fear of attack from military forces loyal to President Assad? If so, how would that work?

To guarantee the safety of the people inside the safe corridor air power would have to be capable of intercepting and destroying any pre-emptive move made by pro-regime military forces to encroach on the area. Inside the safe corridor the international community would have to be able to supply the needs of the people. Food, water, medical aid and shelter would all need to be brought in. It would be a massive humanitarian operation whose end would be difficult to envisage. The lessons from the no-fly zones over Northern and Southern Iraq to protect threatened ethnic minorities from repression by the Saddam regime provide a good example of just how long such missions can last.

The first imperative of any application of air power over the safe corridors from a military viewpoint would be to create a permissive environment. In Libya that saw the Libyan air defence system come under sustained attack in the first four days of the campaign. By the end of those four days senior military commanders went on record to say that its operation had all but been totally neutralized.

The Syrian air defence system is very different. It is more up-to-date than its Libyan counterpart. Suppressing its operations may take any force trying to impose a safe corridor slightly longer. Attacks on command bunkers controlling its operation would inevitably result in civilian casualties. The words of the Danish defence minister would be readily recalled as soon as any pictures started to emerge.

The simple fact is that in such situations air power has its limitations. When any form of military power is used people will die in the crossfire. That is not to sound callous. It is to recognize a reality of war; one that in this era of virtual reality and war games sometimes gets missed.

Until ISTAR assets can provide the pilot with the kind of situational awareness that ensures any attack that places civilians at risk is called off, the application of air power will have attendant dangers. Thinking otherwise is to contemplate nirvana. For the oppressed people of Syria it is to be sincerely hoped that a political way forward is found. If not, NATO's airmen who so carefully undertook the campaign in Libya may be called into action again.

Chapter Eight

Conclusions

T he military application of air power has changed dramatically since its first conception at the start of the 1900s. Those who apply air power have been on a journey that is nothing short of an odyssey. Their adventures have involved many twists and turns and can be likened to a Homeric epic.

Air power's first intensive military use came over the battlefields of Europe between 1914 and 1918. Somewhat tentatively and against a lot of opposition it began to show its potential as a source of intelligence information and to help focus the use of artillery to try to achieve maximum effect. Initially it was not regarded as a panacea.

Cloud cover, navigation issues and limitations on early camera systems limited the contribution that it could make. For those jealously seeking to guard their own positions it was easy to deride what air power could do. However, gradually, as a result of one or two specific times when the vantage point of the air proved decisive, the doubters had to reshape their arguments. If air power was indeed here to stay then they should control its operations and not allow another service to break away.

This attempt to strangle the notion of a separate air force at birth was one that gained some traction. There were still those who looked at the flimsy machines and wondered if they could ever really make a contribution to war. One hundred years later it is easy to note and criticize their narrow-minded views, but at the time they were sincerely held.

The history of the first 100 years of air power is punctuated by a small number of really important events that can be used to mark its emergence from being a nascent capability to being a fully-fledged part of the military instrument of power. There are several particular events that are worthy of note. However, one stands out as the catalyst from which air power grew.

In the First World War the detection from the air of the leading elements of General Alexander von Kluck's plan to initiate the right wheel of the Von Schlieffen plan was one such moment. It showed those who had grown wary of the benefits of air power that it could make a contribution to grand-strategic planning. From that point in time those who had the vision to understand what air power could achieve never looked back.

In the aftermath of the crucible of the First World War in many backwaters of the British Empire across the world air power began slowly but surely to exert its influence. In places like Mesopotamia in the 1920s air power proved itself as an important capability to help police the outposts of empire. The efforts to maintain law and order showed that air power could replace boots on the ground.

The security of the Empire in the 1920s and 1930s could be maintained using air power as a vital lever against fractious leaders trying to lead rebellions. The sight of an aircraft flying over mounted troops still had an ability to create confusion. Today the fast jet that does a low-level fly-past of a Taliban position in Afghanistan without releasing weapons has the same effect. In the crucible that was the far-flung places of the Empire in the period between the two world wars the notions of applying soft power were first considered.

The Evolution of Strategic Air Power

As the world moved inexorably towards its second major military confrontation new ideas emerged as to how air power might be used. By this time many advocates of air power had started to realize that the strategic impact the Zeppelins had over England in the First World War was minimal. The attacks did instil a sense of fear into the British public. The random nature of the attacks caused by navigational issues and poor bomb-aiming accuracy helped create a sense of the attacks being indiscriminate. That added to the psychological impact of the raids, but at this time the attacks were not specifically directed at the public. The Zeppelin raids were not an effort to break the fighting spirit of the British public. That would come later in the Blitz.

As the utility of air power started to develop, the notion of its tactical, operational and strategic application began to enter the lexicon of those formulating doctrine in military schools. It was necessary to try to provide a structure into which air power could be moulded. It was not to prove an easy task.

It led to the emergence of a number of air-power philosophers such as Douhet, Mitchell and Harris who all developed their own take on how and when air power should be applied. The first- and second-generation advocates of air power were quickly replaced by a third generation led by people such as General Curtis LeMay. Each had their views on how air power could be mapped into established doctrinal thinking on the application of military power.

Air power, however, did not neatly fit into the traditional breakdown of military campaigns undertaken by the army and the navy. Its speed and range meant that air power could quickly move from the tactical domain to the strategic. For the army and navy the differentiation of strategic, operational and tactical was relatively easy to understand and to map to military activities. Air power's characteristics meant that creating divisions into which certain applications of air power fitted was not so straightforward. The evolution of tactical air power provides an example of this effect.

In the First and Second World Wars the concern of operating close to one's own formations and creating what today would be called blue-on-blue events restricted the use of tactical air power. It took some time to evolve tactics that enabled air power to be used at the tactical level, whereas its application at the operational and strategic levels was more straightforward.

What was clear and still applies today is the need to secure command of the air. Over Kosovo, Iraq, Afghanistan and Libya command of the air was achieved relatively easily. Against China, in some future scenario based on the Pacific Rim, that will be more difficult. China's rapid investment in its air force shows that it plans to contest the skies.

This differentiation between tactical, operational and strategic applications of any form of military power is made more complicated today. A single bomb delivered in a tactical situation by air, sea or land can have a huge strategic impact if it kills apparently innocent women and children.

In the civil war in Spain the Nazis applied some of this thinking. The bombing of Guernica was a pivotal point in the application of air power. This was an early example of where the concept of air power being applied with due regard for civilian life was lost.

Over time, and through a series of cataclysmic conflicts, that viewpoint altered. While it is hard to suggest a specific catalyst for the emergence of air power, there are some points in history where its next evolutionary step can be clearly identified. One of these events was the bombing of Guernica. The Blitz, the bombings of Dresden, Hamburg, Tokyo, Hiroshima, Nagasaki and Hanoi and the build-up to the start of the First Gulf War all followed from the indiscriminate application of air power over that single city in the Spanish Civil War.

The notion of a chivalrous application of air power that was developed in the First World War as 'men of honour' conducting dogfights in the skies over Europe was consigned to the dustbin of military thinking. If a number of events in history defined points at which air power moved from childhood into adolescence the attack on Guernica could be said to be one of the formative stages in its development.

While the overall death toll was small by comparison with other landmark events such as the fire-bombing of Dresden or the nuclear attacks upon Japan, Guernica was a point at which the Rubicon was crossed. From then on all bets were off. Air power could be used irrespective of any concern for civilian casualties.

The attack on Guernica was to lead to a whole new concept of how air power could be applied to end wars quickly, hence saving human lives in the long run. It is a point of view that even today sparks fierce debate. None more so, perhaps, than when similar arguments were made in favour of using the atomic bombs against Japan in 1945. This was another of the list of pivotal moments in the application of air power.

The Spanish Civil War was also to throw up some misleading insights. The Nazis perhaps understandably overestimated the performance of the Luftwaffe. Over Poland any limitations that its aircraft might have also did not emerge. It was only during the Battle of Britain that the weakness in the Heinkel He 111 became fully apparent.

Even tactical developments like the *Schwarm*, where aircraft were positioned in a formation to provide maximum coverage to each other, did not have a material impact on their loss rates. Over Germany in the daylight bombing campaign conducted by the United States Air Force similar tactical evolutions also did not prove decisive. When fighters were able to get inside the formations and fire upon bombers the latter proved very vulnerable.

Throughout the coming years the strategic application of kinetically-based air power would initially peak over Japan in 1945 before becoming less attractive in the Cold War as the potential of nuclear weapons became clear. In the Cuban Missile Crisis General Curtis LeMay's attitude towards the use of his strategic bombing capability concerned President Kennedy. Over Vietnam President Johnson was reluctant to apply strategic bombing. President Nixon, however, did unleash the B-52s against Hanoi but that was for a limited duration.

Those like LeMay who advocated massive use of air power will go down in history as being frustrated by the constraints placed on them by their political masters. Once the atom bomb had made its debut in warfare the whole nature of the application of strategic air power changed.

For those advocates of air power such as Harris and LeMay, historians will always be able to say that political constraints meant that the full weight of air power's impact could never actually be brought to bear against an enemy. Even Churchill, who harboured doubts about the real achievements of strategic bombing, rationalized away the bombing attacks in 1942 over Germany as being the second front so desired by Stalin. While D-Day was still two years away, Bomber Command could provide the second front.

Nearly sixty years later as American and coalition jets pounded Iraq to force it to leave Kuwait the event where more than 400 civilians died in an attack on a bunker in the Amiriyah neighbourhood of Baghdad was to reignite the debate about collateral damage. The devastating impact of two laser-guided bombs was to create an indelible mark on history. The attack on 13 February 1991 is remembered as the largest single loss of life as a result of the application of air power in contemporary air warfare. Its scars still leave their mark on those who write and lecture doctrine on the use of air power. It was another pivotal event in its history.

This came at a time when images also emerged of what appeared to be indiscriminate use of air power by the Russians in Afghanistan. The combination of the two was to cause a great deal of public disquiet. When the general public begin to challenge the use of military power, political leaders have to listen. As the number of such events grew in military operations in the Balkans in the 1990s it became clear that air power in the future was going to have to be applied with increasing accuracy and precision.

The world had moved through a full circle as far as the wider application of military power was concerned and air forces were in the forefront of the criticism that was emerging. As ever when challenged air forces showed an ability to respond. In Libya in 2011 the results of the developments in those areas was seen in action. It was to dramatically cut the toll of civilian casualties in a war that was conducted to save the Libyans from the threat of genocide by the Gaddafi regime.

Tactical Evolution

Charting the evolution of the strategic application of air power is relatively easy. Its tactical evolution, however, has less readily-defined evolutionary points. Because of the impact of events such as the fire-bombing of Tokyo and the extreme levels of casualties they will always get the attention of historians. Tactical military aviation by its very nature was at the outset of limited impact. As time has gone on, however, and the use of strategic air power to bomb populations has faded as the political landscape has changed, so tactical air power has emerged and has been shown to have a strategic effect.

Looking across the first 100 years it is clear that the application of air power has changed dramatically. So too as a result of technological advances has its ability to conduct a wider range of missions. The combination of speed, range of employment and a varied number of effects has developed significantly over the first century of air power.

As speeds have gone from a mere few tens of knots to several thousand, the range over which air power can be employed now operates on the global scale. A quick comparison with similar technological changes in land and naval warfare shows just how dramatic the impact of these advancements has been on air power.

The American B-2 bomber, although limited in number, has played a part in every major air campaign carried out since its introduction into the inventory. Its ability to apply air power across the globe is quite unique. The range of effects that can now be delivered by air power has also developed significantly. From its use as a passive instrument of war, its first steps into projecting kinetic power while of limited use militarily did point the way to a more significant role in the future. This is a point clearly recognized by the United States Air Force who have recently undertaken a major upgrade to the weapons and systems on board the aircraft to ensure that it retains its precision strike capability.

By using its unique vantage point in the sky air power showed some initial capabilities in helping commanders achieve greater battlefield awareness. The speed with which airmen in particular were able to find ways to ensure they could make a contribution was to lay a foundation that to this day is a hallmark of air forces around the world. Where obstacles existed to air power making a direct contribution to the dynamics of the battlefield, airmen quickly developed innovative solutions. To this day agility, flexibility and versatility remain the watchwords of air power. Those attributes are underscored by its characteristics of speed, range and payload-carrying capacity.

It would be easy to declare many events that occurred in the Second World War as being pivotal. There are, however, a number that do stand the test of time. Of all of the pivotal moments in air power the Battle of Britain could easily be argued as one of the most significant. At that point the islands of the United Kingdom were hugely vulnerable. That the Royal Air Force was able to thwart the efforts of the Luftwaffe is a matter of history. The outcome, however, on several occasions stood on the edge of an abyss and could have easily tipped over. But for the efforts of the commanders involved, husbanding their resources carefully, the world would look so very different today.

The arguments over the ability of the Royal Navy to prevent the Nazis from implementing their planned invasion of the United Kingdom under Operation Sealion will continue. Historians enjoy such debates, retuning to them periodically to add in new dimensions to the debate. One thing is clear: had the Nazis tried to invade the United Kingdom the Royal Navy would have had to intervene and would have been subjected to an intense aerial bombardment as it left its base at Scapa Flow to head down the North Sea to meet the German invasion force as it tried to cross the English Channel.

The outcome of those engagements is difficult to predict but within months a single event thousands of miles away off the coast of Malaya brought a new perspective to just how difficult that intervention in the English Channel might have been.

The destruction of HMS *Prince of Wales* and HMS *Repulse* off the coast of Malaya in 1941 also showed how vulnerable battleships had become to land-based and torpedo bombers and how they needed carrier-based escorts if they were to come into contact with an enemy formation. Forty years later off the coast of the Falkland Islands the Royal Navy was to demonstrate the enduring flexibility of carrier-based aviation operating over 8,000nm away from home in the most challenging of weather conditions. Despite the presence of two aircraft carriers the Royal Navy was to suffer grievous losses to the sorties by the Argentinian Air Force.

The Royal Navy attack on the Italian Fleet at Taranto was pivotal as it altered the balance of power in the Mediterranean Sea. It also provided confirmation to the Japanese that their emerging ideas surrounding an attack on Pearl Harbor might succeed.

At Arnhem towards the end of the Second World War one aspect of air power found its match. The airborne landings around the city failed to achieve their military goals. The failure to appreciate the value of air photographic intelligence which showed the strength of German units in the area was to lead to the withdrawal of the British parachutists from a small enclave they had created close to the city.

The massacre of the Polish Brigade that descended into the landing zones around Arnhem that had been overrun by the Nazis was to mark one of the last few occasions when parachute landings were to form a part of military planning. Today such operations can only be carried out in a relatively benign or permissive environment. In Iraq in 2003 the United States 101 Airborne did deploy by parachute into areas to the north of Baghdad, but that was against the backdrop of a permissive situation on the ground.

Another pivotal event for advocates of air power was the shooting down of Gary Powers in his U-2 spy plane. This was to change the widely-held view that the bomber would always get through. For the Royal Air Force the U-2 incident and subsequent developments in missile technologies brought into sharp relief the vulnerability of the V Force and their ability to deliver Britain's nuclear deterrent.

This gradual shift in recognizing the limitations of air power as missile technologies eroded its ability to reach its target must have also been affected by the events surrounding the Cuban Missile Crisis. During the thirteen days in which the world teetered on the edge of nuclear holocaust the V Force was dispersed by accident rather than by design.

Wary of sending signals to the Russians the British Prime Minister Harold Macmillan told the leadership of the Royal Air Force to take whatever prudent measures were necessary to protect the force from being destroyed pre-emptively. The fact that the Royal Air Force had declared one of its numerous alerts days before the onset of the crisis helped mask its dispersal of the V Force. This was not a pivotal moment for the application of air power. It was one, however, that would leave its mark on those political leaders involved. The need for the national deterrent to remain invulnerable no matter what the situation became an important consideration.

The movement of the responsibility of delivering a nuclear attack upon the Soviet Union in the Cold War to the Polaris submarine was an important point in the development of air power, but it was not pivotal. This was a national decision taken by the British government in recognition of its specific situation. The French were to follow suit. While the United States continued to maintain its triad of forces to ensure it could survive a pre-emptive first strike, the United Kingdom, with its more limited resources, handed the task of delivering the ultimate weapon to the Royal Navy. It was a relatively small yet significant recognition of the limitations of air power.

In looking at pivotal moments in the application of air power one cannot help but acknowledge the achievements of the Israeli Air Force over the last fifty years. They have on many occasions been at the forefront of the development of new ideas and doctrine.

The Six-Day War in 1967 between the Arabs and Israelis should be included in the list of pivotal events. The pre-emptive strike by the Israelis against the Egyptian Air Force was a huge factor in tilting the balance of the war towards the Israelis. It was to show to the world what the pre-emptive application of air power could do to neuter a military force.

Six years later during the Yom Kippur War the fight-back by the Israeli Air Force against the mobile Egyptian SAM belt that took such a toll on the IAF in the early days of the war showed just how important electronic warfare was to become in the delivery of air power. When faced by an advanced SAM belt the attacking aircraft could not rely alone on flying low and fast.

The Israeli Air Force also provided another classic example of applying air power in an innovative way when it mounted the raid on Entebbe Airport to secure the hostages seized by the Palestinian Liberation Organization. Projecting military power over such distances and releasing the Israeli citizens that had been seized was a pivotal moment in the development of air power. It showed what could be done with the right resources, careful planning and professional execution.

Since the end of the Cold War there have been relatively few pivotal moments in the application of air power. The one-sided battle between the Israeli Air Force and the Syrian Air Force over the Bekkar Valley in 1982 was a pivotal moment. It provided the first evidence of the potential of ISTAR to provide excellent situational awareness to one side. From that point on many air forces started to re-write the doctrine about how to use critical elements of air power.

The accidental attack by the United States on the Chinese Embassy in Belgrade was not pivotal. It was the source of huge embarrassment in the Pentagon and the American intelligence agencies but it really did not create a seismic shift in the conduct of warfare. It simply provided another example in the increasing list of intelligence failures that punctuate warfare.

In Afghanistan there have been times when the issue of collateral damage has raised its head and caused major political tensions between NATO and the Afghan government. The attack by a C-130 gunship on a wedding party was one of the more notorious events that showed that intelligence sources in COIN operations can be unreliable and have their own agendas.

None of those events was pivotal in changing the application of air power. They simply provided more evidence of a need to be certain about the sources of information before conducting attacks and the enduring need for the highest possible sensor resolution over the target. By taking such measures any pilot or commander on board an aircraft can be increasingly confident that they are doing their very best to avoid civilian casualties.

The attacks by terrorists on New York and Washington in September 2001 showed an innovative way of using civilian aircraft as cruise missiles. The confused reaction of the American air defence systems on the day showed the scale of the shock of the attacks. It completely disorientated the systems and processes designed to protect the United States from air attack.

Given the relatively benign political and military situation against which the attacks appeared it is perhaps understandable that the air defence systems found it hard to cope. This was a bolt from the blue. Since then every major sporting event including the Olympic Games in London has had to have an air defence presence to address the potential for a repeat attack.

In 2006 the Israeli Air Force made another contribution to the list of applications of air power. Their use of simple bombs without explosives over Gaza in 2006 during Operation Cast Lead showed that they were still capable of innovating. With intense international scrutiny of their every action when they mounted military operations, the Israeli Air Force developed the idea of a simple device that would warn those in buildings on the target list that they had a few moments to get out of harm's way.

It can be argued this was a pivotal moment in the application of air power. This innovation allowed the Israelis to highlight the measures they were taking to avoid civilian casualties in an operation that was conducted against the backdrop of a high-density urban population. While such measures did not eliminate civilian casualties, they did help the Israelis fight the media war that always accompanies any major conflict.

In Libya in 2011 air power arguably reached a new summit in terms of its capabilities. Through its selective application, by a coalition authorized by the United Nations, it was able to create the conditions whereby the people of Benghazi were initially protected and the groups involved in the rebellion could overthrow the Gaddafi regime.

A year later in Syria, however, any vision that the Libyan campaign would set a new benchmark for the international community to come together to overthrow despotic regimes was shown to be fallacious. Russian and Chinese intransigence left many Syrians to die as the Assad regime refused to accept that the majority of its people no longer wanted to live under their control.

The situation in Syria partially undermines an argument that the campaign in Libya was pivotal. However, that would be to ignore the point that the reason why the situation in Syria is so bad is primarily the result of political inertia rather than an indication of a military deficiency.

It is clear that if the United Nations could get a resolution passed to enforce a no-fly zone over Syria there are nations like the United Kingdom, France and others who participated in the Libyan campaign that would again send in their air forces to help the people of cities such as Aleppo.

While the Syrian Air Force and its air defence systems represent a far more challenging target than their Libyan equivalents, the final outcome would see NATO and its allies impose their will and achieve air superiority over the designated areas agreed by the United Nations. It is a mission that could be achieved if the political will were able to be mustered.

At the start of the second century of air power its role in the international security landscape is secure. Its characteristics and attributes are well understood and accepted by those who wield power in the nation-states and those who control non-state actors. As the Turkish Air Force continues to hunt insurgents hiding in northern Iraq, the Israeli Air Force pursues members of Hamas and Hezbollah, and NATO aircraft patrol the skies over Afghanistan the temptation is to define air power through the lens of its use in counter-insurgency operations. That would be to diminish its ongoing significance.

Air power also should not been seen solely through the lens of fast jets and the kinetic application of force. Of all the positive catalysts that have emerged in the first century of air power it is its use to benefit mankind that is often forgotten. The Berlin Airlift was a major event in the evolution of air power. It defined a new sense of air power. It was the forerunner of operations that were to come.

Sarajevo and numerous locations around the world since suffering from the devastation of man-made or natural disasters have seen countless lives saved through the delivery of food, water, medicines, tents, clothes and blankets to those most in need. With air power now able to range over the globe in a matter of hours it is the strategic heavy-lifting capability of humanitarian relief supplies rather than bombs that now are a major effect arising from the application of air power. In this regard payload-carrying capacity, one of the principal characteristics of air power, has gone through a subtle yet important change. That is unlikely to change in the immediate future.

In the first century the application of air power has gone from a single quite specific mission to collect intelligence about enemy formations to a military tool that can be applied in a vast array of ways. The most important area for its continued development is the precision with which it can deliver effects.

In a media-dominated world those effects now have to be seen to be proportionate. Where those who apply air power make mistakes, its effectiveness is questioned. That scrutiny is never more avidly applied than when drones are used to attack targets and result in civilian deaths.

Drones are getting a mixed reaction in the press. There are those who argue strongly that the capabilities they afford the military and political leadership are indispensable. There are others who are vociferous in projecting criticisms of their use. Legal arguments often dominate their commentary. Whatever the rights and wrongs of the arguments, it is clear their use polarizes opinions.

One element of the ways drones are operated is at the heart of the arguments. By removing the pilot from the cockpit those who criticize their use claim that this somehow detaches them from the reality of war. They suggest that by having breakfast with their families before going to war impairs their professional judgement and ability to call off an attack.

The idea that this remoteness adds to a feeling that firing a missile against a target 10,000 miles away is somehow the act of someone playing a computer game is nonsense. It belies all the training that those who operate the drones go through plus the layers of lawyers and commanders that now track their every move. Where mistakes are made, investigations are held. The liberal media's attempts to portray these as cover-ups and whitewashes miss the vital point. Accidents do happen. Not many pilots of drones are revenge-crazed individuals hell-bent on killing innocent civilians.

Those who are quick to judge fail to understand just how the pilots' ability to make these life-and-death decisions depends upon technology. The images they see on the ground do not appear in an instant. Often drone operators track a target for hours if not days on end. Their basic decision-making is driven by the analysis of what they see on the ground as the pattern of life. Where unusual patterns develop, the operators see these and pay attention. Where mistakes are made are on those few occasions where the patterns of life indicators are not totally distinct.

A group of people entering a house in an area known to be frequented by terrorists can be misinterpreted. The resolution of the imagery that is available can allow false deductions to be made. That weakness surrounding the current applications of drones will not readily go away. It will take another step in technology to allow the operators to get even higher-resolution imagery over the target before accidents of that nature can be eliminated. Meanwhile advances in warhead designs will help as their explosive powers and ways of operating seek to reduce still further the risks of collateral damage.

For the foreseeable future it is very unlikely that drone technologies are going to be adapted for use in the next generation of strategic bombers. If public concerns about their applications in specific tactical situations cannot be allayed then their use in a strategic situation to attack a major enemy airbase or city is virtually unthinkable.

The replacement for the B-2, B-1 and B-52 bombers will enter the inventories of air forces from 2030 onwards and if the history of the B-52 is anything to go by will still be in service as the end of the second century of air power comes to a close. The necessity to still be able to penetrate an adversary's air defence system and deliver a high payload against a specific target will not disappear. The one lasting shift in the application of air power is likely to be that as far as bombing is concerned, air power will increasingly be applied with precision against military targets.

While the strategic bombing capabilities of the United States, Russian and Chinese air forces are unlikely to be retired any time soon, it will be in the tactical and operational arenas in which air power will inevitably be focused in the short-term. It is difficult to envisage a scenario where population-centric bombing will ever return, but to state that will never happen is to tempt fate.

Speed will also be another area where air power will benefit from technological advancement. Hypersonic air travel for commercial purposes will inevitably result in military spin-offs. But of all the developments in air power that may well punctuate the second century of its application, the question of manned or unmanned aircraft will be a dominant question. With the F-35 Lightning II aircraft likely to still be in service until 2050 throughout NATO, the issue over the unmanned future of military aviation still has some time to be discussed and sorted. There are a huge number of problems that need to be overcome.

For the traditionalists the need to maintain a pilot somewhere in the command loop will not be easy to let go. Even the film *Star Wars* had manned fighters. As the priority to deliver air power with precision becomes a greater focus the idea that decision-making could be delegated to a robot is almost unthinkable. For those technologists who see a vision of a robotic form of warfare the future may look very different, but it is a pathway that should be followed with some trepidation.

For mankind to delegate warfare to robots seems to be the ultimate technological folly. Hollywood film producers have often tried to portray its consequences, sending out warning signals of what might be to come. War has always been an intensely human endeavour. It allows warfare to be modulated by a sense of what is right or wrong. Limits can be set on what should and can be done to achieve a political aim. If that were ever taken completely away from human beings it would be a very significant development. That might be one the human race would come to regret.

Looking back on the first century of air power it is difficult not to conclude that its application has come a long way in what from a historical viewpoint is a relatively short period of time. For those who advocated its war-winning characteristics the story of the first century is mixed. Douhet, Mitchell, LeMay and Harris's vision of strategic air power has never quite been achieved, its application reined in by nervous political leaders. Yet, that is not the whole story.

The application of air power has developed far beyond the rather narrow views expressed by its major historical advocates. Today air power can not only deliver kinetic effect with precision on the ground and in air-to-air combat: it can also deliver humanitarian relief on a global scale in a matter of hours. One of the enduring aspects of air power in its first century is its ability to be flexible, agile and adaptable to changing technology and geo-strategic viewpoints. In its second century, those enduring characteristics are unlikely to change.

Bibliography

Almond, Peter, *A Century of Flight* (W.H. Smith, 2002)

Bond, S. and Forder, R., *Special OPS Liberators* (Grub Street, 2011)

Bowman, Martin, *Bomber Command: Reflections of War* (Pen & Sword, 2011)

Boyne, Walter J., *The Influence of Air Power upon History* (Pelican, 2002)

Boyne, Walter J., *The Yom Kippur War and the Airlift that Saved Israel* (Thomas Dunne Books, 2002)

Buckley, John, *Air Power in the Age of Total War* (Routledge, 1999)

Cooper, Alan W., *Air Gunner: The Men Who Manned the Turrets* (Pen & Sword, 2009)

Corum, James S. and Johnson, Wray R., *Airpower in Small Wars* (Kansas University Press, 2003)

Creveld, Martin van et al, *Air Power and Maneuver Warfare* (University Press of Pacific, 2002)

Downing, Taylor, *Spies in the Sky* (Little, Brown, 2011)

Hastings, Sir Max, *Bomber Command* (Pan Military Classics, 1999)

Hastings, M., *The Korean War* (Pan, 1987)

House, Jonathan M., *Combined Arms Warfare in the Twentieth Century* (Kansas University Press, 2001)

Lashmar, Paul, *Spy Flights of the Cold War* (Sutton, 1996)

Leinburger, Ralf, *Fighter: Technology, Facts, History* (Parragon, 2008)

Olsen, John Andreas (ed.), *Global Air Power* (Potomac Books, 2011)

Pook, Jerry, *RAF Harrier Ground Attack – Falklands* (Pen & Sword, 2007)

Preston, Paul, *A Concise History of the Spanish Civil War* (Fontana Press, 1996)

Price, Alfred, *Instruments of Darkness: The History of Electronic Warfare, 1939–1945* (Greenhill Books, 2005)

Satia, Priya, *Spies in Arabia: The Great War and the Cultural Foundations of Britain's Covert Empire in the Middle East* (Oxford University Press, 2008)

Wakefield, Alan and Moody, Simon, *Under the Devil's Eye: The British Military Experience in Macedonia 1915–1918* (Pen & Sword, 2004)

Wilson, Jim, OBE, *Launch Pad UK: Britain and the Cuban Missile Crisis* (Pen & Sword, 2008)

Wragg, David, *A Century of British Naval Aviation 1909–2009* (Pen & Sword, 2009)

Index